Scandalous Liaisons

Scandalous Liaisons

CHARLES II AND HIS COURT

R. E. PRITCHARD

AMBERLEY

Then to country dances; the King leading the first which he called for; which was – says he, cuckolds all a-row, the old dance of England.

Samuel Pepys, Diary, 31 December 1662

First published 2015
This edition published 2018

Amberley Publishing
The Hill, Stroud
Gloucestershire, GL5 4EP

www.amberley-books.com

Copyright © R. E. Pritchard, 2015

The right of R. E. Pritchard to be identified as the Author of this work has been asserted in accordance with the Copyrights, Designs and Patents Act 1988.

ISBN 978 1 4456 6036 3 (paperback)
ISBN 978 1 4456 4879 8 (ebook)

British Library Cataloguing in Publication Data.
A catalogue record for this book is available from the British Library.

Typesetting and Origination by Amberley Publishing
Printed in the UK.

CONTENTS

INTRODUCTION: NEW RANTS AND RAPTURES

> Of villains, rebels, cuckolds, pimps and spies,
> Cowards and fools, and stormers of dirt pies,
> Bawds, whores, e'en all that are or would be so,
> Stale Maids of Honour that are wooed or woo,
> Of scouring drunken drabs, foul, old and pocky,
> That cuckold King, captain, knight or jockey,
> I sing –

These lines, the mock-epic opening of the satiric *An Heroic Poem* of 1681[1] cover most of the subject of this book: the loves and lives – the scandalous liaisons – of members of the Court of Charles II, the so-called 'Merry Monarch'. Thomas Carlyle thought of history as the biography of great men; in the history here, each chapter is generally organised around the biographies of one or two by no means great individuals engaged in the sexual catch-as-catch-can of court life. Inevitably, some narrative threads intertwine and overlap, which in turn may suggest how closely these lives were interwoven in this small world. The discussion quotes extensively from contemporary writings: the diary of the inexhaustible gossip-hunter Samuel Pepys, the memoirs and letters of various well-informed and observant foreigners, especially the Frenchman Philibert, Comte de Gramont, the Italian Count

Lorenzo Magalotti, the French ambassadors, gossip-writers and, notably, some of the – frequently indecent – lampoons and verse satires written by courtiers and court hangers-on, invaluable for showing what people really thought about what was happening. As Samuel Butler observed, 'The muse that inspires lampoons is very powerful here, where they admit of no other poesy.'[2]

The period is remarkable for the quantity and quality of writing produced by courtiers and associates, including plays for the new, professional theatres and verse ranging in quality from the highly sophisticated to near doggerel, from charming lyrics of seduction to acute cultural-political satire and mocking, comical bawdry, directed against the perceived sexual and political misdoings of the time. Dryden, ever amenable to the ruling culture, may have described it as a 'laughing, quaffing and unthinking time', but it is clear that there was a great deal of resentment and discontent directed against court values during these unsettled years, as in Butler's 'Satire upon the Licentious Age of Charles the Second'.[3] It has been suggested that 'the Restoration was above all a triumph of the aristocracy and gentry who sought, and secured, the re-establishment of social hierarchy and social order,'[4] but the Civil War and the years of the inter-regnum had ensured that there was no going back to the old ways: Parliament – especially the Commons – the middle and merchant classes, the religious independents, the theatre and women would never be as submissive again. At the heart of it all were the court and the looser ways stirred up during the war and imported by Charles from France.

A recent critic suggests that

> To Pepys, and indeed to every eager consumer of gossip and lampoon, the Court presented a monstrous spectacle of 'wanton talk' and obscene writing, drunken brawling, riot, injury, outrage, window-smashing and wife-snatching, a general state of warfare, both verbal and physical, in which sexuality and disease are the weapons. The age that coined the 'noble savage' also produced the savage noble.[5]

This is to overstate the case somewhat – many of the people at court were just self-willed and irresponsible – and conscientious Pepys was well placed to observe sober work, governing and political activity there – but, indeed, there is some truth in it. Certainly, there was extremely loose sexual behaviour by both sexes, and wild, even brutal conduct by young aristocratic men, feeling themselves to a considerable extent free from the law's restraints and eager to distinguish themselves from the ever-rising, industrious and sober middle classes, chiefly by mocking 'polite' manners as hypocritical and by gross delinquency and adopting the coarse language of the lowest classes (thought of, somehow, as more authentic).

One might cite Charles's eldest illegitimate son, raised to the title of Duke of Monmouth (the 'stormer of dirt pies' absurdly re-enacting his part in the siege of Maastricht), who killed a watchman while raiding a brothel in Whetstone's Park, or the vile 6th Duke of Pembroke, who killed at least two men in fights, or, more harmlessly but also scandalously, Sir Charles Sedley and Charles Sackville, Lord Buckhurst (who had himself already – mistakenly, he claimed – killed a tanner), who were involved in a notorious episode at the Cock Inn on 16 June 1663, when, as Pepys recorded, they went out on a balcony, drunk and naked,

> acting all the postures of lust and buggery ... abusing of scripture and, as it were, from thence preaching a mountebank sermon from that pulpit, saying that there he [Sedley] hath to sell such a powder as should make all the cunts in town run after him, a thousand people standing underneath to see and hear him. And that being done, he took a glass of wine and washed his prick in it and then drank it off, and then took another and drank the King's health.

The overexcited crowd then threw things at them; Sedley was later bound over to keep the peace and Buckhurst, as a lord, got off.

This performance was not just an instance of aristocratic 'sons of Belial, flown with insolence and wine' (*Paradise Lost*, I.502), but an example of 'libertine' self-assertion, showing-off to shock, by spoiled young men stirred up by a new sense of liberty and licence. In general, as James Turner writes, 'The word "libertine" in early modern Europe could denote challenge to orthodox religion, an attempt to construct an authentic self on the basis of the passions, a loosening of family bonds and respect for parental authority, or a deliberate celebration of "loose gallantry".[6] Loosening of behaviour, whether sexual or in general manners, had been growing before 1660, but the Restoration seemed to accelerate it, at court at least, and to some extent elsewhere. Insofar as there was much thinking behind Restoration libertinism, it derived from (mis) readings of Thomas Hobbes's *Leviathan* (1651), interpreted as regarding all authority – state, religious and church, family and sexual laws – as arbitrary, hypocritical and repressive of man's natural impulses; with that went the *De Rerum Natura* of the Roman writer Lucretius, which asserted that the universe was not created by divine power, that religion is organised superstitious delusion and the object of life is pleasure and physical happiness. The names of such writers were flourished in 'gallant' society as evidence of one's intellectual sophistication but not always convincingly. One unimpressed contemporary wrote of the typical libertine:

> His religion ... is pretendedly Hobbian. And he swears that *Leviathan* may supply all the lost leaves of Solomon. Yet he never saw it in his life, and for aught he knows it may be a treatise about catching of sprats, or new regulating the Greenland fishing trade.[7]

In practice, the result was all too frequently merely boozing, fornicating and brawling – but protected by one's social position. The mood of fashionable disillusion was summed up neatly by Sedley, in an adaptation:

> *Out of the French*
> Dear friend, I fear my heart will break;
> In 'tother world I scarce believe,
> In this I little pleasure take;
> That my whole grief thou may'st conceive;
> Could not I drink more than I whore
> By Heaven, I would not live an hour.[8]

It has been estimated that there were some fourteen notable court wits of a libertine persuasion: among the aristocracy were George Villiers, Duke of Buckingham (the oldest); Charles Sackville, Lord Buckhurst (later Earl of Dorset); the Earls of Rochester (the most brilliant poet of his time), Sheffield and Carbery. From the gentry were Sir Charles Sedley, Sir Carr Scrope, Sir George Etherege; William Wycherley, Henry Savile, Fleetwood Shepherd, Henry Bulkeley (on Prince James's staff), Henry Guy and Henry Killigrew (court wit and liar).[9] These were the men whom Alexander Pope had in mind as 'the mob of gentlemen who wrote with ease', when

> In every taste of foreign courts improved,
> All by the King's example lived and loved ...
> ... when all was Love and Sport,
> The willing Muses were debauched at Court.[10]

For all their erotic verses and exploits, most of them prudently married wealthily: Buckingham to Mary, Lord Fairfax's daughter; Sedley to the (later insane) daughter of Earl Rivers; Rochester to 'the great beauty and fortune of the west' (as Pepys described her, on 28 May 1665), Elizabeth Malet (or Mallet); Mulgrave, Earl of Sheffield, first to two wealthy earls' widows and then to the Duke of York's illegitimate daughter; Wycherley to the widow of the Earl of Drogheda – and so on. Apart from their incidental verses, many of them were quite prolific writers for the theatre. Buckingham rewrote part of Fletcher's *The Chances* (1661) and collaborated on *Sir Politick Would-Be* (1663–4), *The Country Gentleman* (1669) and, most effectively, the parody tragedy, *The Rehearsal* (1671). Rochester adapted a Jacobean tragedy, *Valentinian*, and wrote prologues and scenes for others. Etherege's plays included *She Would if She Could* – a good, suggestive title – and, most successfully, *The Man of Mode* (1676). Sedley wrote three plays, including *The Mulberry Garden* (1668), about the fashionable London scene. The most famous of Wycherley's four plays, still enjoyed today, was *The Country Wife* (1678), which gleefully explored the possibilities of energetic cuckolding and women's hypocrisy.

As for the courtiers' wives, they were to provide not love but money and heirs, as Sarah Fyge bitterly complained:

> Most mortally the name of wife they hate,
> Yet they undertake one as their proper fate,
> That they may have a child legitimate,
> To be their heir, if they have an estate,
> Or else to bear their names: so for by ends
> They take a wife, and satisfy their friends, [mistresses]
> Who are desirous that it should be so,
> And for that end, perhaps, estates bestow,
> Which, when possessed, is spent another way.
> The spurious issue do the right betray
> And with their mother strumpets are maintained,
> The wife and children by neglect disdained.[11]

The theme of usurpation of wives by mistresses and their children is also a subject of Rochester's excellent, bitter analysis of contemporary sexual relationships, *Artemisia to Chloe* (1674).[12] Margaret Cavendish, Duchess of Newcastle, also complained that men now

> love the company and conversation of wanton and free women,
> insomuch that a courtesan shall have a greater and stronger power
> ... nay, many men love a whore so much more than an honest and
> chaste woman, as so many make better husbands, and are more
> fond and kinder to their wives if they be libertines, than if they were
> honest and true to their marriage bed.[13]

Aristocratic and upper-gentry men commonly took mistresses, and their wives, often married off by their parents at an early age but with no independent resources, had to put up with it. Many were shunted off to the country (a dreadful fate) to breed and brood, but if they stayed up in town, they often retaliated. A woman's song in Dryden's aptly titled comedy of 1673, *Marriage A-la-Mode*, defended adulterous affairs:

> If I have pleasures for a friend
> And further love in store,
> What wrong has he whose joys did end,
> And who could give no more?[14]

(Fortunately, the 1650 Adultery Act, carrying the death penalty, had quietly lapsed at the Restoration.) Apart from 'the great bawdy-house', the court, there were other opportunities for affairs. Several writers refer to popular 'picking-up' places, such as The Mall in St James's Park. Rochester's satire *A Ramble in St James's Park*[15] describes it as a place for quick sexual encounters, where great ladies (probably masked), footmen, chambermaids, great lords and pimps 'arrive / And here promiscuously they swive'. Ned Ward's *The London Spy*[16] writes of Duke Humfrey's Walk in St James's Park as an ideal place for 'a woman as rich as lewd to furnish herself with a gallant that will stick as close as a crab-louse to her *nunquam satis*'. In Etherege's *She Would if She Could* (1668), Lady Cockwood speaks wistfully of 'the plays, Park and Mulberry Garden', where a wife could 'indulge the unlawful passions of some young gallant'.[17]

The Restoration period marks the high point in half-humorous but essentially anxious references to cuckoldry, reflecting a sense of a weakening of traditional male authority and loosening of norms of social conduct. Popular libertine and cuckold comedies, whether set among the upper classes, such as *The Country Wife*, or Ravenscroft's *The London Cuckolds* (1682), somewhat lower in the social scale, provided a way of coping with unease through laughter. All men were potentially cuckolds (including, as it turned out, the King – by his mistresses), so one might as well laugh about it. If it happened, nothing useful could be done about it. Social disorder spread from the stage to the audience, as actresses – and actors – became the sexual playmates, or even longer-term partners, of the wealthy, while the 'middling sort', such as Pepys, imitated their social superiors in more limited fashion. Comedies and satires presented a Hobbesian world of mutual sexual predation, where 'every man [and woman] is enemy to every man', with 'continual fear'; as Rochester wrote, in *Artemisia to Chloe*, 'A woman's ne'er so ruined but she can / Be still revenged on her undoer, man.'[18]

Verse satire was the fashion – almost a craze – among the wits (or would-be wits), not so much aiming at high moral purpose as scoring off someone else, or relieving an itch:

> I who from drinking ne'er could spare an hour,
> But what I gave to some obedient whore,
> Who hate all satire, whether sharp or dull,
> From Dryden to the Governor of Hull [Marvell, MP for Hull],
> Provoked at length to a poetic rage,
> Resolve to share in railing at the age.[19]

Some men sought to make their names by malevolent gossip-satire about court carryings-on (such as one might read today on Twitter, but with wit and rhyme), such as John Grubham Howe, acolyte of Rochester, one of the grubbier, less witty wits, as a contemporary described him:

> For smutty jests and downright lies, Jack Howe.
> He to this function mightily pretends,
> And satires those the most he calls his friends ...
> His whole design is to be thought a wit;
> Therefore this freedom takes to further it,
> Sends forth his spies; his home-spun sisters too
> Daily inform him what their acquaintance do.
> Then out himself he packs and scouting goes,
> Singles out pairs as he thinks fit, and those
> He handles evilly, then frames his jest,
> Writes what he sees, feigns and makes out the rest.[20]

Most satires and lampoons were handed around among friends, and relatively few from the early 1660s survive, but, increasingly, an unofficial distribution system operated, notably by 'Colonel' Robert Julian, who ran a sort of clearing house, copying and distributing verses by such as Marvell, John Ayloffe and Robert Gould. Buckingham even addressed a verse epistle to him as 'Secretary to the Muses':

> Thou common shore of this poetic town, [dung-heap]
> Where all our excrements of wit are thrown,
> For sonnet, satire, bawdry, blasphemy,
> Are emptied and disburthened all on thee ...[21]

Julian was pilloried for this later, but it had been profitable,

> While our bards e'en famish by their wit,
> Thou, who hast none at all, didst thrive by it.[22]

Generally, one had to be a little careful of the various laws and acts against unapproved printing: many disguised political criticism as sexual-moral criticism of court women associated with one's opponents, especially (chaste) Queen Catherine's entourage and other Catholics. So, of the seventeen cheerily lewd and abusive verses on *The Ladies of the Court* (1663),[23] all the women in the first five verses were members of her court (though most of them had earned such sexual mockery on their own accounts). Likewise, another lengthy, obscene lampoon on court women, *Colin*, began with looking for the release of the King from the malign French influence of Louise de Kéroualle:

> – this is the day
> For which poor England long did pray,
> The day that sets our monarch free
> From buttered buns and slavery.
> This hour from French intrigues, 'tis said,
> He'll clear his Council and his bed ...[24]

A clear example of sexual libel having political reference is *An Essay of Scandal* (1681), where the writer blames the King's financial difficulties on his expensive mistresses:

> Thee and three kingdoms have thy drabs destroyed ...
> Remove that costly dunghill from thy doors [Louise];
> If thou must have 'em, use cheap, wholesome whores,
> Take Temple, who can live on cheese and ale [Philippa Temple,
> Maid of Honour to the Queen],

> Who never but to bishop yet turned tail;
> She's seasoned, fit to bear a double brunt,
> In her arse London, Rowley in her cunt.
> Bishop and King, choose (handy-dandy) either;
> They still club votes, why not club seeds together?[25]

Whatever the Bishop of London's (imputed) sexual proclivities, the target here is political: the alliance for mutual advantage of the bishops in the House of Lords with the King.

Sometimes, of course, the satires against women were simple misogyny, provoked by sexual and social insecurity, sometimes good-humoured, sometimes not. Robert Gould's widely read *Love Given O're* (1680)[26] begins as it means to go on (though his other writings suggest he was capable of more generous response):

> Woman! By Heaven, the very name's a crime
> Enough to blast, and to debauch my rhyme ...

When he writes, with obvious innuendo, of

> Lapdogs! To whom they are more kind and free
> Than they themselves to their own husbands be

Pope in *The Rape of the Lock* (1712), more indirectly, remarks how

> Not louder shrieks to pitying Heav'n are cast
> When husbands or when lapdogs breathe their last.

Gould claims the sexual voracity of

> [...] The womb
> To be as greedy as the gaping tomb.
> Take men, dogs, lions, bears, all sorts of stuff,
> Yet it will never cry, there is enough ...

which in turn leads to the cry in Pope:

> Sooner let Earth, Air, Sea to Chaos fall,
> Men, monkeys, lapdogs, parrots, perish all!

Gould asserted, 'Pride is the deity they most adore', as Pope's Belinda begins 'the sacred rites of Pride'.[27]

Richard Ames, in *The Folly of Love* (1691), anticipates a popular Edwardian music hall comic song (occasionally heard even today: 'After the ball was over, / She took out her one glass eye'):

> Imagine now from playhouse just returned
> A lady, who when there, in fancy burned,
> Uneasy by some disappointment made,
> Preparing now to undress herself for bed;
> Her curled locks (mistaken for her own)
> Are in confusion on her toilet thrown;
> Next her glass eye put nicely in a box,
> With ivory tooth, which never had the pox,
> Her stiff steel bodice, which her bunch did hide,
> Are with her artificial buttocks laid aside ...[28]

With comic exaggeration, sometimes funny, sometimes sour, Ames suggests, perhaps unintentionally, the straits to which upper-class ladies might be reduced in their competition to attract moneyed men (their only source of income).

Apart from conventional, automatic sneers, many versifiers were sympathetic to the less fortunate young women. Alexander Radcliffe knew about the generally unregarded distresses of the minor suppliers of the court's fun:

> *The Poor Whore's Song*
> Good young lecher, cast an eye
> Upon a poor whore's misery:
> Let not my antiquated front
> Make you less free than you were wont,
> But like a noble rogue
> Do but disembogue,
> And you shall have our constant vogue,

For I am none of those
That a-bulking goes, [street-walking]
And often shows
Their Bridewell blows,
Or New Prison lash,
For filing of cash
Or nimming prigsters of their trash. [robbing thieves]

But I at Court have often been,
Within the view of King and Queen;
A guinea to me was no more
Than fifteen pence to a suburb whore;
And when he did tilt,
I did briskly jilt,
And swallowed pego to the hilt;
A pox was very near,
For bubo did appear,
Had not my surgeon then been there ...[29]

(Whores and their clients, from court and town, were equally at risk of venereal infection.)

By no means all the satires and lampoons were directed at women, or political. Libertines themselves were often the subjects, even by themselves against themselves. In about 1663 a poem appeared, *Régime de Vivre*, possibly about the Earl of Rochester and possibly by Charles Sackville, Earl of Dorset, mocking the day of a typical libertine:

I rise at eleven, I dine about two,
I get drunk before seven, and the next thing I do,
I send for my whore, when for fear of a clap,
I spend in her hand, and I spew in her lap;
Then we quarrel and scold, till I fall fast asleep,
When the bitch, growing bold, to my pocket does creep,
Then slyly she leaves me, and to revenge th'affront,
At once she bereaves me of money and cunt.
If by chance then I wake, hot-headed and drunk,

> What a coil I do make, for the loss of my punk.
> I storm and I roar, and I fall in a rage,
> And missing my whore, I bugger my page.
> Then crop-sick all morning, I rail at my men,
> And in bed I lie yawning till eleven again.[30]

After reporting Sedley's and Buckhurst's indecent antics on the balcony of the Cock Inn, on 16 June 1663, Pepys wrote that 'people say that buggery is now almost grown as common among our gallants as in Italy, and that the very pages of the town begin to complain of their masters for it'. It appears that he was not familiar with this fashionable occupation of the smart set, continuing, not wholly convincingly, 'But blessed be God, I do not to this day know what is the meaning of this sin, nor which is the agent and which is the patient.' At the time, taking the active role in this modish practice, whether with women or page boys (as in Rochester's *The Imperfect Enjoyment*[31]), was in vogue among aristocratic rakes and libertines, as marking the peak of masculine, 'macho' self-assertion.[32]

Perhaps the best – if comically exaggerated – pictures of the lower reaches of libertine courtier life were provided by Alexander Radcliffe, as in his rumbustious *The Ramble*:

> While duns were knocking at my door,
> I lay in bed with reeking whore,
> With back so weak and prick so sore,
> You'd wonder.
> I roused my doe, and laced her gown,
> I pinned her whisk, and dropped a crown, [neckerchief]
> She pissed, and then I drove her down
> Like thunder.
> From chamber then I went to dinner,
> I drank small beer like mournful sinner,
> And still I thought the devil in her
> Clitoris.
> I sat at Muskat's in the dark,
> I heard a tradesman and a spark,
> An attorney and a lawyer's clerk

Tell stories.
From thence I went, with muffled face,
To the Duke's House, and took a place [theatre],
In which I spewed, may't please his Grace,
Or Highness.
Should I been hanged I could not choose
But laugh at whores that drop from stews,
Seeing that Mistress Margaret Hughes [actress, mistress of
Prince Rupert] So fine is.
When play was done, I called a link;
I heard some paltry pieces clink
Within my pockets, how d'ye think
I employed 'em?
Why, sir, I went to Mistress Spearing [gaming-house],
Where some were cursing, others swearing,
Never a barrel better herring
Per fidem.
Seven's the main, 'tis eight, God damn me,
'Twas six, said I, as God shall sa'me,
Now being true, you could not blame me
So saying ...
As luck would have it, in came Will,
Perceiving things went very ill,
Quoth he, you'd better go and swill
Canary ...
[The speaker gets involved in drunken brawls, until a
    constable arrives, whom he buys off.]
At last, I made the watchmen drunk,
And then away to bed I slunk
To hide it.
God save the Queen! – but as for you,
Who will these dangers not eschew,
I'd have you all go home and spew,
As I did.[33]

It was customary, in these circles, to visit brothels – Rochester took
the King along incognito, where gossip said they both got robbed

of their clothes. The Duke of Monmouth, a frequent visitor, and his friends wrecked one brothel, where a friend had been infected. The Count Magalotti described visits to upmarket brothels, where rooms were well furnished with tables laden with wine, oranges and cakes, where the girls were paraded for a selection to be made and prices started at a pound.[34] Another 'ramble' poem (the term meant a sexual prowl), *The Last Night's Ramble* (1687), provides another humorous view of wealthy courtiers and aristocrats at a brothel:

> I took last night a ramble being drunk
> To visit old acquaintance bawd and punk.
> 'Twas Madam Southcot near old Dunkirk Square,
> That house of ease for many a rampant peer,
> For only the lewd quality f—k there.
> The first divertissement I found was this,
> I heard the treble note of yielding Miss,
> Whispering, 'Lord, Sir, what pleasant tales you tell!
> You'll find th'enjoyment worth your money well.'
> Then in bass viol voice I heard him swear,
> 'Damn me, a guinea, madam's, very fair,
> The utmost fee I ever gave to swive.'
> She answered, 'How d'ye think that we can live?
> I'll swear Sir William R— ch, sir, gave me five.'
> While thus I listened I observed at last,
> Though she asked more, she held the guinea fast.

Our eavesdropper-voyeur then hears another impatient customer:

> 'You know me (bawd) I am not used to wait.
> At Grayden's such a damned defeat I've had [gaming-house],
> With Lady Mary Ratcl— I am mad,
> And must the flame that's kindled by her eyes
> Quench 'twixt some common vulgar beauty's thighs,
> And to advance my gust of lechery,
> Just in the act, 'Dear Ratcl—' I will cry,
> Fancying at least I swive with quality.'

> By that same cocked up nose (thought I) and mien
> That haughty spark should be Lord Chamberl— ...

The writer names names to give an air of verisimilitude to his narrative, reflecting common gossip (true or not). In another room,

> who the devil do you think I found?
> But one (oh frailty) of the reverend gown,
> Stinking-mouthed Chest—, to my best discerning,
> Who gravely was a fine young whore confirming.[35]

The Bishop of Chester was not the only cleric subject to such derision. Marvell also cites Gilbert Sheldon, Archbishop of Canterbury (and patron of the Sheldonian Theatre in Oxford), as 'indifferent to have a wench in bed' and preferring to meet with the court Beauties Boynton or Middleton.[36] Pepys was told (29 July 1667) that Sheldon 'doth keep a wench and ... is as very a wencher as can be', and that Sir Charles Sedley had got one of the archbishop's wenches away from him. Such stories are reflective of the cynical ethos of the time, whether true or false.

No public figures were treated with reverence, let alone much respect. While some people clung to the apparently re-established social forms and structures, these were increasingly hollowed out by a turbulent, sceptical and what might even be called a sexualised culture, largely the consequence of the dubious practices of Charles and his cronies, reinforced by a more pronounced cultural shift, producing a growing sense of moral uncertainty and distress.

In conclusion, a wry survey of the wider society and milieu in which the characters discussed in the following pages lived is provided by Alexander Radcliffe's *As Concerning Man* (where 'Man' means, particularly, men at court or in town):

> To what intent or purpose was Man made,
> Who is by birth to misery betrayed?
> Man in his tedious course of life runs through
> More plagues than all the land of Egypt knew.
> Doctors, Divines, grave disputations, puns,

Ill-looking citizens and scurvy duns,
Insipid squires, fat bishops, deans and chapters,
Enthusiasts, prophecies, new rants and raptures;
Pox, gout, catarrhs, old sores, cramps, rheums and aches;
Half-witted lords, double-chinned bawds with patches;
Illiterate courtiers, Chancery suits for life,
A teasing whore, and a more tedious wife;
Raw Inns of Court men, empty fops, buffoons,
Bullies, robust, round aldermen, and clowns;
Gown-men which argue, and discuss, and prate,
And vent dull notions of a future state;
Sure of another world, yet do not know
Whether they shall be saved, or damned, or how.
'Twere better then that Man had never been
Than thus to be perplexed: God Save the Queen.[37]

In 1660, Dryden's *Astraea Redux* had welcomed the return with Charles of the goddess of Justice and a new Golden Age: 'Now – O, brave new world, that has such people in't! Welcome to Restoration London and its court!' Radcliffe's disenchanted lines were written about thirty years after Charles's accession to the throne; to that, and the preceding years that did so much to shape his character, his behaviour and so his rule and court, we now must turn.

BEFORE DOVER: THE FIRST BUTTERED BUNS

On 4 March 1645, in Oxford, fourteen-year-old Charles Stuart said goodbye to his father, King Charles, for the last time, and rode off to become the figurehead commander of the Royalist forces in the West Country, in the Civil War. His headquarters were originally supposed to be in Bristol, where in fact his council made the decisions for him. In 1645 they moved to Bridgewater in Somerset; here things were much more enjoyable for him, with his passionately affectionate reunion with his former nurse (a less hands-on position than it might seem), Christabel, Lady Wyndham, who met him with open arms.[1] Now in her early thirties, a very attractive and forceful woman, she had been the first woman to show him much physical affection as a boy (more than his mother, Queen Henrietta Maria, who was more demonstrative to her pet midget, Jeffrey Hudson, who first appeared, as a surprise present, out of a pie). Now, the warmth of their relationship was remarked on – despite court formalities, sometimes 'she would run the length of the room and kiss him'; Edward Hyde (later Lord Clarendon) wrote stiffly that Charles felt 'fondness, if not affection' for Christabel.[2] Others later suggested that she might well have decided to 'make a man of', and do a favour to, this rather lonely, gangling youth (while also possibly doing herself and her family some good in later years, as Clarendon wrote[3]). It is possible; certainly, her close familiarity and fondness with the prince led her to encourage him to act more independently and irresponsibly, while she, in effect, showed off and put herself about in court. Very soon, the council had to separate them, and Charles was moved away, further west.

Later, he was in Exeter,[4] where he may have met again pretty young Lucy Walter, the same age as him, first briefly encountered in South Wales in 1641. Soon, however, he was moved on again, to Launceston, in Cornwall, and then, in March 1646, to the greater security of the Scilly Isles. The greater security was only apparent, for on 11 April a Parliamentarian fleet showed up, but Charles and his party were able to slip away to Jersey, Charles himself steering his ship for a couple of hours, to his great enjoyment.

Here, he was warmly welcomed by cheering crowds, and generously entertained by the Royalist Lieutenant-Governor Sir George Carteret. (It would have been expensive for Sir George: the prince's entourage would have numbered some 300.) Here, too, according to legend, Charles also enjoyed the governor's twenty-year-old daughter, Marguerite.[5] There is no reliable evidence for such an affair, though in 1668 a James de la Cloche (Marguerite's surname on her marriage in 1656), describing himself as the son of Charles and Marguerite, presented himself as a novitiate for the Jesuit order, but died the following year. Charles never acknowledged any such parentage, but gave grateful donations to the Carteret family (and later made Sir George Treasurer to the Navy – a very lucrative position).

Any such affair could only have been very brief, as his mother was demanding that he join her in Paris at the French court. (Charles's chief adviser, Hyde, was opposed to the move, fearing that Charles might be converted to Catholicism or become identified with French political interests.) The pressure was persistent, even including sending a large party of courtiers, including the Queen's adviser, Henry Jermyn, to Jersey, eventually forcing his surrender and agreement to join his mother in St Germain in summer 1647. Here he was received by the King, welcomed to the court's various entertainments and introduced to the politicking among the English factions (notably, Hyde, Charles's adviser, against Henry Jermyn, or Prince Rupert against George, Lord Digby).

Now he was exposed to his mother's various schemes for him. Her initial idea was to marry him to some wealthy princess, who would provide diplomatic support among continental royalty, much-needed money to support a court in exile and soldiers in England. Her first target was Louis XIV's first cousin, the enormously wealthy Anne-Marie Louise d'Orléans, Duchesse de Montpensier, known, for both her grandeur and her stature as 'La Grande Mademoiselle'.[6] Nineteen to his sixteen, tall, blonde, blue-eyed, big-built, magnificent, determined and Catholic, she had her mind on greater matches – the Holy Roman Emperor might do – and was quite beyond his reach. The young man hardly spoke a word to her, claiming to know little French; neither was much impressed.

For all that, he did well at court, with his pleasant manner, skill in dancing and riding and responsiveness to French manners. Chief among the English courtiers was handsome Henry, Baron Jermyn, Earl of St Albans, Henrietta Maria's Master of Horse and particularly close favourite – to the extent that gossip suggested they were long-time lovers (and even young Charles's parents). There was one story relating to an incident in about 1628, of the poet, Thomas Carew, then 'Gentleman of the Privy Chamber, [who,] going to light King Charles into her chamber, saw Jermyn Lord St Albans with his arm round her neck; – he stumbled and put out the light; – Jermyn escaped; Carew never told the King, and the King never knew it. The Queen heaped favours on Carew.'[7] Gossip also suggested that after Charles I's death, they were secretly married (as Samuel Pepys heard[8]). Avuncular Jermyn spent time playing and encouraging the young man in the gay, expensive French court.

While Charles was otherwise occupying his time, developments in England in summer 1648, had a direct effect on his life, as Royalist fortunes seemed to improve in the war. With an eye to convenience for sailing to Scotland, where hopeful negotiations had been taking place, the Queen agreed that Charles should move to Holland. Then English sailors stationed in the Downs mutinied, put their officers ashore, declared for the King and sailed to the harbour of Helvoetsluys to offer their services, initially to the Lord High Admiral, Charles's younger brother, James, Duke of York, recently escaped from England. To follow this up, Charles went there, displacing his brother and agreeing to lead the little fleet in forays against the English coast while awaiting an answer from the Scots.[9] Then came news that a Parliamentarian fleet was approaching, and a brief skirmish ensued, Charles excitedly waving a pistol, until the Royalist fleet had to withdraw to Helvoetsluys for supplies. Once there, almost everything went wrong, quarrels broke out and Charles fell ill with smallpox. When he recovered, he was happy enough to stay at The Hague, with another interest.

It is generally agreed that it was at The Hague, that summer, that Charles began his first serious romance – with Lucy Walter. This young woman was the daughter of good gentry parents, the family one of the many unsettled by the war and its upheavals. They had lived in King Street in London, a very good address near Whitehall, with good neighbours – the Earl of Oxford, Sir Kenelm Digby, the artist Sir Peter Lely and the (unrespectable) dramatist Thomas Killigrew. Whatever their social hopes, Lucy's parents' marriage broke up, and in 1641, when Lucy was eleven, the couple separated, which led to court proceedings and bitter mutual accusations of infidelity. Mr Walter withdrew to his Welsh estate, while Mrs Walter stayed in London with her sister, Mrs Gosfright, the wife of a Dutch merchant. The Lords awarded the children to the father, as his property; in 1647, when she was at an age when she might otherwise have been expecting her parents to be helping her to a husband, Lucy, child of a broken home and with poor prospects, ran away.

While she was in London she had fallen in with Algernon Sidney, a younger son of the Earl of Leicester, and a vigorous Parliamentarian soldier (wounded at Marston Moor). In her unfortunate situation, he would have seemed a godsend to an attractive girl with only her physical charms to see her through. A couple of years later, John Evelyn shared a ride with her in the Earl of Rochester's coach and described her as 'brown, beautiful, bold but insipid',[10] the last word suggesting that this not very bright, sexually active teenager did not make much conversation with a slightly prissy older gentleman.

Sidney later claimed to have bought her 'for five broad pieces', presumably from her mother, but before he could properly enjoy what he had paid for, he was recalled to his regiment in Ireland. So Lucy went off again, this time to Holland and Uncle Gosfright, but carrying a letter of recommendation to Algernon's younger brother, Robert, a colonel of the English regiment there, and chamberlain to Charles's sister, Mary, Princess of Orange. By the spring of 1647, Lucy was established as his mistress and trophy. Some of this last story derives from writings by Hyde and James, both of whom had strong political reasons for discrediting her, and so her son. (Not everyone believed that Charles was the father; 'when [the boy] grew to be a man, he very much resembled the colonel, both in stature and countenance, even to a wart on his face.'[11]) James claimed to have had her while at The Hague, and Hyde asserted that he believed that she had been sent there to seduce the less-experienced Charles. In any case, now calling herself Mrs Barlow (a family name), she became Charles's mistress very quickly, certainly by the summer of 1648.[12]

It seems very probable that he was for some time in love with Lucy, whom his contemporaries, however, would have dismissed as 'a buttered bun' (a woman very recently possessed by another man (or men), which was to prove the pattern of most of his sexual life). In her *Memoirs*, the Baronne d'Aulnoy expressed it more romantically:

> Her beauty was so perfect that when the King saw her in Wales [or wherever: the Baronne had heard stories of an earlier beginning] where she was, he was so charmed and ravished and enamoured that in the misfortunes which ran through the first years of his reign he knew no other sweetness or joy than to love her. The surroundings that he gave her; the care that he took to please her; the delight that he displayed in her went so far that, as he was so very young, and this was his first passion, and as, when a heart is truly possessed there is no engagement which it is not capable of taking, the world thought that he had promised this beautiful girl to marry her.[13]

This was just what Hyde and the other Royalists most feared: an inappropriate marriage with a commoner of dubious reputation. That summer, when Charles was lodged in the Stadtholder's palace with James and his aunt, Elizabeth of Bohemia (another dispossessed royal), her son and three daughters, there was some flirtation with the youngest, Sophia. She later recalled walking with Charles, who told her that she was handsomer than Mrs Barlow and that he hoped to see her in England. Nothing came of it; Charles was presumably emotionally engaged with Lucy, and Sophia went on to marry the Elector of Hanover. Politically and financially useful marriages were very much the main business. Then and later, various German princesses were wheeled out, in person or in portraits, of whom he observed, with his favourite oath, "Ods fish! They are all dull and foggy.' 1648, with Lucy and most of his family around, was proving a good time.

Then, early in February 1649, came the shocking news from England. Mary, informed before Charles, was unable to control herself and gave the responsibility to his chaplain, Dr Stephen Goffe, who went to Charles's room and began, hesitantly, with the awful words, 'Your Majesty ...'. Hyde recalled how 'the barbarous stroke so surprised him that he was in all the confusion imaginable, and all about him were almost bereft of their understanding.'[14] It is hard to decide how grieved Charles was after the initial shock, when he burst into tears; it was four years since he and his father had last met, and, in that royal court, they had never been, as the phrase has it, close. Now, suddenly, a terrible responsibility had descended on the young man. Later, he was to make little show of his feelings; within a few months his boyhood companion, the Duke of Buckingham, the aristocratic jester, was entertaining him with mocking mimicry of the late king. The dashing Buckingham, who had chosen exile with Charles, was at that time a notable influence on the younger man.

According to the Revd Gilbert Burnet, Buckingham was then 'a man of noble appearance and of a most lovely wit, wholly turned to mirth and pleasure', and 'possessed the young king with very ill principles both as to religion and morality, and with a very mean opinion of his father, whose stiffness was with him a frequent object of raillery.'[15] From now on, Charles was to cover his true thoughts and feelings, a youthful openness and warmth replaced by an indifferent affability and easiness, an inner coldness.

Then, on 9 April 1649, Lucy's son was born in Rotterdam – though Clarendon later said it was at The Hague – James, known as Barlow (later, the Duke of Monmouth), presumably conceived in mid-July 1648, just before Charles sailed away. The relationship was a somewhat intermittent affair, with many separations. Charles was delighted with the child and was always to show fondness for his first son. As was usual, the baby was put out to nurse – but away in Schiedamm, some way off – while Lucy returned to the good times with Charles.

Two questions now became urgent: what was Lucy's status, wife or mistress, and what was James's, bastard or legitimate and so heir to the throne? There was talk of there having been an earlier marriage, and again, years later, by Lucy's mother (to paraphrase Mandy Rice-Davies, well, she would, wouldn't she?). In 1679, during the furore connected with the Bill to exclude the Duke of York, Charles was forced to deny the marriage, first, to his close advisers, then in full council, and then in a statement printed in the *London Gazette*, in the spirit of Lewis Carroll's Bellman, 'What I tell you three times is true'. For some years there were stories of a 'black box', containing the certificate of a marriage performed in 1648 by Bishop Cosin, then the Protestant chaplain to Henrietta Maria, concealed for fear of the damage it might cause if opened. Pandora's box was supposed to have eventually reached one of Monmouth's descendants, the Duke of Buccleuch, at some time in the late nineteenth century, who then destroyed it. While Lucy was seen with Charles in public and travelled with him, her status remained unclear; she was part of the entourage but, being 'insipid', was of no apparent importance.

The dual standard operated: fidelity was only required of the woman. A king, even an impoverished and landless king, was in himself attractive; there is no knowing how many court ladies decided to make him offers he was unlikely to refuse. Of those named, the first to give him his second child was Elizabeth Killigrew, eight years older than Charles, wife of Francis Boyle,

Earl of Cork and later Viscount Shannon, one of Henrietta Maria's attendants. Her mother had a reputation for being 'long versed in amours' (*DNB*); it may have been due to her brother, Thomas Killigrew, that she was brought to Charles; the ribald wit that characterised his plays made him welcome to Charles, and after the Restoration he was granted one of London's two theatres. Her affair with Charles took place in 1649, as, in Paris in 1650 she gave birth to a girl, significantly and optimistically christened Charlotte Jemima Henrietta Maria. More prolific, and longer-lasting than Betty Boyle, was Catherine Pegge, the beautiful daughter of another Royalist exile, whom he encountered in Flanders in 1657–8, and by whom he had two children, Charles Fitzcharles, commonly known as 'Don Carlos' when in Whitehall Palace, and a girl, also named Catherine. When king, he gave her a pension and a house in Pall Mall; in 1667, she married Sir Edward Greene, Bart. There was also Eleanor Needham, a young widow who became the second wife of John, Baron Byron (who died in 1652); on 26 April 1667, Samuel Pepys quoted John Evelyn bitterly referring to her as 'the King's seventeenth whore abroad'. While Charles was always generous to those who had served him in one way or another, she was considered notably rapacious and managed to get an estimated £15,000 out of him during his exile when he was relatively poor, with a promise of £4,000 worth of silver after the Restoration ('Thanks be to God, she died before she had it').

In thinking of these young women who so readily laid themselves down for their king, it should be remembered that they had found themselves dragged off to a foreign country by husbands who were probably not of their free choice, their homes and estates forfeited, possibly forever, in uncertain and difficult financial circumstances – some of the English courtiers were now really poor – and in a court of generally relaxed morals. In these circumstances, it is not surprising that they took their chance with the young king. As to whether Charles should be considered especially promiscuous for that time, there seems little evidence for much in the way of wild living. Reports speak of his attendance at dances and assemblies, but also of riding, hunting, billiards and brisk walks, while he had little spare money for seduction. Of Evelyn's snarl about seventeen whores, one modern commentator, dividing seventeen by fifteen years of exile, remarked coolly, 'Many men who consider themselves relatively abstemious have as many'; one wonders whom he had in mind.[16]

Charles's philandering did not imply loss of affection for Lucy and his son; 'Mrs Barlow' remained with him. In the early summer of 1650, he had to go off to Scotland, but arranged a position for her in his mother's household, where the boy was put in the care of one of the maids,[17] and for a friend of his, Theobald, Viscount Taaffe, to look out for her.

This is not the place to repeat accounts of his unhappy time in Scotland, nor of his military defeats and the disastrous Battle of Worcester on 3 September 1651. After this debacle, he escaped, as is well known and as he never tired of relating, accompanied for some of the time by Henry Wilmot, in disguise, with his face blackened and suffering agonies in shoes that were too small. On the way they met a Colonel Lane and came up with a scheme whereby Charles would be disguised as a servant travelling with his mistress, the colonel's unmarried sister, Jane Lane, who had a permit to travel. Off they went, the 'servant, William Jackson' in the saddle of the one horse, with his mistress holding his waist and riding behind. The original plan was to get away through Bristol, but they were warned that it was too guarded; in the end it was agreed that their cover story should be that Jane had received news that her father was gravely ill, and they would have to go back, while actually diverting southwards to Royalist friends near Sherborne, Dorset. This they reached the next day, and Jane went on alone; Charles's adventures were not yet over, before he eventually sailed away with Wilmot in the brig *Surprise*, on 15 October 1651.

As for Jane and her brother, hearing worrying rumours about how Charles had escaped, the colonel thought it best for them to slip out of the country quietly, and, in early December, they arrived in France. They sent word ahead to Paris, where Charles and Henrietta Maria came to welcome them. Though the colonel went back to England, only to be captured and interrogated, Jane stayed on in Paris, where she entered the service of Mary, Princess of Orange. Inevitably, gossip started up about a possible romance between Charles and Jane during those days and nights of physical closeness and danger. In Paris, gossips characteristically assumed that she was, or had been, his mistress. During the years of exile, they corresponded, Charles signing himself her 'affectionate' or 'assured and constant' friend. After the Restoration, the Lane family members were very generously rewarded. Intriguingly, there is a portrait that Jane commissioned then, which shows her holding a veil over a crown, symbolising her hiding her king from his enemies. In the top left corner is a scroll, reading, *sic sic iuvat ire sub umbra*, meaning, 'thus, thus it pleases me to go into the shadows', indicating a modest withdrawal into obscurity. However, it could suggest more: these are the words spoken in Virgil's *Aeneid* by Dido, who, having fallen in love with the wandering prince Aeneas, commits suicide on learning of her lover's abandoning her on his way to obtaining a kingdom. Thus she goes into the shadows, betrayed and abandoned.[18] Nevertheless, with her reward money, Jane made a good marriage to Sir Clement Fisher and died in 1689.

Charles was away in Scotland and England for some sixteen months; when he got back, in October 1651, Lucy, disastrously for her, confronted him with another baby, Mary, the father presumed to be Lord Taaffe (who later adopted the child). Lucy had had no certainty of Charles's return or continued affection; she may have been casual, or lonely – or making a sort of provision for an uncertain future. How Charles felt is not known. While starting to detach himself from her, he kept his friendship with Taaffe. As was to be usual with him, he attempted to be generous; some money was found and more promised.

In Paris, with little money, and making another futile bid for La Grande Mademoiselle,[19] Charles amused himself with various ladies, much to the annoyance of Hyde, who expressed fears that 'his immoderate delight in empty, effeminate and vulgar conversation is become an irresistible part of his nature and will never suffer him to animate his own designs and others' actions with that spirit which is requisite for his quality and much more to his fortune.'²⁰ (He was not to know of the King's later skilful negotiations with Louis XIV.) Lucy was now on the outer fringes of his concern. There was talk of a promising relationship with the celebrated beauty Isabelle-Angélique de Montmorency, Duchesse de Châtillon, but he was only one of many admirers, including several Englishmen. By the end of 1653, Lucy was looking elsewhere for protection, while pestering Charles for hand-outs. He arranged for a pension of 5,000 livres for her, but with the instalments to be paid in Antwerp to keep her away.²¹ In Brussels, she began some sort of affair with Charles's official representative there, Sir Henry de Vic, and apparently got him to go with her to Cologne to ask his permission to marry – which was refused. While this argues against a previous marriage with Charles, proponents of that story point to letters to Charles from his sister, Mary, Princess of Orange, at The Hague, notably one in June 1655:

> Your wife desires me to present her humble duty to you, which is all she can say. I tell her 'tis because she thinks of another husband, and does not follow your example of being as constant a wife as you are a husband: 'tis a frailty they say is given to the sex, therefore you will pardon her I hope.²²

The ironies seem obvious, while 'wife' was easily used to refer to a long-term mistress.

By the beginning of 1656, she was living with a member of the princess's household, Thomas Howard (who was also, unfortunately, an agent of Cromwell, retailing the dirt back to England). Word was also getting back to Charles about her wild behaviour, so he sent his own agent to find out what was going on. This was Daniel O'Neill, a trusted agent for Charles I, who, married to Lady Stanhope, had now arrived in Paris, where he was highly regarded by Hyde as 'a great observer and discerner of men's natures and humours ... very dextrous' and nicknamed 'Infallible Subtle'.²³

O'Neill soon reported the relationship with Howard, such as it was, and then on 14 February 1657 wrote suggesting a general moral collapse on Lucy's part, driven by a despairing sense of abandonment. It was only by buying off her maid that he had been able to prevent major public scandal:

> Her maid, whom she would have killed by thrusting a bodkin into her ear as she was asleep, would have accused her ... of miscarrying of two children by physic, and of the infamous manner of her living with Mr Howard, but I have prevented the mischief, partly with threats, but more with a 100 guilders I am to give her maid. Her last miscarriage was since Mr Howard went, as the midwife says to me that I employ to her. Doctor Rufus [not known, but possibly Dr Fraser who was later to be very helpful to embarrassed young women at Charles's Court in Whitehall] has given her physic, but it was *always* after her miscarrying; and though he knew anything, it would be indiscreet to tell it ...
>
> Though I have saved her for this time, it's not likely she'll escape [disgrace] when I am gone; for only the consideration of your Majesty has held Monsieur Heenvliet and Monsieur Nertwick not to have her banished this town and country for an infamous person and by sound of drums. [24]

He went on to advise Charles to be firmer, to acknowledge the child and then command Lucy to give him up. He had read Lord Taaffe's recent encouraging letter to her, telling her that Charles was especially concerned for her and that the next money Charles could 'get or borrow' would be sent to her. 'While your Majesty encourages any to speak this language, she'll never obey what you will have. The only way is to necessitate her, if your Majesty can think her worth your care.'

Such severity seems to have been too much for Charles, who even paid her a brief visit and, according to the maid, spent a day and night with her. Perhaps it was then that it was agreed for her and the children to go back to England and off his hands. Off they went that summer, with her brother and maid, under the name of Barlow – though as Howard was also of the party, Cromwell would have known immediately – with a pearl necklace worth £1,500 and some other funding.

She was promptly arrested as a suspected spy and put in the

Tower. Here, under questioning, she could tell them nothing of any use, but said that the children were not Charles's but by a Dutch husband, now dead, and that her son by Charles was also dead. After the authorities had got some propaganda value out of her, as showing the kind of people Charles was associating with, they contemptuously returned her to Flanders, for the Dutch, or Charles, or anybody, to deal with.

So back to Brussels she went, where she was again the focus of critical comment. In one incident, Lucy, having been dumped by Thomas Howard, sent someone – another 'friend' – to stab him in the street. Later, Howard charged her with theft of important papers, which could be harmful to him if they got into the wrong hands. Blackmail was always available as a potential weapon.

Once again she turned to Charles for help, who lodged her with the family of Sir Arthur Slingsby, secretary to the Earl of Bristol, where she started making suggestions of revealing some of Charles's papers. After a few weeks Slingsby employed the stratagem of complaining of unpaid bills for board and lodging, and so tried to have her sent to the local jail. When the officers tried to seize her eight-year-old son, the real object of the exercise, she set up such a commotion in the street, running out screaming, in showers of tears, tearing her hair and shouting for help that the whole street was aroused in this mother's cause and drove off the men.[25] It is impossible to know whether this was genuinely outraged maternal feeling or recognition of the danger of losing her principal weapon against Charles and his advisers. With her rackety way of life, with different lovers and travels, she may not have had much time to care properly for young James: an agent reported that, though very willing, he was not literate and could count only up to twenty.

One of those disturbed during this brouhaha was the former Spanish ambassador to England, who put her in the safety of another house, and wrote a very stiff letter to the Duke of Ormonde. Ormonde apologised, but he and Bristol now put on diplomatic pressure. Lucy's rooms were searched and papers removed. Once again, she was pressed to give up James; when she went to her room to find a document, Charles's assistant, Edward

Progers, simply took the boy and hurried him out of the house. James was taken off to Paris, where he was brought up in the household of the recently ennobled Lord Crofts, under the name of James Crofts, and under the overall, if distant, supervision of Henrietta Maria. Later he was to become his father's favourite and, as Duke of Monmouth, his uncle's greatest menace.

As for Lucy, she remained for a while in Brussels, making a pathetic nuisance of herself with the Royalists. Tradition has it that she moved to Paris, perhaps to be near her son, or to where she might better scrape a living. In November 1658, not very long before the Restoration and her former lover's triumphant return to England, she died suddenly, possibly of – as James, Duke of York, put it, with characteristic insensitivity – 'the disease incident to her profession'. Never a professional, Lucy Walter was never more than a bewildered amateur, caught up in an unstable world, used and abused by more powerful men. It is not easy to be severe with Charles: he began naïvely, with genuine feeling; he could not have kept on with her and could not adequately compensate her, financially or any other way.

Further potentially significant amorous relationships were to come his way. In October 1659, Charles's advisers approached the great Cardinal Mazarin for the hand of his beautiful, young, immensely wealthy niece, Hortense Mancini, a brilliant, lively and unpredictable teenager, who, as Queen Hortense, would certainly have changed the course of British history. As it was, the royal situation was profoundly unappealing to the calculating eyes of the cardinal, and, unsurprisingly, the proposal fell through. Years later, however, after unsatisfactory marriages and a lot of notches on their bed-posts, Hortense and Charles were to meet again. In the meantime, Charles retired to fly his hawks at partridges in Hoogstraten and fancied himself in love again, with the twenty-year-old Princess Henrietta Catherine, third daughter of the Dowager Princess Amelia of Orange. In 1657–8, while his courtiers were attempting to disentangle him from Lucy, Charles was making discreet visits to Henrietta, even though his mother was still trying to snaffle a Catholic princess for her son, despite the opposition of the Hyde Protestant faction.

The courtship seemed to be going very well, despite the lurking presence of a rival suitor. On the news of the death of Oliver Cromwell in September 1658, Charles felt he could approach Henrietta's mother formally. The initial response was favourable, but the Dowager Princess soon decided that Charles's political prospects had not improved significantly, while his sexual record was not one that a careful mother could approve. The courtship came to an end, Henrietta married her German prince and Charles was left to swallow his wounded pride.

Comfort, however, was not long in coming: in February 1660 appeared Mrs Barbara Palmer, née Villiers, his next great amour. Her back story is not without its own interest. Barbara Villiers was a member of one of the most widely successful families of the century. Born in the winter of 1640–1, the daughter of Lady Mary Bayning and William, Viscount Grandison (whose sister was also a Barbara Villiers), she was first cousin once removed of George Villiers, 2nd Duke of Buckingham and son of James I's notorious favourite. Her father, fatally wounded in the siege of Bristol, died in Oxford in 1643. In 1648, Lady Mary remarried, to yet another Villiers, her late husband's cousin, Charles, 2nd Earl of Anglesey. After Charles I's execution, Royalist fortunes (political and financial) slumped. Money and estates gone, some families went overseas, while others stayed on, on the understanding that they would be left alone if they kept their heads down.

The Angleseys stayed in London, in Ludgate Hill, associating with other Royalist families. It was reported that pretty young Barbara – blue-eyed, auburn-haired, with a forward manner – first appeared in 'a very plain country dress', but was soon to be seen in more fashionable clothes, when, 'the gaiety and mode of the Town ... adding a new lustre to that blooming beauty of which she had as great a share as any of her sex, she became the object of divers young gentlemen's affections.'[26] Among these young gentlemen was Philip Stanhope, 2nd Earl of Chesterfield.

Born in 1633, he had spent time at courts in both The Hague and Paris with his widowed mother, improving his languages and style if not his morals. Good-looking, with a fine head of hair and a reputation as a ladies' man, he was very likely to cause a flutter among the young ladies when he arrived in England. Hot-tempered, he had fought the first of his many duels at the age of sixteen, wounded his opponent and got away to Italy. In 1652 he came back to England to petition Parliament for the return of sequestered estates. Although this was unsuccessful, in that June he married wealthy Lady Anne Percy, of the great Northumberland family. When she died of smallpox in 1654 he returned to France and Italy, where he appears to have wrought havoc among the young women there, 'where all women shave, or where they shave all, which you please, for both are true', he reported in a later letter.[27]

While he was abroad, an uncle seized his estate over an alleged debt of £10,000, but in 1656, his grandfather, the 1st Earl, died, so he came back, made up with his uncle, and took on the estates and title of the Earldom of Chesterfield. He also got engaged to marry Mary Fairfax, the daughter of the great Parliamentary general, Lord Fairfax, owner of both his own and other sequestered estates in Yorkshire. The banns had been called three times in St Martin in the Fields, in London, when the even more glamorous George, Duke of Buckingham, arrived on the scene to sweep Mary and her father off their feet, and regain his sequestered estates adjoining the Fairfaxes'. Amazingly, her father approved, and in 1657 the two estates and young people were united.

Buckingham had had a busy few years. After the assassination of his father, George (born in 1623), like his brother and sister, had been brought up with the royal children. When the war broke out both brothers rushed to join up, but were sent abroad, where they learned about life, Italian style. They returned in 1648 and took up arms, when Francis was killed in action. George was soon captured, but escaped; the young man was offered a pardon, but got away to Charles in Jersey in 1649.

At that time he was a close friend and privy counsellor of Charles and was with him in Scotland, where he threw a tremendous sulk when, despite his high rank, he was refused overall military command. Like Charles, he escaped after the Battle of Worcester and went into hiding. The Baronne d'Aulnoy has a story about how he hid in London:

trimmed with a fox's brush and a merry cock's feathers. Sometimes, his face was covered by a mask; at others with flour, or blackened, whichever he deemed the most suitable. He established a theatre in the square at Charing Cross, and himself took the leadership of a company of musicians and buffoons. Every day he composed songs on such events of the moment as he could remember; he sang before an audience of three thousand persons; he sold antidotes for poisons, and plasters, and in this great city, surrounded by enemies, he lived in complete security.[28]

Meanwhile, his sister, Mary, married to James, Duke of Richmond and Lennox (a cousin of Charles), was under watch in Whitehall, and asked to be reunited with her husband, himself under similar guard at Windsor. George found out, and 'pitched his little stage on the road she would take; and as she passed, he cried out to the populace that he must have a little fun at the expense of the Duchess of Richmond and her family'. So he got the carriage stopped, and sang his songs, and then insisted that he should present her with the manuscripts. 'In approaching her, he lifted the piece of black silk which covered one of his eyes ['It is I …'], and his sister recognised him.'[29] With the songs came a packet of letters and other papers. Remembering that some years later his friend Rochester also disguised himself as a charlatan, selling potions to the people of London, one has to wonder whether Rochester recalled this exploit, or whether the baronne's friends transferred Rochester's jape to Buckingham. It is not impossible that it happened: amusing cheek was very much part of his repertoire.

After this, he got away to Rotterdam, and later continued negotiations about his sequestered estates, and even about a Restoration, slipping into England and debating with John Lilburne, the leader of the Levellers; the rest of the Royalists around Charles saw him as unprincipled and unreliable and his influence fell away. He was always wild in his behaviour, and, as a young man, arrogant and careless in his ways. John Aubrey has a characteristic little 'snigger-story' dating from about 1649, when the mathematician-philosopher Thomas Hobbes was in Paris, how the young man asked him to teach him geometry, which he picked up quickly: 'His Grace had great natural parts, and quickness of wit; Mr Hobbes read, and his Grace did not apprehend, which Mr Hobbes wondered at; at last, Mr Hobbes observed that his Grace was at mastrupation (his hand in his codpiece).'[30]

In 1652 there was talk that he wanted to marry the widowed Princess of Orange: the royal family was outraged, Queen Henrietta Maria declaring that she would tear her daughter in pieces with her own hands if she thought she would degrade herself with such a match. Undeterred, but still keen for money – exile, and the sequestration of his property had cost him dear – he came back to England, charmed Lord Fairfax and snapped up Mary Fairfax and the estates. Cromwell suspected a plot and ordered him to be arrested, but George went into hiding again. Fairfax appealed for his son-in-law, and he was allowed to reside in York House, under a kind of house arrest; when he left it, he was promptly put in the Tower, when Cromwell's death may have prevented his execution. In February 1659 he was released on a security payment of £20,000 by Fairfax, whom he joined in taking part in the activity that led to the overthrow of the Rump Parliament. When Charles landed at Dover, George was there to greet him.

To return to Chesterfield, who, no doubt considerably chafed in spirit after his outrageous almost pre-marital cuckolding, was now at a loose end. In no time he challenged a relative of Barbara's to a duel but was arrested and confined for a while; but with his title, looks and reputation for readiness with his weapon, the young women found him even more attractive. Soon, he was involved in flirtations with Barbara and her friend Lady Anne Hamilton. One of the girls' letters gives a good impression of giggling teenagers besotted with their charmer:

My Lord, My friend and I are now abed together a-contriving how to have your company this afternoon. If you deserve this favour, you will come and seek us at Ludgate Hill about three o'clock at Butler's shop, where we will expect you, but lest we should give you too much satisfaction at once, we will say no more, expect the rest when you see, Your etc.[31]

Chesterfield kept almost all his correspondence with his various lady friends throughout his life. His early letters, to Barbara among others, are characterised by courtly artifice – style over sincerity – whereas Barbara's spill out her heart:

> My Lord, I would fain have had the happiness to have seen you at church this day but I was not suffered to go, I am never so well pleased as when I am with you, though I find you are better when you are with other ladies, for you were yesterday all the afternoon with the person I am most jealous of, and I know I have so little merit that I am suspicious you love all women better than myself. I sent you yesterday a letter that I think might convince you that I loved nothing better besides yourself, nor will I ever although you should hate me ...[32]

She had not been allowed to go to church where she might see him: perhaps her parents were becoming uneasy. Her friend was sent off to Windsor, away from danger (Anne was to marry Robert Carnegie, later Earl of Southesk, and to take the Duke of York as lover, among others: of that more – sensationally – anon). Chesterfield's reputation for wildness was worsening, matched almost by Barbara's recklessness; she wrote:

> It is ever my ill fortune to be disappointed of what I most desire, for this afternoon I did promise to myself the satisfaction of your company; but I fear I am disappointed, which I assure you is no small affliction to me; but I hope the fates may yet be so kind as to let me see you about five o'clock; if you will be at your private lodgings at Lincoln's Inn Fields, I will endeavour to come.[33]

This was going too far: for a young lady to be alone in a man's private lodgings was socially taboo and could mean 'only one thing'. It seems that her parents' watchfulness may have been in vain:

> My Lord, The joy of being with you this last night has made me do nothing but dream of you, and my life is never so pleasant to me

but when I am with you or talking of you, yet the discourses of the world must make me a little more circumspect ...[34]

The circumspection proved inadequate; her mother and step-father were now sufficiently alarmed and action had to be taken before Barbara was publicly ruined.

Now, in the nick of time, they found Roger Palmer, a year younger than Chesterfield, of a good Catholic Royalist family, of Eton, King's College, Cambridge, and the Inner Temple, who was, moreover, in love with the lovely Barbara. They were delighted; his father, Sir James, was not, who

> having strong surmises of the misfortunes that would attend this match, used all the arguments that paternal affection could suggest to dissuade his son from prosecuting his suit in this way, adding that if he was resolved to marry her, he foresaw he should be one of the most miserable men in the world.[35]

Barbara's feelings about this enforced marriage can be imagined, how they made her do it can only be guessed, but on 14 April 1659, in the church of St Gregory by St Paul's, the Angleseys transferred responsibility for their headstrong daughter to their naïve new son-in-law, Roger Palmer.

Marriage did not diminish Barbara's passion for Chesterfield; within a few weeks, she was writing to her beloved:

> Since I last saw you I have been at home and I find the mounser [monsieur: her husband, lord and master; spelling was never her forte] in a very ill humour, for he says that he is resolved never to bring me to town again and that nobody shall see me when I am in the country [It is like an episode in Wycherley's *The Country Wife*]. I would not have you come today, for that will displease him more. But send me word presently what you would advise me to do. For I am ready and willing to go all over the world with you and I will obey your commands, that am, whilst I live, Yours.[36]

Not surprisingly, Chesterfield did not take up this offer and was soon moving on to other engagements. It was not long before he was in trouble again, after another duel; the cause was another young woman, as he explained in his memoirs:

> A young lady having drawn me for her Valentine, I presented her with a porcelain chamber pot and a looking glass fitted to the bottom of it with the inscription,
>
> *Narcissus se mirent en l'onde* [Narcissus admiring himself in the water]
> *Vit la plus belle chose du Monde* [Saw there the most beautiful thing in the world]
>
> which was ill resented, and I had a quarrel with Captain Whaley, who in a duel I wounded and disarmed, for which I was sent prisoner to the Tower ...[37]

Suspected of involvement in a Royalist plot, he was released only on surrendering £10,000 as security.

At some time that summer, Barbara fell seriously ill with smallpox and wrote to him, pathetically:

> My dear life, I have been this day extremely ill, and the not hearing from you hath made me much worse than otherways I should have been. The doctor doth believe me in a desperate condition, and I must confess that the unwillingness I have to leave you makes me not entertain the thoughts of death so willingly as otherways I should, for there is nothing besides yourself that could make me desire to live a day.[38]

Although Chesterfield had earlier survived an attack of smallpox, he did not rush to visit her. At least Barbara survived, now immune, apparently unmarked, her beauty unimpaired.

Now, with tensions developing between the Army and the Rump Parliament, the Royalist party began to feel more hopeful. General Monck had begun his march south from Scotland with his troops, though nobody knew what his intentions were. ('I remember in the main,' wrote John Aubrey, 'that they were satisfied he no more intended the King's restoration, when he came into England ... than his horse did.'[39]) Now was the time for all good, or shrewd, men to rally to the cause.

Roger Palmer loyally donated £1,000, a considerable sum out of his resources, but possibly a good investment. Furthermore, his sister, Catherine, had as a brother-in-law Henry Darrell, a principal clerk in the Council of State. Barbara's cousin, Alan Brodrick, persuaded Darrell to transfer secret information to Catherine, who was easily able to pass it on to Roger. Brodrick could now get important information back to Charles – if a suitable messenger could be found. He wrote to Hyde about Palmer's help – and needs:

> I must presume to whisper to your Lordship: a gay wife and great expense to a slender fortune in possession, the main of his estate being in lease for some years to come.
>
> To the King, he suggested, 'that you may in more than ordinary expressions of kindness own this meritorious act of theirs.'[40]

The King's court was now in Brussels, where there had been a severe outbreak of smallpox, so it was important to find messengers from England immune to the disease – such as Roger Palmer's 'gay wife'. Roger presumably stayed back to receive any further information, but soon enough Barbara had crossed over, on the rebound from Chesterfield and ready for more life; before long she was at court and in bed with her king. At some time he wrote to Palmer to express, 'how much I am beholding to you in several respects ... You have more title than one to my kindness.'[41]

The question is, whether this happened spontaneously, or whether her Villiers relations got her there, believing in the power a mistress could have. George Savile, Marquess of Halifax, later wrote:

> A mistress, either dextrous in herself or well instructed by those that are so, may be very useful to her friends, not only in the immediate hours of her ministry, but by her influence and insinuations at other

times. It was resolved generally by others whom he should have in his arms, as well as whom he should have in his councils. Of a man who was so capable of choosing, he chose as seldom as any man that ever lived.[42]

However discreet they may have been, word got around, nevertheless. Chesterfield heard, far away in France, and wrote reproachfully:

Madam, My letters have equally with more thoughts attended you from all the considerable parts of my journey ... but Madam the news I have from England concerning your ladyship makes me doubt of everything; and therefore let me entreat you to send me your picture, for then I shall love something that is like you and yet unchangeable ...[43]

Word, presumably, also got back to Roger. Where Barbara was in the crucial early months of 1660 is not known. The general opinion is that she went back to England before the King; had some interesting conversations with her husband, who, knowing her as he had come to, may have been shocked but not very surprised, reconciling himself to his (inevitable) fate as a cuckold; and then prepared herself for the King's triumphant return and arrival in London on his thirtieth birthday, when she would still be only nineteen.

2

THE KING, THE QUEAN AND THE QUEEN

How shall I speak of that triumphant day
When you renewed th' expiring pomp of May?
(A month that owns an interest in your name:
You and the flowers are its peculiar claim.)[1]

On 25 May 1660, Charles arrived in Dover aboard *The Royal Charles* – so very recently the Parliamentarian *Naseby* – accompanied by, among others, Samuel Pepys and an incontinent dog 'which shit in the boat, which made us laugh and me think that a King and all that belong to him are but just as others are', wrote Pepys (25 May 1660), who would learn more of the King's common humanity. At Dover, General Monck handed his sheathed sword to the King and the mayor presented him with a very rich Bible, which he said was the thing that he loved above all things in the world. Charles and Monck then sat in the royal coach, facing forward; the royal Dukes of York and Gloucester sat opposite; and Buckingham, who had been present on the beach, climbed onto the boot, over the back wheels. When the others transferred to horseback, he rode behind them in unwavering pursuit, to be present at Barham Downs when the King reviewed soldiers he and the Earls of Oxford, Derby and Northampton had gathered together.

On went the royal party, to Canterbury, Rochester and Chatham, met by cheering crowds (those less enthusiastic stayed away, biding their time). At Blackheath, on his thirtieth birthday, 29 May, Charles was confronted by 30,000 soldiers of the Parliamentary army, who symbolically laid down their weapons before taking them up as loyal soldiers of the King. His triumphant progress into the City of London was not merely spontaneous but carefully overseen, with an eye to triumphal arches, pageants and loyal readings. A speech to the House of Lords declared his determination to restore the nation 'to freedom and happiness ... by the advice of my Parliament'. Finally, there was a ceremonial dinner; when at last he could withdraw, he remarked that he now realised that it must have been 'my own fault that I have been absent so long, for I see nobody that does not protest he has ever wished for my return'.[2]

Where he then went, to lay his weary head, is not known, but one person who was waiting impatiently for him was Barbara Palmer. Legend has it that he spent the night with her; be that as it may, nine months later, on 25 February 1661, Barbara gave birth to her first child, Anne. Charles was to acknowledge the child, though Roger Palmer also claimed her; some people thought she resembled Philip Chesterfield.

A satirist (possibly Andrew Marvell) wrote in *An Historical Poem* (1678) how

> Of a tall stature and of sable hue,
> Much like the son of Kish, that lofty Jew
> [Saul, son of Kish, was 'a choice young man and a
> goodly ... from his shoulders and upward he was
> higher than any of the people': 1 Samuel IX],
> Twelve years complete he suffered in exile
> And kept his father's asses all the while.
> At length by wonderful impulse of Fate
> The people call him home to help the State,
> And what is more they send him money too,

> And clothe him all from head to foot anew;
> Nor did he such small favours then disdain,
> But in his thirtieth year began to reign.
> In a slashed doublet then he came to shore,
> And dubbed poor Palmer's wife his royal whore.[3]

In some respects, 'poor' Palmer was not too badly off; he had taken a house in fashionable King Street (where Lucy Walter's parents had lived, earlier), convenient for Whitehall and Westminster. It was next to the house of the Earl of Sandwich, member of the Navy Board and patron of Samuel Pepys. Working late one night, on 13 July 1660, Pepys and the Earl stood at the door listening to the music coming from next door, 'the King and Dukes there with Madam Palmer, a pretty woman that they have a fancy to make her husband a cuckold'. James and Henry had already been noticed as regulars in St James's Park, soon to become notorious as an active 'pick-up ground'.

On 14 October, when Pepys was at chapel in Whitehall, he 'also observed how the Duke of York and Mistress Palmer did talk to one another very wantonly through the hangings that part the King's closet and the closet where the ladies sit'. The Duke's amorous activities were not greatly hindered by his (as yet, secret) marriage on 3 September to Anne Hyde, the daughter of the Chancellor. Soon enough, it came into the open, with great scandal; meanwhile, Barbara's liaison with the King was being kept fairly quiet – not even the relentlessly curious Pepys had realised it yet. In the early months, she would be brought to his rooms in Whitehall. The visiting Italian courtier Lorenzo Magalotti later told of an incident when the King was in bed with her when a fire broke out near his room:

> ... and they found themselves surrounded by the guards and all the Court, who had run to extinguish it. Meanwhile the lady was in the King's bed, and he found it advisable to put her, naked, into the hands of [Charles] Gerard, who thought of a place to stow her safely away, also profiting from his opportunity, according to some people.[4]

It would not be long before she had earned that reputation.

Meanwhile, she learned of Chesterfield's proposed marriage to Elizabeth Butler, daughter of the Marquis of Ormonde, and angrily broke off with him. 'After so many years service, fidelity and respect,' he wrote,

> to be banished for the first offence is very hard ... Let me not live, if I did not believe that not all the women on earth could have given me so great an affliction as I have suffered by your displeasure. [It is to be hoped that his intended did not see this.] ... if you will neither answer my letters nor speak to me before I go out of Town, it is more than an even lay that I shall never come to it again.[5]

That was all over now.

On 20 April 1661, the King dubbed sixty-eight Knights of the Bath to attend his coronation and promoted six noblemen to earldoms, including his Chancellor, Baron Hyde, who became the Earl of Clarendon. That evening, Pepys went to the theatre, where his pleasure was to see 'many great beauties, but above all Mrs Palmer, with whom the King doth discover a great deal of familiarity'. On St George's Day the coronation took place, with great magnificence and pageantry, followed by heavy rain, thunder and lightning and a heroic quantity of popular drinking – Pepys 'wondered to see how the ladies did tipple' and wrote how, when he woke, 'I found myself wet with my spewing. Thus did the day end, with joy everywhere.'

Now that Charles was crowned King, he needed a queen, and, as soon as Parliament met, he announced his intended marriage to the Infanta Catherine of Braganza, of Portugal. After protracted negotiations and reviewing of other possible candidates, Catherine had been chosen with a view of the effect of the marriage on Spain, France and the Netherlands. Furthermore, the dowry included Tangier, with its access to the Mediterranean, the island of Bombay, not expected to be of great value, privileges for British merchants in the Portuguese Empire and about £30,000 (which, disappointingly, came to be paid in instalments and some of it in kind). There was about a year to pass before the young princess could arrive and be married – a year to make arrangements for Barbara.

In May, she caused alarm and scandal in court by announcing that she intended to give birth in Hampton court Palace – where at about that time the royal honeymoon might be expected to take place. Her relationship with the King was by now common knowledge: on 23 July, Pepys, at the theatre, remarked, 'Only, I sat before Mrs Palmer, the King's mistress, and filled my eyes with her, which much pleased me' (this seems to mark the beginning of his obsession with her). Now seemed the time to acknowledge her formally.

The King wanted her in Whitehall, with a title. Unfortunately, it was known that Clarendon, who detested her, would not, as Lord Chancellor, approve an English title. On October 16, the King requested a warrant for Mr Roger Palmer to be an Irish earl.

Barbara's choice was the earldom of Castlemaine and barony of Limerick: her father and uncle had been viscounts of Limerick, so any son of hers would have the title of Lord Limerick. On November 8, Charles demanded a warrant for Roger Palmer for these titles. On 7 December, Pepys saw the patent at the privy seal office and noted that it was only Lady Castlemaine's heirs who were to be honoured, 'the reason whereof everybody knows'. Palmer took his time before assuming his tainted title, while Clarendon was established as her deadly foe.

Others at court were hostile to this blatant sexual misconduct, despite the King's obvious commitment. On 22 January 1662, Pepys wrote, 'There are factions (private ones at court) about Madam Palmer. What it is about I know not, but it is something about the King's favour to her now that the Queen is coming.' On 6 April, he heard the canon at Whitehall Chapel preach to the King on the sin of adultery, and on 21 April he recorded that the Duchess of Richmond, Buckingham's widowed eldest sister, had denounced Barbara to her face as 'Jane Shore, and did hope to see her come to the same end'. (Edward IV's mistress died in poverty, her body thrown on a dunghill.)

On 13 April Catherine sailed from Lisbon; the journey was stormy, and she was seasick, never leaving her cabin (though perhaps attempting a little English). In expectation, the royal apartments were being refurbished for her with a crimson velvet bed lined with cloth of gold, a looking glass given by the Queen Mother, many pictures and a chapel with a raised altar and silvered altar rails.[6] On 15 May, she arrived at Portsmouth. 'At night all the bells rang, and bonfires made for the joy of the Queen's arrival', but there was no bonfire outside Lady Castlemaine's house in King Street, where Charles was visiting, as usual. As Sarah, Lord Sandwich's housekeeper, told Pepys, after remarking on Barbara's bulk late in her pregnancy, she and the King 'sent for a pair of scales and weighed one another; and she, being with child, was said to be the heaviest.'

Every night that week the King dined with Barbara, no doubt making promises; Parliamentary business took up the day until late in the evening of the 19th, when he drove down. On the 20th, Pepys saw Barbara at the theatre, although his pleasure was spoiled 'to see her look dejectedly and slighted by people already'.

On the 21st, Charles was able to give Catherine only a chaste kiss, as she had a sore throat. He was relieved at her appearance and assured Clarendon that there was nothing about her 'that in the least degree can shock one' (praise indeed; what had he been led to expect?), though with her hair dressed in tight corkscrews on each side of her head, 'at first sight,' he later confided, 'I thought they had brought me a bat, instead of a woman.'[7] She was short – though so was his mother – (Magalotti wrote later, 'small for a woman and a shade tall for a dwarf'[8]) dark, her face somewhat pointed and her teeth rather protuberant (but then, so were his mother's, though Van Dyck's portraits concealed that: Princess Sophia of Hanover described Henrietta Maria as 'a little woman with long arms, crooked shoulders, and teeth protruding from her mouth like guns from a fort'[9]). Later, he wrote, 'I think I must be the worst person living (which I hope I am not) if I be not a good husband.'

There were problems from the very beginning, as Charles was required to be married by the Church of England rite, but Catherine insisted that only a Roman Catholic priest would do. In the end, a secret, Catholic ceremony took place in her chamber, followed by a service conducted by the Archbishop of Canterbury, which she detested. To Clarendon he wrote, 'It was happy for the honour of the nation that I was not put to the consummation of the marriage last night, for I was so sleepy by having slept but two hours in my journey as I was afraid that matters would have gone very sleepily.'[10] The next day, he wrote to his sister:

> I was married the day before yesterday, but the fortune that follows our family is fallen upon me, car Monsieur Le Cardinal *m'a fermé la porte au nez*, and though I am not so furious as Monsieur was [Minette's husband, the Duc d'Orléans], but am content to let those pass over before I go to bed to my wife, yet I hope I shall entertain her at least better the first night than he did you.[11]

As for Barbara, she saluted her monarch's wedding day in her own fashion: Pepys, walking through the Privy Garden in Whitehall, saw her laundry, 'the finest smocks and linen petticoats of my Lady Castlemaine's, laced with rich lace at the bottom, that ever I saw', billowing in the breeze: they had the air of battle flags.

Catherine, on the other hand, was not well equipped for a contest with the glamour queen of the court – she was no more than pleasant-looking, unfashionably dressed, brought up devoutly in a Catholic convent and 'inclined to piety, or rather superstition', according to Magalotti.[12] With her came a squad of monks and a train of lady attendants generally regarded at court as ugly, who insisted on wearing old-fashioned farthingales, with skirts projecting widely at each side (inconveniently taking up twice the space in the coaches ordered to bring them from Portsmouth). Their concern for propriety meant that they could not sleep in a bed which had previously been occupied by a man. Some of their complaints seem not unreasonable: 'Yesterday,' Chesterfield reported, 'they complained that they cannot stir abroad without seeing in every corner great beastly English pricks battering against every wall, and for this and some other reasons they are speedily to be sent back to their own country.'[13] The 'other reasons' were part of the King's reprisals against Catherine's resistance to Barbara.

Before that, the honeymoon took place at Hampton Court.

Charles, affable and experienced, helped with learning English, teased and spent the nights with her – possibly the only virgin he was ever to have – which did much to reconcile her and bring her to love him. Naturally, there was always prurient speculation; later, Magalotti was to sum up court gossip, to the effect that Catherine was 'more than usually sensitive to pleasure'.

> She finds the King provided by nature with implements most suitable for exciting it [Apropos of the King's 'implements', on 15 May 1665, Pepys was told that Charles was genitally well endowed. Rochester wrote, with satiric hyperbole, that 'his sceptre and his prick are of a length'; the sceptre was two feet ten and a half inches long[14]], and it is said that her ecstasy is then so extreme that after the ordinary escape of those humours that the violence of pleasure presses even from women, blood comes from her genital parts in such great abundance that it does not stop for several days.[15]

Catherine's reaction sounds much more like the condition that was thought to have afflicted her earlier, before her marriage ('the extraordinary frequency and abundance of her menses'[16]). In later years, perhaps,

> with all this, it may be so much because of her care not to harm her chance of having children that she very often refuses the embraces of the King, who sleeps with her every night; and when she does get ready to receive them, she prepares herself with an unusual diet, and in the act itself she manages to avoid all those refinements that others seek in order to stimulate more vehemently the heat of wantonness.[17]

This, to compete with 'my Lady Castlemaine [who] rules him; who [it is said] hath all the tricks of Aretino that are to be practised to give pleasure'.[18] Some two and a half weeks after their arrival, a messenger reported to the King that Barbara had been delivered of a boy, whom she had named after him.

This gave the cuckold husband, Roger Palmer, an occasion for a sort of revenge: recently converted to Catholicism, he got the child to a Catholic priest, who administered the baptismal rites. Enraged, Barbara sent word upriver to the King, who hurried back with Lady Suffolk (Barbara's aunt) and Aubrey de Vere, Earl of Oxford, and promptly had the child baptised by the Anglican rites at St Margaret's, Westminster. The boy was now Charles Palmer, Lord Limerick.

The double baptism provoked a violent quarrel between husband and wife; in one of the spectacular rages for which she was to become notorious, she stormed off to her uncle's place at Richmond, taking with her almost everything in the King Street house – furniture, cloths, dishes, all her plate, jewels and her servants – leaving an empty house and one porter. Palmer's response was to secure his position by executing a bond with his wife's family, the Earl and Countess of Suffolk and her uncle, Lord Grandison, binding them with the sum of £10,000 to indemnify him from any and all of his wife's debts. With him gone, she could return at leisure, whenever she wished; meanwhile, Richmond was only four miles from Hampton – and soon the King set her up in an apartment there.

Now the time had come for Barbara's appointment as Lady of the Bedchamber to the Queen. What Charles thought Catherine would make of it, is not known; perhaps he thought she did not know about Barbara – but the affair had been known about in Portugal before Catherine sailed. Part of the problem consisted in the fact that the appointment had to be approved by the Queen, who did not wish to have her husband's whore about her. When he handed her a list including Barbara's name, she promptly struck it off; the King equally promptly restored it. When the Queen was in her reception room in Hampton Court Palace, the King led in a tall, auburn-haired woman, whom he presented to her as 'My Lady Castlemaine'. After a moment's shock, Catherine sat down, white-faced; tears gushed from her eyes and blood from her nose and she fainted. Courtiers carried her into a more private chamber. The King did not follow his wife; instead, he escorted Lady Castlemaine to her coach, furious at what he saw as Catherine's public defiance.

He was absolutely determined to have his way, at any cost to his wife. When, on 22 July, he wrote to his sister in France, where they were familiar with court mistresses, giving his view of events, she replied with a mixture of amusement and reproach, 'Alas! How can one possibly say such things? I, who know your innocence, marvel at it. But, jesting apart, I pray you tell me how the Queen takes this. It is said here that she is grieved beyond measure, and, to speak frankly, I think it is with reason.'[19]

Now he turned to his oldest counsellor, Clarendon, hardly the best choice. Clarendon (who recorded the whole sorry business[20]) himself felt it was too delicate a task for him, who had already told the King that whatever he had seen in Louis' court, such practices would be regarded very differently in England. The King then declared:[20]

I have undone this lady and ruined her reputation, which was fair and untainted until her friendship with me, and I am obliged in conscience and honour to repair her to the utmost of my power. I will always avow a great friendship for her, which I owe as well to the memory of her father as to her own person; and I shall look upon it as the highest disrespect to me in anybody who shall treat her otherwise than is due to her own birth and dignity to which I have raised her.

I like her company and conversation, from which I will not be restrained, because I know there is and will be all innocence in it. My wife shall never have cause to complain that I broke my vows to her if she will live towards me as a good wife ought to do, in rendering herself grateful and acceptable to me, which it is in her power to do. But if she continue uneasy to me I cannot answer for myself that I shall not endeavour to seek content in other company.

I have proceeded so far in the business that concerns my Lady Castlemaine, and am so deeply engaged in it, that she will not only be exposed to all manner of contempt if it succeeds not, but my own honour will suffer so much that I shall become ridiculous to the world and be thought too in pupillage under a governor.

And therefore I shall expect a conformity from my wife herein ... Upon the whole I shall never secede from any part of the resolution I have taken and expressed to you. And therefore I require you to use all those arguments to the Queen which are necessary to induce her to a full compliance with what I desire.

An impressive display of cant and hypocrisy, with remarkable views of Barbara's reputation and his honour. One wonders whether he felt he had been too much 'in pupillage' to his mother, in Paris. Clarendon still had to talk to the Queen. Tactlessly, he said that, coming as she did from a southern country, she could not be unfamiliar with similar sexual liaisons and could not expect her husband to have no sexual experience, but all that was behind him now, and if she would respond, all would be well. However, when he assumed that she would approve Castlemaine as a Lady of the Bedchamber, she was furious, and said she would rather put herself on any little vessel and go back to Lisbon. He in turn bluntly reminded her she had no control over her actions and could not even leave the house without the King's permission.

Clarendon persisted, but in vain, and asked to be relieved of this unpleasant task. The King warned him against permitting any gossip or discussion about the whole business. As it happened, Sir Allan Brodrick, who only two years earlier had asked Clarendon to persuade Charles to reward Roger Palmer for his generosity, had just been appointed Provost Marshal of Ulster; he had something to say, now. The King wrote to Clarendon to warn Brodrick to say nothing about the affair, and ' to let him have a care how he is the author of any scandalous reports, for if I find him guilty of any such thing I will make him repent it to the last moment of his life'. He went on to threaten Clarendon:

And I wish I may be unhappy in this world and the world to come if I fail in the least degree of what I have resolved; which is of making my Lady Castlemaine of my wife's Bedchamber; and whosoever I find use any endeavour to hinder this resolution of mine (except it be only to myself) I will be his enemy to the last moment of my life.

You know how true a friend I have been to you. If you will oblige me eternally, make this business as easy as you can, of what opinion soever you are. For I am resolved to go through with this matter, let what will come of it: which again I solemnly swear before Almighty God. Therefore, if you desire to have the continuance of my friendship, meddle no more with this business, except it be to bear down all false scandalous reports and to facilitate what I am sure my honour is so much concerned in. And whosoever I find to be my Lady Castlemaine's enemy in this matter, I do promise you upon my word to be his enemy as long as I live.

He was not always a merry monarch.

Another threat by Catherine to go home to Portugal was met with the banishment of her spiritual confessors and almost all her Portuguese ladies in waiting (as Chesterfield reported), though Buckingham snapped up one of them.[21] The effective isolation of the desperate young queen was intended to break her will. She sat alone, disconsolate in her chamber; in the Great Hall at Hampton, the King did not speak to her, while courtiers and ladies crowded around him. At night, or rather, in the early hours before dawn, he would return to bed. At some time, she broke, and gave in. Utterly alone, utterly helpless; there was nothing to be done. If she was to have any life, here in this distant foreign country, she had to concede. As Clarendon – to continue with him – recorded, with, no doubt, mixed feelings, 'The Queen on a sudden let herself fall first to conversation and then to familiarity, and even in the same instant to a confidence with the Lady [whom he could never refer to by name]; was merry with her in public, talked kindly of her, and in private used nobody more friendly.' Castlemaine became a Lady of the Queen's Bedchamber; when the Queen went to the first Mass allowed her by the marriage treaty, the Lady Castlemaine was in attendance.

On 23 August 1662, the King and Queen left Hampton Court for Whitehall by barge, in a magnificent waterborne spectacle, 'with 10,000 barges and boats,' thought Pepys, 'for we could see no water for them.'

But that which pleased me best was that my Lady Castlemaine stood over against us upon a piece of Whitehall – where I glutted myself with looking on her. But methought it was strange to see her Lord and her upon the same place, walking up and down without taking notice one of another; only, at first entry, he put off his hat and she made him a very civil salute – but afterwards took no notice one of another. But both of them now and then would take their child,

which the nurse held in her arms, and dandle it. ... Anon, there
came one there, booted and spurred, that she talked long with. And
by and by, she being in her hair, she put on his hat, which was but
an ordinary one, to keep the wind off. But methought it became her
mightily, as everything else do.

She made a glamorous picture, her auburn hair ruffled under the
broad-brimmed hat; it was the last time she and Roger were seen
together in public, but already she was looking away, for the
coming of her lover and his wife.

Soon enough, the new set-up was in place at Whitehall, where
the young Queen entered her gilded cage. On 7 September, Pepys
was in the Queen Mother's presence-chamber, where he saw the
Queen herself – 'a good modest and innocent look' – and where he
also saw Castlemaine, together with Charles's son by Lucy Walter,
'a most pretty spark', now nearly thirteen, named James Crofts,
who, he perceived, 'doth hang much upon my Lady Castlemaine
and is always with her', while she and the Queen 'were mighty
kind to him'. He recorded how the King and Queen were 'very
merry, and how he would have made the Queen Mother believe
that his Queen was with child, and said that she said so; and the
young Queen answered, "You lie"; which was the first English
word that ever I heard her say.'

When they left, the King, Queen, Castlemaine and young Crofts,
went together in one coach. Soon, the King made his precocious
son the Duke of Monmouth, while also promoting his marriage
– or getting him away from Barbara (whose character was too
notorious for 'her real design' in her 'commendations and caresses
... to be mistaken', wrote the Comte de Gramont[22]) – to Lady Ann
Scott, the twelve year-old heiress of the Earl of Buccleuch. The
Baronne d'Aulnoy observed that

She was one of the richest heiresses in the Kingdom of Scotland;
all that could be wished for to make a person amiable met in her;
virtue, intelligence, great possessions, birth; and, although she was
not extraordinarily beautiful, and although she limped a little [but
not at this time: she dislocated her hip while dancing, in 1668], she

was ever full of liveliness. Perhaps if the Duke had been obliged to exert himself to achieve the conquest and had found it difficult, and so to his glory to win, he might have thought himself but too happy to succeed in espousing her; but he received her from the hands of the King; she never cost him a tear or a sigh; and this, what should have been his happiness, proved but his embarrassment and his affliction ... In addition, he was disinclined to submit to the fetters Hymen imposes.[23]

The wedding was in April 1663, though Charles pulled them out of bed after ten minutes because he considered the bride too young.[24]

The court went on its way. Sir Charles Berkeley was made Privy Purse – 'a most vicious person', wrote Pepys on 17 October, who offered the wife of Pierce (or Pearse), the Duke's surgeon, £300 to be his mistress. Berkeley and Sir Henry Bennet were in cahoots with Castlemaine, 'whose interest is now as great as ever ... Mistress Hazlerigg, the great beauty, is got with child and was brought to bed, and lays it to the King or the Duke of York.' She could not be sure, it could be either; both disavowed it, unconvincingly. The Duke thought that at the relevant time he had been pursuing Jane Middleton (of whom, more later), while Charles was then sleeping with Winifred Wells, a Maid of Honour, described by Gramont as 'a tall girl, exquisitely shaped ... [who] walked like a goddess' but whose face made her look like a sheep. 'Her father having faithfully served Charles the First, she thought it her duty not to revolt against Charles the Second.'[25] Others suggested that His Majesty 'had to complain of facilities less pleasing', which prompted Buckingham to write a verse punning on Wells:

Quand le roi de ce puits sentit l'horreur profonde,
Progers, s'écria-t-il, que suis-je devenu! [the King's Groom of the
   Bedchamber]
Ah! Depuis que j'y sonde
Si je n'avais cherché que le centre du monde
J'y serois parvenu.[26]

A loose translation, better it who can:

When the King plumbed this frightful well,
Progers, he cried, where am I, tell!
Since these depths I have sounded,
If I'd sought of the earth's shell
The centre, by now I'd have found it.

Pepys also heard that Barbara was pregnant again, while also taking an interest in Harry Jermyn, nephew and heir to Henry Jermyn, Lord St Albans, no *beau garçon* but a fashionable favourite with the court women because of his reputed 'implement' (as Magalotti would have put it). He was interested in Jane Middleton, but was temporarily banished from the court. Her pregnancy was inconvenient for her husband, as Pepys noted on 3 November, 'though it be the King's, yet her Lord being still in town and sometime seeing of her, though never to eat or lie together, it will be laid to him': in practice, it was a politic lie imposed on the husband.

Pepys was able to get in to see the court's New Year's Eve Ball, in Whitehall, attended by the King and Queen, the Duke and Duchess of York 'and all the great ones', including young Monmouth and Lady Castlemaine:

Then to country dances; the King leading the first which he called for; which was – says he, *Cuckolds all a-row*, the old dance of England.[27] Of the ladies that danced, the Duke of Monmouth's mistress and my Lady Castlemaine and a daughter of Sir Harry de Vic's were the best.[28]

The age-old dance of cuckoldry was certainly all the fashion at Charles's court. Shortly afterwards, Sarah, Lady Sandwich's housekeeper, told Pepys how

the King sups at least four or five times every week with my Lady Castlemaine; and most often stays till the morning with her and goes home through the garden all alone privately, and that so the very sentries take notice of it and speak of it. She tells me that about a month ago she [Barbara] quickened at my Lord Gerard's at dinner and cried out she was undone; and all the lords and men were fain to quit the room, and women called to help her. In fine, I find that there is nothing almost but bawdry at Court from top to bottom.[29]

The 'quickening' was, if anything, a miscarriage; her next child, Henry, was not born until 20 September.

Shortly afterwards, at another ball during the New Year festivities,

> A child was dropped by one of the ladies in dancing; but nobody knew who, it being taken up by somebody in their handkerchief. The next morning all the Ladies of Honour appeared early at Court for their vindication, so that nobody could tell whose this mischance could be. But it seems Mistress Wells fell sick that afternoon and hath disappeared ever since, so that it is concluded it was her.[30]

(Winifred was back at court by the 23rd, and remained on the reserve team of mistresses for some years.) The father was tacitly assumed to be the King. On 17 February, Pepys was told that the shocking story was true,

> and that the King had it in his closet a week after, and did dissect it; and making great sport of it, said that in his opinion it must have been a month and three hours old and that whatever others think, he had the greatest loss (it being a boy, he says), that had lost a subject by the business.

Meanwhile, Barbara flirted with her clique – she was seen, through open windows, going to bed while Sir Charles Berkeley watched – and kept an eye on Charles's latest passion, the recently arrived young Frances Stuart. Her thinking, presumably, was that if he were quickly successful, he would be less likely to bother about what she herself was up to with Harry Jermyn (when he returned to court) or anyone else. Her strategy was to be particularly friendly to the rather naïve fifteen year old, having her round for sleepovers and spending the night in her bed. When the King called round in the morning, he would find two lovelies to greet him, which he came to look forward to. One night, Barbara pushed matters on a little further, arranging a mock marriage-night ceremony with Frances, playing the bridegroom herself and with the King arriving to take her place. However, he got no further with Frances than Barbara had. The tactic having failed, by July she felt that she could do without Frances's company every night, but Charles insisted that if she were not there, he would not come.

He was very loyal – or obedient – to Barbara. When Lady Gerard invited the King and Queen, but not Barbara, to dinner, Barbara spoke beforehand to the King. The King and Queen arrived at their hosts', but before the meal, Charles left the house and went to Barbara's and spent the night there; it was as crude an insult as could readily be imagined (and what of poor Catherine?). Afterwards, there was an exchange of views, and when, at a ball, Lady Gerard requested him as a partner, he led her out then left her, and, as Pepys recorded on 7 March, dismissed her as Lady of the Bedchamber to the Queen. On 25 April, Pepys heard that the Queen was 'much grieved of late at the King's neglecting her, he having not supped once with her this quarter of a year, and almost every night with my Lady Castlemaine, who hath been with him this St George's feast at Windsor and came home with him last night'. He was also sorry to hear, 'though I love her much', that she had been given rooms in Whitehall, over the Tudor Holbein Gate, convenient for the King.

Sometimes Catherine was able to score a little. On 4 July, Pepys recorded how Barbara, as Lady of the Bedchamber and waiting for the Queen, found the Queen still with her dresser and remarked, 'I wonder your Majesty can have the patience to sit so long a-dressing'. 'Oh,' the Queen replied, 'I have so much reason to use patience, that I can very well bear with it.' Pepys's informant thought 'it may be the Queen hath commanded her to retire', but Pepys thought it unlikely. Then, on 13 July, the King and Queen rode in St James's Park, where Pepys thought that she

> looked in this dress, a white laced waistcoat and a crimson short
> petticoat and her hair dressed *à la negligence*, mighty pretty; and

the King rode hand in hand with her. Here was also my Lady Castlemaine amongst the rest of the ladies, but the King took methought no notice of her; nor when they [alighted] did anybody press (as she seemed to expect, and stayed for it) to take her down, but was taken down by her own gentleman. She looked mighty out of humour, and had a yellow plume in her hat (which all took notice of) and yet is very handsome – but very melancholy; nor did anybody speak to her or she so much as smile or speak to anybody.

Pepys was charmed; ominously, he now thought that Frances Stewart was more attractive. 'Nor do I wonder if the King changes, which I verily believe is the reason of his coldness to my Lady Castlemaine.'

Barbara withdrew for a while, 'upon some slighting words from the King', but was soon back and in command. On 21 July, the Duke of Buckingham invited the King and Queen to dinner; again she dealt with it. Hearing of it at the home of her aunt, Lady Suffolk, she remarked, 'Well, much good may it do them, and for all that I will be as merry as they,' went home and ordered a great supper to be prepared. Next day, Pepys recorded, 'After the King had been with the Queen at Wallingford House, he came to my Lady Castlemaine's and was there all night'. Not only another snub to would-be friendly hosts, but another public humiliation for Catherine. (It is a wonder that the King and Queen were ever invited out.)

Catherine rallied; the court went to Tunbridge Wells, where it was thought the waters might help her conceive. The spa town was, as Gramont observed, the meeting place 'of all the gay and handsome of both sexes', where 'constraint is banished, familiarity is established upon the first acquaintance, and joy and pleasure are the sole sovereigns of the place'.[31] A doctor friend of Pepys told him on 11 August how the Queen was 'grown a very debonair lady and now hugs him and meets him galloping upon the road, and all the actions of a fond and pleasant lady that can be', while Charles, for his part, was no doubt making every effort to ensure that the visit was not wholly wasted. Rochester saw a more effective means than spa water of making the various ladies pregnant:

> For here walk Cuff and Kick,
> With brawny back and legs and potent prick,
> Who more substantially will cure thy wife,
> And on her half-dead womb bestow new life.
> From these the waters got the reputation
> Of good assistants unto generation.[32]

He may well have had a point: as it was, the waters, while ineffective on Catherine, were apparently all too potent with some of her ladies, as the French ambassador reported, 'For they nearly ruined the good name of the maids and the ladies (those I mean who were there without their husbands). It took them a whole month, and some more than that, to clear themselves and save their honour; and it is even reported that a few of them are not quite out of trouble yet.'[33]

Barbara never needed spa water; on 20 September 1663, she gave birth to a son, Henry (possibly named with a fond remembrance of her admirer of some nine months earlier, 'Harry' Jermyn). Two days later the Queen required her to ride up to Oxford with her, to join the King's party there, which must have been quite an ordeal. When the royal party returned to London, there was a rapprochement between the King and Barbara, and when he came back from Bath, where Catherine had been taken for the waters, she gave him supper. When the tidal Thames started to flood into the kitchen, as happened sometimes, the cook told her that the great chine of beef could not be roasted there; she answered, 'Zounds, she must set the house on fire, but it must be roasted.' So it was taken to Sarah's husband's house and roasted there.[34]

Then, suddenly, that October, Catherine fell seriously ill with a high fever and delirium. The King spent days at her bedside, as she rambled on about the children she believed she had just had, wondering 'that she should be delivered without pain and without spewing or being sick, and was troubled that her boy was but an ugly boy. But the King, being by, said, "No, it is a very pretty boy." "Nay," says she, "if it be like you, it is a fine boy indeed, and [I] would be very well pleased with it."'[35] In the evenings, Charles went for his supper to Barbara's, and during the day, at court, continued his ardent wooing of Frances Stuart, whom everybody – including, no doubt, Frances and Barbara – saw as Catherine's replacement.

The Queen's condition deteriorated, despite the physicians' best efforts (including live pigeons applied to the feet) and she was not expected to survive. As Gramont wrote,

> The few Portuguese women who had not yet been sent back to their own country filled the Court with their doleful cries ... She loved him tenderly, and, thinking it was the last time she should ever speak to him, she told him that the concern which he showed for her death was enough to make her quit life with regret; but that not possessing sufficient charms to merit his tenderness, she had at least the consolation, in dying, to give place to a consort who might be more worthy of it, and to whom heaven perhaps might grant a blessedness that she had been refused. [Remarkably polished prose in the circumstances, if Gramont is to be believed.] At these words, she bathed his hands with some tears which, he thought would be her last. He mingled his own to hers, and, without supposing that she would take him at his word, he conjured her to live, for his sake. She had never yet disobeyed him; and, however dangerous sudden impulses may be when one is between life and death, this transport of joy, which might have been fatal to her, saved her life; and the King's wonderful tenderness had an effect for which every person did not thank heaven in the same manner.[36]

Her recovery was slow, although for some time her first waking thought was to ask for her children, and for a while she had difficulty in walking and was deaf. The New Year saw her much better, and on 4 January the next year, Doctor Pierce was able to tell Pepys that Charles had recently lain with her.

Nevertheless, there was no coming back into the King's affections; he continued his wooing of Frances and his relationship with Barbara and her children. The final surprise of 1663 came in December, when Barbara converted to the Catholic faith – 'which the Queen for all doth not much like, knowing she doth it not for conscience sake,' wrote Pepys on the 22nd. The Reverend

Stillingfleet, chaplain to the King, observed, 'If the Church of Rome has got by her no more than the Church of England has lost, the matter is not much.'[37] Her relatives were deeply shocked; while cousin Buckingham believed in religious toleration, his sympathies were always with the Protestants and Independents. As for the King, more interested in women's bodies than their souls, when he was approached to prevent this change, he replied, according to the French ambassador, Cominges, '*galamment que, pour l'âme des Dames il ne s'en mêlait point, mais bien de leur corps quand leur civilité se vouloit contenter de ses peines et des soins.*'[38] He did, however, persuade Catherine to come to dinner with him at Barbara's, in a gesture of reconciliation. Conversation might not have flowed easily between the wife, the mistress and the man whose desires were known to be directed to a third woman, Frances.

On 20 January 1664, Pepys was told that Barbara was 'not at all set by the King, but that he doth dote upon Mistress Stuart only … and to the open slighting of the Queen,' although he did not disown Barbara, while '[Charles Berkeley] my Lord Fitzharding and the Hamiltons, and sometimes my Lord Sandwich, they say, have their snaps at her. But he says my Lord Sandwich will lead her from her lodgings in the darkest and obscurest manner and leave her at the entrance into the Queen's lodgings, that he might be the least observed.' Pepys knew that Sandwich had become part of her circle, even content to lose money to her, gambling, and so was prepared to believe this. Gossip was starting to circulate again, some of which would have come to Charles's ears, so that Barbara had to take steps to establish her position. On 1 February, Pierce told Pepys how, when the King was at the theatre, to see Dryden's *The Indian Queen*, Barbara was in the next box before he arrived,

and, leaning over other ladies a-while to whisper with the King, she ris [rose] out of that box and went into the King's and set herself on the King's right hand between the King and the Duke of York – which he swears put the King himself, as well as everybody else, out of countenance, and believes that she did it only to show the world that she is not out of favour yet – as was believed.

It may not have been a convincing performance and annoying to the King, who nevertheless continued to visit her.

Soon enough, they were on terms again, and Charles spent the night of his thirty-fourth birthday at her court lodgings in the Holbein Gate, the fiddlers performing 'all night almost, and all the world coming by taking notice of it', which Pepys was 'sorry to hear' – as must have been Catherine, not many yards away in the palace, sleeplessly awaiting her husband's return. That summer, she, Barbara and Frances all had their portraits painted. The court artist Sir Peter Lely painted Barbara – as usual (he was almost as obsessed with her as was Pepys, her features somehow fusing with those of his other women sitters: a contemporary wrote that 'he put something of [Barbara]'s face and her languishing eyes into everyone's picture'), Jacob Huysmans painted Catherine as an improbably finely dressed shepherdess; as a Catholic, he was associated with Catherine, though he also painted Frances, curiously, in soldier's dress.[39]

The hostilities against the Dutch proceeded that summer, with the capture in America of New Amsterdam, renamed, in James's honour, New York, and of nearby Fort Nassau, renamed Albany. The French, who had signed a defensive treaty with the Dutch, strove to influence the English court against going to war, by means of bribes, which Barbara was happy to accept. She gave a great party for the French ambassador on 4 September and, the next day, gave birth to her fourth child, Charlotte. When she was up and about again, one night early in October she visited the Duchess of York; walking home through St James's Park, with only a maid and a page, she was accosted by three masked gentlemen, who abused her as a whore, again forcefully reminding her of Jane Shore's dunghill death. She escaped to the palace, and the King had the park gates closed and whoever was in the park arrested and questioned, but to no avail.[40]

With the advent of the war, Parliament voted a considerable sum of money, which incidentally enabled the King to reward his mistresses. The fleet was got ready under the command of the Duke of York. In May 1665, the courtier volunteers set sail, pens gallantly in hand; to quote Sir Charles Sackville, Earl of Dorset, with the Duke on board the *Royal Charles*:

To all the ladies now at hand
We men at sea indite ...

For though the Muses should prove kind,
And fill our empty brain,
Yet if rough Neptune rouse the wind
To wave the azure main,
Our paper, pen and ink and we
Roll up and down our ships at sea,
With a fa, la, la, la, la ...

To pass our tedious hours away,
We throw a merry main;
Or else at serious ombre play; [cards]
But why should we in vain
Each other's ruin thus pursue?
We were undone when we left you.
With a fa, la, la, la, la ...[41]

Such lyrics (his best known) might not have produced great expectations, but the Battle of Lowestoft was nearly a great success – the sound of gunfire was heard away in London – which could have been decisive, if Henry Brouncker, the Duke's Gentleman of the Bedchamber, had not taken it upon himself to instruct the pursuing English fleet to shorten sail (gossip said, so as not to disturb the Duke's sleep), so allowing the Dutch to escape and prolong the war.

Worse, on 7 June 1665, Pepys saw 'two or three houses marked with a red cross upon the door, and "Lord have mercy upon us!" writ there; which was a sad sight to me'; the Great Plague had arrived, with all its horrors. The theatres closed, and the court retreated to Hampton, though Barbara refused to go, concentrating instead on improving her financial affairs, chiefly with the 'full and unwithdrawing' help of her creature, Baptist 'Bab' May, newly appointed Keeper of the Privy Purse. The King, of course, remained her chief banker, the provider of thousands of pounds to pay for her expenses in huge gambling debts, horses, coaches, jewels and clothes.

As the corpses mounted in the streets (3,000 a week in August), the court moved on, first to Salisbury and then to Oxford, where they did not make themselves welcome. Anthony Wood wrote in his *Life and Times* that

> The greater sort of the courtiers were high, proud, insolent and looked upon scholars no more than pedants or pedagogical persons … Though they were neat and gay in their apparel, yet were they very nasty and beastly, leaving at their departure their excrements in every corner, in chimneys, studies, coalhouses, cellars. Rude, rough, whoremongers; vain, empty, careless.[42]

The King, the Duke and the Duchess took up occupation in Christ Church, while the Queen and Barbara were – surprisingly – both in Merton College (where pregnant Henrietta Maria had been quartered in 1641). Here Barbara gave birth to her fifth child, George, on 28 December 1665. Someone scholarly put up a notice on her door that commented on her escape from the ducking-stool, the traditional punishment for loose women: '*Hanc Caesare pressam a fluctu defendit onus*', helpfully translated as, 'The reason why she is not ducked? / Because by Caesar she is —'.[43] A very substantial reward of £1,000 was offered for information as to the author, but in vain. The King went back in January, leaving the Queen behind, and in Merton College, on 4 February 1666, she miscarried a son – a cause for hope, of sorts, suggesting she could conceive, though her women told Charles that it was only a false conception, so that he was now convinced she could never bear a child.[44]

The bitterness following upon this may have been the cause of some mild asperity on her part towards Barbara, provoking a row with the King. Pepys recorded, on 10 June, how, a few days earlier,

> the Queen, in ordinary talk before the ladies in her drawing-room, did say to my Lady Castlemaine that she feared the King did take cold by staying so late abroad at her house. She answered, before them all, that he did not stay so late abroad with her, for he went betimes thence (though he doth not before 1, 2 or 3 in the morning), but must stay somewhere else. The King then coming in, and

overhearing, did whisper in the ear aside and told her she was a bold
impertinent woman, and bid her be gone out of the Court and not
come again till he sent for her – which she did presently.

Apparently, 'she did in her anger say she would be even with the
King, and print his letters to her'. A few days later, she sent a note
from her place in Pall Mall, asking if she might take away her
belongings from her room in the palace. The King replied that she
should first come and view them, 'and so she came, and the King
went to her, and all friends again.'

Another quarrel was provoked by the Duke of Buckingham's
difficulties, caused by the machinations of his inveterate enemy, Sir
Henry Bennet, Earl of Arlington, as a result of which he had been
dismissed from his post of Gentleman of the Bedchamber and as
Privy Councillor, and sentenced to the Tower. However, the Duke
simply went into hiding, before surrendering himself at a time of
his choosing, when he was able to outwit and defeat Arlington
before the King in council.

While the Duke was on trial, Barbara spoke out for him, so
much so that she and the King fell out, 'and parted with very foul
words,' wrote Pepys on 12 July,

> the King calling her a whore, and a jade that meddled with things
> she had nothing to do withal. And she calling him fool; and told
> him, if he was not a fool, he would not suffer his business to be
> carried by fellows that did not understand them, and cause his best
> subjects, and those best able to serve him, to be imprisoned.

By 29 July, Pepys heard news more alarming than merely shocking,
that

> my Lady Castlemaine hath, before the late breach between her and
> the King, said to the King that he must rule by an army or all would
> be lost. And that Bab May hath given the like advice to the King, to
> crush the English gentlemen [especially the Whig MPs and 'Country
> Party'], saying that £300 a year was enough for any man but them
> that lived at Court' [such as himself].

Apparently, the King felt that some useless expenditure would cheer up the court and instituted a new fashion of black and white, described by Pepys on 15 October as 'a long cassock close to the body, of black cloth and pinked with white silk under it, and a coat over it, and the legs ruffled with black ribbons like a pigeon's leg.' Pepys liked the fashion, and hoped the King would keep it, but within a few weeks Louis XIV had fatally mocked it by dressing his footmen in similar garments. Meanwhile, the Queen held a birthday ball with everyone extravagantly dressed in black and silver. Pepys was particularly enchanted with the sight of Frances Stuart, in black and white lace, dressed with diamonds. Barbara was there, not dancing, but with a sour eye on Mistress Stuart. Soon enough, she had engineered the breakup of her relationship with the King, followed by Frances's marriage to the Duke of Richmond, to the King's extreme chagrin.

On 21 October Pepys was told that young Harry Killigrew, brother of the theatre owner and friend of Rochester, had been banished from court,

> for saying that my Lady Castlemaine was a little lecherous girl when she was young, and used to rub her thing with her finger or against the end of forms, and that she must be rubbed with something else. This, she complained to the King of – and he sent to the Duke of York, whose servant he is, to turn him away. The Duke hath done it, but takes it ill of my Lady that he was not complained to first.

In December, Pepys was mournfully reviewing the great costs of the Plague, the war and the Great Fire of September, and recorded a neat thrust at the King by Tom Killigrew (Harry's brother), on the 8th, who told the King publicly

> that his matters were coming into a very ill state, but that yet there was a way to help all – which is, says he, 'There is a good honest able man that I could name, that if your Majesty would employ and command to see all things well executed, all things would soon be mended; and this is one Charles Stuart – who now spends his time

in employing his lips and his prick about the Court, and hath no other employment. But if you would give him this employment, he were the fittest man in the world to perform it.'[45]

It is perhaps to Charles's credit as a man – if not as a king – that witty friends could tease him like this and get away with it, but, as Pepys remarked, 'the King doth not profit by any of this.' Indeed, four days later, he heard that the King had paid £30,000 'to clear debts of my Lady Castlemaine's – and that she and her husband are parted for ever, upon good terms, never to trouble one another more.'

The year 1667 saw the war and the half-hearted peace negotiations with the Dutch proceeding unsatisfactorily, culminating in the raid by the Dutch on 13 June into the Thames and up into the Medway, where they burned fourteen ships of the line (laid up to save money) and towed away the flagship, the *Royal Charles*. (The royal coat of arms from the ship is still displayed in the Rijksmuseum in Amsterdam.) Gossip – as recorded by Pepys on the 21st – had it that on that evening 'the King did sup with my Lady Castlemaine at the Duchess of Monmouth's, and there were all mad with hunting a poor moth.' The shock to national morale was great, with criticism directed, unjustly, at Clarendon, when the mob attacked the house he was having built in Piccadilly and set up a gibbet outside. The King was also criticised, with more justice, as in the satire, *Fourth Advice to a Painter*:

> As Nero once with harp in hand surveyed
> His flaming Rome and as that burned he played,
> So our great Prince, when the Dutch fleet arrived,
> Saw his ships burned, and as they burned he swived,
> So kind he was in our extremest need,
> He would those flames extinguish with his seed.[46]

The King needed a scapegoat, and it was obvious who it would have to be. By 30 August, the great Lord Clarendon, who had served Charles for so many years, had been dismissed from office, and by November had fled to Calais.

Pride, lust, ambition and the people's hate,
The kingdom's broker, ruin of the state,
Dunkirk's sad loss, divider of the fleet,
Tangier's compounder for a barren sheet:
This shrub of gentry, married to the crown,
His daughter to the heir, is tumbled down.[47]

Court and national politics, popular hostility, the King's resentment at his moralistic criticisms, what the King believed was his involvement in Frances Stuart's elopement and the machinations of his great enemy, Lady Castlemaine, all combined to bring him down. Pepys reported the general belief that 'this business of my Lord Chancellor's was certainly designed in my Lady Castlemaine's chamber.' When the old man left the King, he went past her residence, when

she was in bed (though about 12 o'clock) and ran out into her aviary looking into Whitehall garden, and thither the women brought her her nightgown [*peignoir*] and stood joying herself at the old man's going away. And several of the gallants of Whitehall (of which there was many staying to see the Chancellor's return) did talk to her in her bird cage; among others Blankford [commander of James's army] telling her she was the Bird of Paradise.[48]

According to one witness, Clarendon looked up and saw her: 'O, Madam, is it you? Pray remember that, if you live, you will grow old.'

Apart from the overthrow of Clarendon, the year had produced mixed results for Barbara. Being, as Gramont phrased it, 'a woman lively and discerning', she had pursued an affair with Harry Jermyn, and later, 'though undeceived of a reputation which promised so much and performed so little, she nevertheless continued in her infatuation.'[49] It made for a busy summer: once, as Pepys was told on 30 July, 'the King had like to have taken him a-bed with her, but that he was fain to creep under the bed into her closet.' Marvell, in his *Last Instructions to a Painter*, written between that

June and November, wrote of another of her brief flings, an affair with one of her footmen, when

> She through her lackey's drawers, as he ran,
> Discerned love's cause and a new flame began.
> Her wonted joys thenceforth and court she shuns,
> And still within her mind the foot man runs:
> His brazen calves, his brawny thighs – the face
> She slights – his feet shaped for smoother race ...
> [In Exodus XXXII, the Israelites idolatrously worshipped
>   a brazen calf]
> Stripped to her skin, see how she stooping stands,
> Nor scorns to rub him down with those fair hands,
> And washing (lest the scent her crime disclose)
> His sweaty hooves, tickles him 'twixt the toes ...
> [In Luke VII, a sinful woman washed Christ's feet. Here,
>   the hooves suggest either a satyr or centaur. Now,
>   when the man grew too indiscreet,]
> Justly the rogue was whipped in porter's den,
> And Jermyn straight has leave to come again.[50]

This footman was more fortunate than another of her lovers: soon after, John Ellis's boasting of his success was cruelly cut short when he was castrated, as Pope later recorded:

> What pushed poor Ellis on th'imperial whore?
> 'Twas but to be where Charles had been before.
> The fatal steel unjustly was applied,
> When not his lust offended, but his pride.
> Too hard a penance for defeated sin,
> Himself shut out, and Jacob Hall let in. [a rope-dancer][51]

There were no consequences for Barbara; she could do whatever she wished.

On 29 July Pepys heard that she was with child, and the King said he did not beget it, as he had not lain with her for months. (Pepys was also told that 'for a good while the King's greatest

pleasure hath been with his fingers, being able to do no more.')
'With that, she made a slighting "puh!" with her mouth and went
out of the house and never came in again'. At last, the King went
to where she was staying, at Sir Daniel Harvey's house in Covent
Garden (whose wife, Elizabeth, was one of the Duke of York's
mistresses), and made it up with her. This was done by giving
in, when, as Pepys heard on 7 August, 'She made him ask her
forgiveness upon his knees, and promise to offend her no more so,
and that indeed, she did threaten to bring all his bastards to his
closet door and hath nearly hectored him out of his wits.'

Pepys was told that she was in love with Harry Jermyn, 'who
hath of late lain with her oftener than the King, and is now going
to marry Lady Falmouth [Sir Charles Berkeley's widow – though
he did not]. The King, he is mad at her entertaining Jermyn, and
she is mad at Jermyn's going to marry from her, so they are all
mad; and thus the Kingdom is governed.'[52]

When the King repeated that the child was not his, she insisted,
'God damn me, but you shall own it,' and threatened that, if he
did not, she would bring it into Whitehall and dash its brains out
before his face. It was no wonder that Mr Povey, the Duke of
York's treasurer and Pepys's friend, said that she hectored the King
to do whatever she wanted, and that, as Gramont wrote, 'Beautiful
as she was, she resembled Medea less than her dragons, when she
was thus enraged.'[53]

Things could not go on like this indefinitely.

3

JAMES, THE MARRIED MAN

On 7 October 1660, the Earl of Sandwich told Pepys that 'the Duke of York hath got my Lord Chancellor's daughter with child, and that she doth lay it to him, and that for certain he did promise her marriage and hath signed it with his blood'. As the story came out, it transpired that when the court-in-exile was based in Brussels, the twenty-six-year-old Duke had had a secret affair with one of the Princess of Orange's Maids of Honour, the pleasantly plump twenty-two-year-old Anne Hyde, and agreed a marriage contract with the lawyer's daughter on 24 November 1659. In the early spring of 1660 she became pregnant, and matters could no longer be wholly concealed, while Anne wanted James to honour his promise. A stout father might not realise the condition of a plump daughter, but other women would, soon enough.

As embarrassed father-to-be, James soon began to have doubts about this socially disadvantageous marriage to a commoner, which wrecked his chances of marriage to royalty or nobility. Now, suggested Gramont, 'he remembered that [Henry] Jermyn had not engaged him in an intimacy with Miss Hyde until he had convinced him, by several different circumstances, of the facility of succeeding'[1]. Was it possible to get out of it? He asked the advice of Sir Charles Berkeley (Lord Falmouth) – not very bright, but always agreeable, a natural pander – who told him that he was not married as any marriage he undertook without the King's consent was invalid. Sir Charles also told him that he had had predecessors, whom he helpfully collected: the Earl of Arran, Jermyn, Talbot and Henry Killigrew – 'all men of honour who infinitely preferred the Duke of York's interest to Miss Hyde's and who, besides, were greatly dissatisfied, as well as the whole court, at the insolent authority of the chief minister.'[2]

So, the Earl of Arran declared that, in the gallery at Hounslaerdyke, when Lady Ossory, his sister-in-law, and Jermyn were playing ninepins, Anne claimed to feel unwell and withdrew into a room at the end of a corridor; he had followed her and, 'having cut her laces to give a greater probability of her suffering the vapours [often the consequence of over-tight lacing], had acquitted himself to the best of his abilities both to assist and to console her.' Talbot said that she had 'made an appointment with him in the Chancellor's cabinet, while he was in Council, and that, not paying so much attention to what was upon the table as what they were engaged in', they had knocked a bottle of ink over an important document (and that the King's monkey was blamed for the accident). Jermyn indicated several occasions when he had 'received a long and favourable audience.'

Killigrew, Groom of the Bedchamber to the Duke, and later to become notorious at court, wished to improve on these feeble depositions:

He was of a sprightly and witty humour, and had the art of telling a story in the most entertaining manner, by the graceful and natural turn he could give it. He affirmed that he had found the critical moment in a certain closet, built over the water for a purpose very different from giving ease to the pains of love; three or four swans, he added, had been witnesses to his happiness, and might perhaps have been witnesses to the happiness of many others, as the lady frequently repaired to the place, and was particularly delighted with it.[3]

Whether or not he believed these stories (Pepys did not, when he heard them on 10 December), James went to his brother and told him how he had married below himself socially and without permission and asked him if the marriage should be acknowledged? The King consulted his councillors Ormonde and the Earl of Southampton. Eventually it was agreed that the marriage was legal and could not be overthrown, and that, in Charles's phrase, James must 'drink as he had brewed', especially as Anne's father was needed, as Chancellor, for important constitutional work and could not be disgraced or forced out of office; so, off they went, to break the news to him.

The disclosure of his daughter's condition was a terrible shock for Hyde – portly, gouty, pompous and moralistic. He swore that 'as soon as he came home he would turn her out of his house as a strumpet, to shift for herself, and would never see her again'. Having been told that she was already married,

> he fell into new commotions, and said that if that were true he was well prepared to advise what was to be done ... in which he hoped their lordships would concur with him, that the King should immediately cause the woman to be sent to the Tower, and to be cast into a dungeon, under so strict a guard that no person living should be permitted to come to her, and then that an Act of Parliament should be immediately passed for the cutting off her head, to which he would not only give his consent, but would very willingly be the first man that should propose it.[4]

Apart from his shock at his daughter's behaviour, which was genuine, his exaggeratedly violent and improbable recommendation may have been a blocking move against others' propositions. He feared that people would suggest – as many did – that this affair had been part of a plot to get closer to the royal family and the succession (a son would be second in line to the throne), but the King was kind and reassuring. Charles was firm with James; the Duke, upset, asked Falmouth and Ossory to come with him to confront his father-in-law. They found him in his daughter's room. 'A few tears trickled down her cheeks, which she endeavoured to restrain. The Chancellor, leaning against the wall, appeared to them to be puffed up with something, which they did not doubt was rage and despair.' The Duke then invited them to be 'the first to have the honour of paying your compliments to the Duchess of York; there she is'.[5] When Hyde went home, he shut up his daughter in her room, but his wife quietly let James in at night.

Later, around eleven o'clock on the night of 3 September, in a room in Worcester House in the Strand, the home of the Lord Chancellor, in the presence of Lord Ossory, the Duke's chaplain (re)married him and Anne. It was a quiet ceremony; the bride's father was not present. As for public opinion, many were not greatly out of agreement with the Earl of Sandwich, who told Pepys, 'That among his father's many old sayings was one: "That he that doth get a wench with child and marries her afterward, it is as if a man should shit in his hat and then clap it on his head."'[6]

The Duke's family was not pleased. His mother, Henrietta Maria, 'hearing that her son / Was thus enamoured of a buttered bun,'[7] was furious, sending the King word that she was on her way to England 'to prevent with her authority so great a stain and dishonour to the Crown', as Clarendon later recorded, and arrived declaring, in true comic mother-in-law fashion, 'Whenever that woman is brought into Whitehall by one door, I go out by another, never to return.' (Of course, this was not true: she was reconciled soon enough, and returned to France to marry her other daughter, Minette, to the bisexual Comte d'Orléans.) The Princess Royal let it be known she would never yield precedence to her former lady-in-waiting. Henry, Duke of Gloucester, sneered that Anne 'smelt so strong of her father's green [lawyer's] bag that he could not get the better of himself whenever he had the misfortune to be in her presence'.[8] However, he did not have to endure this for long: on 13 September, he died of smallpox. Princess Mary of Orange, the widowed Princess Royal, who had come to England to pressure her brothers about her son, also contracted smallpox (gossip suggested that she then married her reputed lover, Harry Jermyn, nephew of Henry Jermyn) and died in December. That left Charles and James, one clever, devious and relaxed, the other, plodding, earnest and stiff-necked. Buckingham summed them up neatly: 'The King could see things if he would and the Duke would see things if he could.'[9]

Meanwhile, Anne's baby, little Charles, was born on 22 October 1660 and died on 5 May 1661. (Two daughters died in infancy, but two – Mary and Anne – survived, and became Queens of England.) As one might have expected, 'the *petits-maîtres* [coxcombs]' as Gramont called them, 'who had spoken against her, seeing their intentions disappointed, were not a little embarrassed,'[10] and reasonably expected a campaign of revenge from her, which never came; she never spoke ill of them. Her situation at court was very difficult: she had to be pleasant and also properly dignified. The French ambassador, Cominges, described her in 1668 'as worthy a woman (*aussi brave femme*) – the word "*honnête*" is not strong enough – as I have met in my life, and she upholds with as much courage, cleverness and energy the dignity to which she has been called as if she were of the blood of kings.'[11] Gramont wrote that she behaved with 'such prudence and circumspection as could not be sufficiently admired: such were her manners that she appeared to have found out the secret of pleasing everyone.'[12] Later she began 'to take state on her too much', as one commentator put it, with a sense of her status which, as the years passed, increased with her girth. Unable to ignore her husband's continual philandering, she took to comfort eating. Gramont observed:

> The Duchess of York was one of the highest feeders in England: as this was an unforbidden pleasure, she indulged herself in it, and as an indemnification for other self-denials. It was really an edifying sight to see her at table. The Duke, being incessantly in the hurry of new fancies, exhausted himself by his inconstancy and was gradually wasting away; whilst the princess, gratifying her good appetite, grew so fat and plump that it was a blessing to see her.[13]

Andrew Marvell, in his *Last Instructions to a Painter*, in 1667, described her rather surrealistically (though perhaps with sexual innuendo):

> With Chancellor's belly and so large a rump,
> There – not behind the coach – her pages jump.[14]

Others resented the social and sexual disorder at court, of which she was now an instance. One bitter ballad began,

> Good people, draw near,
> If a ballad you'd hear,
> It will teach you the new way of thriving,
> Ne'er trouble your heads
> With your books or your beads,
> The world's ruled by cheating and swiving.
>
> Old Fatguts himself,
> With his tripes and his pelf,
> With a purse as full as his paunch is,
> Will confess that his Nanny
> Fopdoodled her Jemmy,
> And his kingdom is come to the haunches.[15]

The deaths of the Duke of Gloucester and the Princess Royal briefly sobered the court, especially Sir Charles Berkeley, who now declared that the stories of Anne's promiscuity were false. The deaths also provoked other responses from the usual conspiracy addicts, that Anne and Clarendon were responsible, clearing the way for her descendants.

> Then Culp'per, Gloucester, ere the Princess, died: [Lord
>   Culpeper, king's counsellor]
> Nothing can live that interrupts an Hyde [Anne Hyde].[16]

Likewise, in *An Historical Poem*, the writer remarks of James, how

> ... the best times have ever some mishap:
> His younger brother perished by a clap;
> And his Dutch sister quickly after died ...
> Bold James survives, no dangers make him flinch,
> He married Mynheer Falmouth's pregnant wench.[17]

As for James, with the marriage settled and Barbara Palmer,

despite her flirtatious ways, already spoken for, he reverted to type, looking for fresh entertainment, of a familiar kind. Having appeased his conscience by marrying, he 'thought that he was entitled by this generous effort to give way a little to his inconstancy,' wrote Gramont. 'He therefore immediately seized upon whatever he could first lay his hands upon: this was Lady Anne Carnegie [née Lady Anne Hamilton, the teenage Barbara Villiers's friend], who had been in several other hands. She was still tolerably handsome, and her disposition, naturally inclined to tenderness, did not oblige her new lover long to languish.'[18] (On 19 March 1665, Pepys refers to her as 'said to have given the Duke a clap on his first coming over'.)

Gramont has a good story about this affair. The Duke took precautions against discovery by the husband by apparently only visiting the lady formally, making a polite, social call, accompanied by a third person. On one occasion, the cover was provided by Richard 'Dick' Talbot, who left the couple together while waiting in an antechamber. Happening to look out of the window, he saw a man arrive in a carriage and enter the house. Talbot, who had been abroad, did not know that Carnegie, an old friend, was now the new Earl of Southesk. 'Welcome, Carnegie, welcome, my good fellow. Where the devil have you sprung from? ... What business brought you here? Do you, likewise, wish to see Lady Southesk? If this is your intention, my poor friend, you may go away again; for I must inform you, the Duke of York is in love with her, and I will tell you in confidence, at this very time, he is in her chamber.'

The dumbfounded Earl was hustled downstairs, out of his own house and into his coach again, cheerily advised to try his luck elsewhere (where he went, the story does not relate). Talbot went back, impatient to tell the couple the entertaining story of the visitor. 'He was very much surprised that the story afforded no pleasure to those who had the principal share in it; and his greatest concern was that Carnegie had changed his name as if only to draw him into such a confidence.'[19]

Regrettably, this story cannot be altogether true: apparently, the affair between the Duke and Lady Carnegie took place in 1662, and her husband did not succeed to the title of Earl of Southesk until some years later. Writing his memoirs some years later still, Gramont was not very reliable about chronology, concentrating more on what made for an amusing story. He also provided a follow-up to this affair, a story repeated by Pepys on 6 April 1668, how the husband,

> finding her and the Duke of York at the King's first coming in too kind, did get it out of her that she did dishonour him; and so he bid her continue to let him, and himself went to the foulest whore he could find, that he might get the pox; and did, and did give his wife it on purpose, that she (and he persuaded and threatened her that she should) might give it the Duke of York; which she did, and he did give it the Duchess; and since, all her children are thus sickly and infirm – which is the most pernicious and foul piece of revenge that ever I heard of. And he this day owns it with great glory, and looks upon the Duke of York and the world with great content.

Gramont varied the story by claiming that the Duke had finished with Lady Carnegie by the time that the Earl had infected himself, and that 'after he had gone through every remedy to get quit of his disease, his lady did but return him his present.'[20] The story, though widely circulated, seems improbable; interestingly, a similar story had been told previously about François I of France, and a Spanish husband[21] – which, of course, does not affect its truth one way or the other.

James then turned his attention to Lady Letitia Robartes, who would have been quite willing, but for her husband, 'an old, snarling, troublesome, peevish fellow [about fifty-seven], in love with her', who was always on the watch. It was suggested to him what titles and honours might come his way if his wife were to become a lady-in-waiting at court; however, at this, 'he did not rest until the highest mountains in Wales were between his wife' and the Duke.[22]

Next, it was the turn of pretty Margaret Brooke; unfortunately, the King was also interested, until Lady Castlemaine got wind of it and nipped that in the bud. So Miss Brooke had to wait, until 'it should please heaven to dispose of her otherwise', which came about very soon, when, on 25 May 1665, Sir John Denham, aged about fifty, having been a gambler in his youth, gambled against the odds by taking to wife pretty, young Mistress Brooke, aged about nineteen. For his loyal service during the Civil War, Sir John had been appointed Surveyor of Works and was a good poet – his politico-landscape poem, *Cooper's Hill* (1642), was much admired and influential in the eighteenth century. Aubrey describes him as

> of the tallest, but a little incurvetting at his shoulders, not very robust. His hair was but thin and flaxen, with a moist curl. His gait was slow, and was rather a stalking (he had long legs) ... In the time of the Civil War, George Withers, the poet ... was taken prisoner, and was in danger of his life, having written severely against the King, &c. Sir John Denham went to the King, and desired his Majesty not to hang him, for that, whilst G.W. lived, he should not be the worst poet in England.[23]

Known as 'the limping bard', he was perhaps not the ideal husband for a pert nineteen-year-old. A couplet of the time observed trenchantly: 'O Denham, thou had'st better bin brained with a brick, / Than marry a young C. without a stiff prick.' (Bodleian MS. Don. b.8)

The Duke now 'rekindled his ardour', while she encouraged him in hopes of an 'approaching bliss which a thousand considerations had opposed before her marriage.'[24] Once again, however, there was someone else, a stronger player, who had been after the Duke before (as the Duchess had complained to the King in November 1662): Lady Elizabeth Chesterfield, wife of Barbara Villiers's old flame. So, for a while they had to content themselves with making eyes at each other, while the Duke got on with his affair with Lady Chesterfield.

Gramont introduces the Chesterfields:

> He had married [perhaps on the rebound from Barbara's relationship with the King] without loving her, and had lived with her in such coolness as to leave her no room to doubt of his indifference. As she was endowed with great sensibility and delicacy, she suffered

at this contempt; she was at first much affected with his behaviour, and afterwards enraged at it; and when he began to give her proofs of his affection, she had the pleasure of convincing him of her indifference.[25]

She was very charming, with large, blue eyes and a fair complexion. 'Her manners were engaging, her wit lively and amusing; but her heart, ever open to tender sentiments, was neither scrupulous in point of constancy, nor nice in point of sincerity.'[26]

At the time, there was a craze at court for playing the guitar. 'Lady Chesterfield,' writes Gramont, 'had the finest guitar in England', as her intimates knew. The Duke was keen to play with her instrument, and Lord Arran, her brother, kindly took him round to visit her at the Duke of Ormonde's house, where they also, unexpectedly, found her husband, who was not pleased. For some time, Lord Arran, a good guitarist, played a sarabande, while Lady Chesterfield and the Duke discreetly played up to each other, to her husband's suppressed fury. In the end, he had to leave them to it, having been summoned by the Queen to attend a visiting Muscovite deputation (this would have been in the winter of 1662–3). Scarcely had he got there when Lord Arran joined him – leaving the couple together at their play and convincing him that Arran was in on the plot.

The next day, still seething, he went to court, and there met James Hamilton, and persuaded him to walk with him in Hyde Park, where he told him about his doubts about his wife's behaviour. He went on to remark how, while husbands are conventionally the last to know of such affairs, he was not stupid enough to see nothing. He reported how the Duke and Lord Arran had called on his wife, and that Arran had left them together. He went on:

Hear me and judge ... Lady Chesterfield is amiable, it must be acknowledged; but she is very far from being such a miracle of beauty as she supposes herself. You know that she has ugly feet; but perhaps you are not acquainted with, is that she has still worse legs ... They are short and thick, and, to remedy these defects as much as possible, she seldom wears anything other than green stockings.

He went on to relate how, on the previous day he was

> with Mistress Stuart after the audience with those damned
> Muscovites; the King arrived then just before me and had just
> come in and, as if the Duke had sworn to pursue me wherever I
> went that day, he, too, just after me. The conversation turned on
> the extraordinary appearance of the ambassadors. I do not know
> where that fool Crofts [the Duke of Monmouth] had heard that
> all these Muscovites had handsome wives, and that their wives had
> all handsome legs. Upon this, the King maintained that no woman
> ever had such handsome legs as Miss Stuart, and she, to prove the
> truth of his Majesty's assertion, with the greatest imaginable ease,
> immediately showed her legs above the knees. Some were ready
> to prostrate themselves in order to adore their beauty; for, indeed,
> none can be handsomer; but the Duke alone began to criticise
> them. He contended that her legs were too slender, and that, as for
> himself, he would give nothing for a leg that was not plumper and
> shorter, and concluded by saying no leg was worth anything unless
> it was clothed in a green stocking. Now this, in my opinion, was a
> sufficient demonstration that he had just seen green stockings and
> had them fresh in his remembrance.[27]

Hamilton thought he was probably right, but tried to reassure him
by saying that, however polite she had been to the Duke, she was
unlikely to have been 'willing to indulge him in any greater liberties
to engage him'. Hamilton then went off to write a reproving letter
to her, who was his cousin and whom he himself was pursuing.
A few days later she replied, telling him he was being foolish and
to be thankful 'for a groundless jealousy which diverts to another
quarter the attention he [Chesterfield] might pay to my attachment
for the most amiable and dangerous man in all the court'.[28] Taking
the last phrase to apply to himself, he settled to write her a tender
letter, when her husband burst in, to report a shocking scene: one,
he said,

> no less public than the room where the Queen plays at cards,
> which, while her majesty was at play, was, God knows, pretty well

crowded. Lady Denham was first to discover what they thought would pass unperceived in the crowd; and you may very well judge how secret she would keep such a circumstance. The truth is, that she addressed herself to me first of all, as I entered the room, to tell me that I should give my wife a little advice, as others might take notice of what I might see myself, if I pleased. Your cousin was at play, as I before told you. The Duke was sitting next to her. I know not what was become of his hand, but I am sure no one could see his arm below the elbow [presumably in her placket, the slit-opening in the side or back of the skirt; a facetious etymology derived it from the Latin, *placet*, it pleases]. I was standing behind them, in the position that Lady Denham had just quitted. The Duke, turning round, perceived me, and was so much disturbed at my presence that, in pulling away his hand he almost undressed my lady. I know not whether they perceived that they were discovered; but of this I am convinced, that Lady Denham will take care that everybody shall know it.[29]

In jealous anger, Chesterfield agreed with Hamilton that, to save his wife from herself, and to get her away from the predatory Duke, he must immediately take her away into the country. At first, she could not believe that he was determined on this; finding that all her relatives were 'serious and cold', she turned to Hamilton for help, 'but she was expecting pity from a crocodile'. She expressed bewilderment as to why she was being 'dragged into the wilderness' – Bretby Hall, near Repton in the Peak District – in the middle of winter, but away she was taken. As for general court opinion, Gramont observed that 'they looked with astonishment upon a man who could be so uncivil as to be jealous of his wife; and, in the city of London it was a prodigy, till that time unknown, to see a husband have recourse to violent means, to prevent what jealousy fears and what it always deserves.'[30] Gramont concurred: 'Every man who believes that his honour depends on that of his wife is a fool ... Precaution is vain and useless before the evil, and revenge odious afterwards.'[31]

It is worth following the rest of the Chesterfields-Hamilton story. Some time later, Hamilton received a letter from Lady Chesterfield, lamenting her plight at Bretby: 'Surrounded by impassable roads, out of one window I see nothing but rocks, out of another, nothing but sheer precipices; but, wherever I turn my eyes within doors, I meet those of a jealous husband.'[32] She begged him to visit her, if only once: her husband would be away at a lawsuit in Chester for eight days.

Off galloped her admirer; before dawn, mindful of the rocks and precipices she had mentioned, he walked a last short distance. Following instructions, he came to a small cottage by the park wall, where he was put up for the night. Exhausted, he slept until nearly midday and spent the rest of the day preparing himself for the rendezvous. As night came, a servant arrived, who escorted him for half an hour through the park to a garden-room on the ground floor. Here he waited and waited. It was winter, and he was getting colder and colder. He walked up and down, to warm himself; shortly before dawn, he gave up and went back to the cottage to warm himself before a fire, and then went to sleep. Two hours later, he was awoken by a tremendous noise of hunting horns and hounds. His host explained that Lord Chesterfield was now hunting the hare, in his park. (It seems like an episode straight out of *Gawain and the Green Knight*, set not many miles away.)

At first, fearing the entry of Lord Chesterfield, riding whip in hand, he hid under the bedclothes. After a while, he decided that it was the unexpected return of his lordship that was the cause of the previous night's fiasco. Now the same servant appeared and handed him a letter – from his sister, Elizabeth, who, it transpired, was staying with the Chesterfields. She revealed that his being there was the result of a trick that they had played on him. It was during their reconciliation that Lady Chesterfield was told that Hamilton had recommended her husband to take her away into the country, which had infuriated her. Elizabeth advised him, 'Console yourself for the hatred of a person whose heart never merited your tenderness. Return.' She, herself offended, would also be leaving soon.[33]

After his initial shock, mortification and fury had passed, he quickly got on his horse and set off back, 'bearing a very pretty cold'. When he looked back, he saw no precipices or crags, but a very handsome mansion (designed by Inigo Jones, but pulled down in 1780), set in delightful grounds.

In 1665, the Duke, always keen to be busy, resumed his negotiations with young Lady Denham, who made it a condition that she should be made a Lady of the Bedchamber to the Duchess (which Anne was unwilling to grant). On 10 June 1666, Pepys was told:

> The Duke of York is wholly given up to his new mistress, my Lady Denham, going at noonday with all his gentlemen to visit her in Scotland Yard, she declaring she will not be his mistress as Miss [Goditha] Price [a Maid of Honour, plain but willing], to go up and down the Privy Stairs, but will be owned publicly, and so she is. Mr Brouncker it seems was the pimp to bring it about, and my Lady Castlemaine, who designs thereby to fortify herself by the Duke, there being a falling-out the other day between the King and her.

Meanwhile, her husband was becoming more and more anguished at this public cuckolding and humiliation – many mocking verses did the rounds. On 26 September 1666, Pepys saw the Duke 'taking her aside and talking to her in the sight of all the world, all alone ... Mr Evelyn cries out against it, and calls it bitchering, for the Duke of York talks a little to her, and then she goes away, and then he follows her like a dog'. For a while Denham went mad, and 'went to the King and told him he was the Holy Ghost', according to Aubrey. Some people attributed this to his grief over his cuckolding, though others said that 'formerly having taken the fluxing pills in Holland, and they not working, they rubbed his shins with mercury, but ... they supposed it lodged in the nerves till the harsh strokes caused it to sublimate.'[34]

In a poem published in 1668, he had his friend Thomas Killigrew advise on the treatment of syphilis:

> Yet be of comfort, I shall send a
> Person of knowledge who can mend a
> Disaster in your nether end-a ...

> Nor shall you need your silver quick Sir, [mercury]
> Take *Mongo Murry's Black Elixir*,
> And in a week it Cures your P— Sir.[35]

Lacking a distant country mansion in which he could confine his wife, 'the old villain', as Gramont phrased it, 'made her travel a much longer journey without stirring out of London. Merciless fate robbed her of life, and of her dearest hopes [the Duke?] in the bloom of youth.'[36] She suffered a protracted and painful illness, dying in early January 1667, two years after she married. In her final agonies she claimed that her husband had poisoned her by means of a cup of chocolate. 'Some suspect her poisoned,' wrote Pepys on 7 January, 'but it will be best known when her body is opened, which will be today.' The post-mortem found no trace of poison – of course – but the story of poisoning by chocolate was widely circulated. In his *Last Instructions*, Marvell hinted that the Duchess was responsible:

> Express her study now if China clay
> Can, without breaking, venomed juice convey,
> [It was believed that china vessels could not endure
>   contact with poison.]
> Or how a mortal poison she may draw
> Out of the cordial meal of the cacao. [37]

Some suspected Anne's lady in waiting, as well as Sir John. The author of *An Historical Poem*, commenting on James's only partial victory over the Dutch in the Battle of Lowestoft in June 1665, neatly combined it with the Carnegie and Denham stories:

> The dreadful victor took his soft repose,
> Scorning the pursuit of such recreant foes.
> But now York's genitals grew over hot
> With Denham's and Carnegie's infected pot.[38]

There was popular outrage at the rumoured murderer, palliated eventually by him providing a grand funeral, with lavish supplies of drink. Denham recovered his spirits, socialised as never before and published his poems in 1668. In one, preferring the single life to marriage, he wrote,

> May not a Prison, or a Grave
> Like Wedlock, Honour's title have?
> That word makes Free-born man a Slave.
>
> How happy he that loves not, lives!
> Him neither hope nor Fear deceives,
> To fortune who no Hostage gives.[39]

James was upset at her death, for a while, and declared he would never have a public mistress again (a vow he was not able to keep); there was also a story of how the Duchess was 'troubled with the apparition of the Lady Denham, and through anxiety bit off a piece of her tongue.'[40]. As it happened, the year before, in July 1665, his earlier fancy, the beautiful Countess of Chesterfield, also died, away in Derbyshire, also rumoured to have been poisoned; the widower remarried in 1669. The story was that Chesterfield had forced his wife to take an oath of her innocence with the Duke upon the Sacrament and that the wine was poisoned. His daughter-in-law, Lady Gertrude Stanhope, supposedly never dined with him afterwards without bringing her own cup, wine and water.[41]

The Duke tended to view his wife's Maids of Honour rather like a taxi rank, to be called upon when other court ladies were not available – though with varying degrees of success. One was Frances Jennings, described by Gramont as having

> the fairest and brightest complexion that ever was seen: her hair was of a most beauteous flaxen: there was something particularly lively and animated in her countenance ... her conversation was bewitching when she had a mind to please: piercing and delicate when disposed to raillery; but, as her imagination was subject to lights, and as she began to speak frequently before she had done thinking, her expressions did not always convey what she wished.[42]

In the summer of 1665, the Marquis de Lionne's nineteen-year-old son, the Marquis de Berni, was sent to England to 'see the world', and soon started wooing her with strawberries, every day. However, her 'kindness' was limited, when they fell out when she refused to have her hands kissed. He then transferred to young Mistress Boynton, which resulted in her having fainting fits.[43]

The Duke pursued Miss Jennings more seriously, but 'he did not find her inclined to enter into his service, though she had engaged in that of the Duchess'. Determined on a respectable marriage, she put up a skilful resistance. Little glances, bold ogling, earnest speeches, all went in vain. Then he tried ardent love letters, smuggled either into her dress pocket or her muff, which she simply dropped on the floor, unread – except by others. Everyone was intrigued, including the King, who wondered how she could have imbibed such severe precepts from the prudence of her mother, who had never tasted anything more delicious than the plums and apricots of St Albans.'[44] He was going to try for himself, but Frances Stuart would not permit it.

Then there was Elizabeth Hamilton, one of the celebrated beauties of the court, whose portrait by Sir Peter Lely in 1663 was one of the 'Windsor Beauties' assembled by the Duke and Duchess and hung at Hampton Court. Her brother wrote that Lely admitted he had enjoyed painting it; the Duke enjoyed looking at it and ogling the original.[45] He seems, however, to have been unusually timid in his approach; Gramont's account of his wooing (of Gramont's future wife) is devastating.

> He did not think it proper to declare such sentiments as were not fit for Miss Hamilton to hear; but he talked to her as much as he could, and ogled her with great assiduity. As hunting was his favourite diversion, that sport employed him one part of the day, and he came home much fatigued; but Miss Hamilton's presence revived him, when he found her visiting the Queen or Duchess. There it was that, not daring to tell her of what lay heavy on his heart, he entertained her with what he had in his head; telling her miracles of the cunning of foxes and the mettle of horses; giving her accounts of broken legs and arms, dislocated shoulders and other curious and

entertaining adventures; after which, his eyes told her the rest, till such time as sleep interrupted their conversation; for those tender interpreters could not help sometimes composing themselves in the midst of their ogling.[46]

Following James's involvement in the Battle of Lowestoft, when, after the Earl of Falmouth was killed standing next to him (to nobody's great regret, except that of the King, whose favourite he was, 'Such was his rise such was his fall, unpraised: / A chance shot sooner took than chance him raised. / His shattered head the fearless duke distains, / And gave the last-first proof that he had brains.[47]), the Duke was forbidden to go to war at sea any more. With the beginning of the development of the plague in London in 1665, the Duke and Duchess of York went on a progress north – to York.

About now, 'a tall creature, pale-faced, and nothing but skin and bone, whom she had taken for a Maid of Honour, became the object of her jealousy'[48] as the Duke's latest fancy. The lady in question was Arabella Churchill, the seventeen-year-old daughter of Sir Winston Churchill and sister to John Churchill (one of Barbara's lovers, and later Duke of Marlborough). In reaction, her eye wandered in the direction of 'handsome' (as he was known) Henry Sidney, fourth son of the Earl of Leicester. (Handsome, but not as handsome does: he never married, but had many illegitimate children, for whom he made no provision. A long-term mistress, Grace Worthley, a widow, he simply dumped; when Diana, Countess of Oxford, asked for money, he paid her £12 10s each quarter.) The Duchess was 'wounded before she was aware of her danger,' wrote Gramont, while Sidney responded with amorous glances. Another maid, Miss Hobart, encouraged her to give him hope, which the Duchess was uneasy about, especially at the risk of her reputation, and which she thought a poor response to the Duke's honouring her by marriage. Hobart insisted that the Duke had continually flaunted his many infidelities, and urged:

Is it still your intention to persevere in a state of indolence and humility, while the Duke, after having received the favours, or suffered the repulses, of all the coquettes in England, pays his addresses to your Maids of Honour one after another, and at present places his whole ambition and desires in the conquest of that ugly skeleton, Churchill? ... there is not a princess in the universe who would refuse the homage of a man like Sidney, when her husband pays his addresses elsewhere.[49]

The Duchess took note, but waited. When Edward Montagu, Master of Horse to the Queen, was killed at the Battle of Bergen, his place was taken by Ralph Montagu, whose place was in turn taken by Sidney. This pleased Miss Hobart, who had many conversations with him, which led the Duke to remark how odd some people's tastes were that Sidney was drawn to such a plain woman. The Duchess riposted that he was well qualified to speak, having considered Miss Churchill (generally thought plain) as a mistress. The Duke now paid Miss Churchill less attention for a while, until she had a fall when they were out riding (as young court ladies did, remarkably often). Far from doing her any harm,

it gave the lie to all the unfavourable suppositions that had been formed of her person in judging from her face. The Duke alighted, in order to help her; she was so greatly stunned, that her thoughts were otherwise employed than about decency on the present occasion [of course]; and those who first crowded around her, found her rather in a negligent posture. They could hardly believe that limbs of such exquisite beauty could belong to Miss Churchill's face. After this accident, it was remarked that the Duke's tenderness and affection for her increased every day; and, towards the end of the winter, it appeared that she had not tyrannised over his passion, nor made him languish with impatience.[50]

With this relationship settled, back to London they all went, with the Duchess particularly dissatisfied, as the Duke now banished Sidney from his court, on suspicion (on 19 October 1666, Pepys was told that 'there really was amours between the Duchess and Sidney'). The Duke and Duchess were not on speaking terms, the Duchess sulking, the Duke otherwise engaged.

Nevertheless, it appears that most of the time they managed reasonably well, though she was hurt by his blatant infidelities. On 24 June 1667, Pepys was told that the Duke had failed to get Jane Middleton (or Myddelton), 'a very great beauty', blonde and golden, frequently admired by Pepys and previously ardently wooed by Gramont (with scented gloves and pocket mirrors from Paris) and the Earl of Ranelagh (with earrings, diamonds and brilliants), before reputedly 'coming into the same place' as Castlemaine in 1668, and becoming moderately notorious.[51] Thomas Povey, treasurer to the Duke, told Pepys that the Duke said, 'He wants not her, for he hath others and hath always had, and that he [Povey] hath known them brought through the Matted Gallery at Whitehall into his closet. Nay, he hath come out of his wife's bed and gone to others laid in bed for him. That Mr Brouncker is not the only pimp, but that the whole family is of the same strain, and will do anything to please him.'

The Duke had no reputation for sensitivity in any of his affairs, as Magalotti remarked, about that time:

He has not much penetration into political affairs, because his rough and impatient spirit does not let him stop for long to examine things. In his inclination towards sensuality he is the opposite of the King, since he cares little for the more innocent preparations for tenderness, and longs for the occasions for the release of a vicious brutality. [52]

Magalotti was also very severe on Anne in her later years:

Obstinate, proud ... worshipping gluttony and amusements ... They say she has been very beautiful, and this is indeed likely ... But now the superfluous fat that she keeps putting on day by day has so altered the proportions of a very fine figure and a most lovely face, that it is very hard to recognise them in her tallness, in the delicacy of her complexion (because her cheeks are a little roughened by some pock-marks) and her bosom, and in the splendour of her chestnut hair.[53]

For all that, Anne's intelligence and common sense gave her an ascendancy over James, as Mr Povey told Pepys on 30 October 1668, 'that the Duke of York, in all things but his codpiece, is led by the nose by his wife.' On 30 July 1667, he reported a neat little joke that linked Charles and James and their relationships with their respective mistress and wife:

The King, speaking of the Duke of York's being mastered by his wife, said to some of the company by, that he would go no more abroad with this Tom Otter [a hen-pecked husband in Ben Jonson's *Epicoene*] (meaning the Duke and his wife). Tom Killigrew, being by, answered, 'Sir,' says he, 'pray, which is the best for a man to be, a Tom Otter to his wife or to his mistress?'

(On 13 February 1668, Pepys wrote that Killigrew was 'the King's fool or jester; and may with privilege revile or jeer anybody, the greatest person ...') At one incident, on 4 June 1669, when Pepys himself was present, one wishes he could have been fuller in his account of going to the treasurer's house, where he found 'the Duke of York and Duchess with all the great ladies, sitting upon a carpet on the ground, there being no chairs, playing at "I love my love with an A because he is so and so, and I hate him with an A because of this and that;" and some of them, but particularly the Duchess herself and my Lady Castlemaine, were very witty.' The duke would have been incapable of wit, but the two women were capable of real barbs.

In that same year, following the Test Act requiring all holders of public office to declare allegiance to the Church of England, James had to reveal his conversion to the Catholic faith, which not only cost him his place as Admiral of the Navy and membership of the Privy Council, but also revealed him as a potential threat to the position of the Church of England in the country – though Anne remained a Protestant, as did his daughters.

However, there was not much time left for Anne, as, aged only thirty-four, cancer wore her down. On 31 May 1671, after a characteristically good meal at Burlington House, she collapsed after her prayers and was obviously dying. Bishop Blandford asked her, 'I hope you continue in the truth,' meaning, in the Church of England, to which she replied, in Pontius Pilate style, 'What is truth?'[54] A doctor later wrote,

> The Duke sent for the Bishop of Oxford out of the chapel, who came, but her senses were first gone. In the meantime the Duke called, Dame, do you know me? twice or thrice. Then with much stirring she said, Aye. After a little respite she took a little courage and, with what vehemency and tenderness she could, she said, Duke, Duke, death is terrible. Death is very terrible. Which were her last words. I am well assured she was never without three or four of her women, so that it was impossible a priest could come to her.[55]

He is concerned to insist – though only 'well assured' – that a Catholic priest could not have given her the last sacraments, which the Duke later said that he did.

With Anne gone, James was now in the marriage market for appropriate royalty and aristocracy, and discreet enquiries and embassages were made. Meanwhile, there were new mistresses to be pursued with a freer hand. There was the widowed Lady Belasys (or Bellasis), a woman, according to Bishop Burnet, 'of much life and great vivacity, but of a very small proportion of beauty: the Duke was often observed to be led by his amours to objects that had no extraordinary charms,'[56] though her portrait suggests average attractiveness. There were suggestions that James was quite keen (he made her a baroness and later a lady-in-waiting to the Duchess), and that the King had to prevent him from marrying her. Mary Bagot, the young widow of the Earl of Falmouth, was briefly in the running, but her reputation (including involvement with the King) disqualified her. Meanwhile, enquiries had narrowed down to the fifteen-year-old Mary of Modena – or, even, possibly, her thirty-year-old aunt, Leonora. When Henry Mordaunt, Lord Peterborough, was sent over to finalise the contract, a blank was left in the place in the document for the bride's name. Both ladies were devout Catholics, professing an interest in entering nunneries; more to the point, Mary, the daughter of the Duke of Modena and Princess Mary Louise d'Este, was the preferred choice of Louis XIV, her mother was related to Cardinal Mazarin and she came with a substantial dowry of 400,000 crowns. On being informed of her forty-year-old fate, it was reported that pretty little Mary 'cried her eyes out.'[57]

She might have been even more distressed had she known of a poem by the Duke's Gentleman of the Bedchamber, Harry Savile, a cheery drinker and friend of Rochester, who was always falling out with his royal master. *Advice to a Painter to Draw the Duke By* is understandable in the context of widespread fears of the growth of Popery and Continental-style arbitrary government. In it, he attacked James for 'adoring Rome' and for saying

> I'll have old England know
> That common sense is my eternal foe:
> I ne'er can fight in a more glorious cause
> Than to destroy their liberty and laws.
> More to the point, here, is his account of Mary:
> Then draw the princess with her golden-chestnut locks
> Hastening to be envenomed with the pox,
> And in her youthful veins receive the wound
> That sent Nan Hyde before her under ground,
> The wound of which now tainted Churchill fades,
> Preserved in store for the new set of maids.
> He advised her to marry elsewhere, in hopes to live longer,
> Than in false hopes of being once a Queen,
> Die before twenty, or rot before sixteen.[58]

The marriage took place by proxy, in September 1673; in October, Parliament tried to have the marriage annulled; the bride and her retinue arrived in London on 26 November. On 5 November, the London apprentices had burned the Pope in effigy, in protest at the Catholic marriage to an Italian.[59] She had to make the best of it.

Over the New Year, Rochester celebrated her arrival in his own way – and perhaps did something to defuse the tension – with a merrily indecent ditty, *On Signior Dildo*,[60] beginning,

> You ladies all of merry England,
> Who have been to kiss the Duchess's hand,

> Pray, did you not lately observe in the show
> A noble Italian called Signior Dildo?

The imputation was that such instruments were, like the Duchess, the products of un-English Continentals.

> This signior was one of the Duchess's train,
> And helped to conduct her over the main;
> But now she cries out, 'To the Duke I will go,
> I have no more need of Signior Dildo.'

The poem tells the eager ladies of the court where such dildoes might be acquired,[61] before listing all the delighted users, including Lady Southesk, Lady Elizabeth Howard (who ran away to marry Thomas Felton, before embarking on a vigorous sexual career), the Countesses of Falmouth and Northumberland and (of course) Barbara, Countess of Cleveland – and many others. The poem was popular, added to by others and widely read.

Meanwhile, the Duke kept Arabella Churchill in play (four children between 1667 and 1674) until 1674, when they parted, amicably enough; she went on to marry Francis Godfrey and bear him three children (incidentally becoming an ancestor of Lady Diana Spencer). The Duke then returned to fishing in the Maid of Honour pool and brought up Mall (or Moll) Kirke and her sister Diana (who later married the Earl of Oxford). In 1674, Mall was the object of both John Sheffield, Earl of Mulgrave and the Duke of Monmouth, who even waylaid Mulgrave on the way from Mall's house and got him locked up. Soon she was in the flattering, if tricky position, of having to juggle three lovers, James having now got involved. Nine months later she had a stillborn child; her brother accused Mulgrave of being responsible and wounded him in a duel in July 1675 (mockingly recorded in Rochester's *A Very Heroical Epistle*[62]). Mall tried to escape her admirers by entering a nunnery – in vain – and eventually married Sir Thomas Vernon of Hodnet, far away in Shropshire.

Sometime after this, these ladies were all replaced by Catherine Sedley, daughter of Sir Charles Sedley, the notorious rake and wit. She seems to have taken after her father: when Evelyn met her when she was fifteen, he remarked, 'None of the most virtuous, but a wit.'[63] She was considered unsuitable as a Maid of Honour to the sober Queen, but placed in the train of the Duchess – within range of the Duke. She began her court career with several disadvantages: her mother was known to be mad, and she would have only a moderate marriage portion. (Sir Winston and Lady Churchill briefly considered her as a wife for their son John, who went on to marry Sarah Jennings.) More important, she was thought unattractive, with a long nose, big mouth, a slight cast in one eye and she was also far too thin for the taste of the time, but she had intelligence, wit and a sharp tongue.[64] Charles Sackville, Lord Buckhurst, Earl of Dorset, mocked her wit and squint (rather surprisingly – he had been a good friend of her father):

> Dorinda's sparkling wit, and eyes,
> Uniting cast too fierce a light,
> Which blazes high but quickly dies,
> Pains not the heart but hurts the sight.
>
> Love is a calmer, gentler joy:
> Smooth are his looks, and soft his pace;
> Her Cupid is a blackguard boy,
> That runs his link full in your face. [torch][65]

Nevertheless, soon enough, she followed Arabella as another conventionally unattractive mistress to the Duke. As she remarked of his taste in women, 'we are none of us handsome, and if we had wit, he has not enough to discover it'.[66] Sackville followed up on this crack of hers:

> Sylvia, methinks you are unfit
> For your great lord's embrace;
> For tho' we all allow you wit,
> We can't a handsome face.

> Then where's the pleasure, where's the good,
> Of spending time and cost?
> For if your wit ben't understood,
> Your keeper's bliss is lost.[67]

(One wonders whether James knew that people at court thought of him as a bit thick.)

When the House of Commons passed an Exclusion Bill against James in March 1679, the King sent the Duke and Duchess away, to Brussels, until things calmed down, before moving them on to Scotland; Catherine was pregnant at the time. The baby was named Catherine Darnley, and was acknowledged by James, though the news made his young wife unhappy. There were suggestions at the time (perhaps to spare Mary's feelings, perhaps to provide an at least partly Protestant successor) that the father was Colonel James Graham, another member of the Duke's household; in later years, Lady Catherine Darnley was thought to resemble the Colonel's legitimate daughter.

In 1680, Sackville (Dorset) returned to the attack on Catherine, accusing her of ageing (she was all of twenty-three, though apparently getting even thinner):

> Tell me, Dorinda, why so gay,
> Why such embroidery, fringe and lace,
> Can any dresses find a way
> To stop th' approaches of decay,
> And mend a ruined face? ...
>
> So have I seen in larder dark
> Of veal a lucid loin,
> Replete with many a brilliant spark,
> As wise philosophers remark,
> At once both stink and shine.[68]

(It does seem excessively savage. In *An Allusion to Horace*, Rochester remarked about Dorset, 'For pointed satires I would

Buckhurst choose, / The best good man with the worst-natured muse.'[69])

Nevertheless, in September 1685, she bore a second child to the Duke, James Darnley, who, like her others by James, did not live long; the child was now an embarrassment, as, in February of that year, King Charles had died. James was now King and attempting to turn over a new leaf. He wrote to her, telling her to retire to the country, or go abroad: he would see her no more.

Catherine fought a vigorous rearguard action, and her campaign is worth following. She would not go; eventually, James weakened, and she was installed in a house formerly belonging to Arabella Churchill, with a pension of £4,000. When little James Darnley died on the eve of the coronation, he was buried in Westminster Abbey; soon she was active again as the King's mistress, before being made Countess of Dorchester and Baroness Darlington, much to the annoyance of the Queen, who would not receive her. More efforts were made to get rid of her, and she was briefly in Dublin, before returning to court in November 1686, with a house near Weybridge.

James's pig-headed intransigence in pushing the Catholic cause led to the Glorious Revolution and his expulsion; he and Mary slipped out of London as his daughter, Mary, and William of Orange arrived. Queen Mary was not inclined to look kindly on her father's former mistress, but Charles Sedley had been active in the Williamite cause and quipped, 'Well, I am even in point of civility with King James, for as he made my daughter a Countess, so I have helped make his daughter a Queen.'[70] She would not be overlooked. After writing an indignant letter about how other former mistresses such as Mazarin, Cleveland and Belasys were received, Catherine was eventually received at court. Not that she spared Mary, telling her that if she herself had broken one commandment (against adultery), Mary had broken another (in supplanting her father) – 'and what I did was more natural.'[71]

Finally, in 1696, aged thirty-eight, she married Sir David Colyear, a Scots soldier and supporter of William, to whom she bore two sons. Characteristically blunt, she told them, 'If anybody calls either of you the son of a whore you must bear it, for you are so; but if they call you bastards, fight till you die, for you are an honest man's sons.'[72] She attended the court of Queen Anne; at the coronation of George I, in 1714, when the Archbishop of Canterbury ritually demanded the consent of the congregation, she was heard to say, 'Does the old fool think that anybody here will say no to his question, when there are so many drawn swords?'[73] She died in October 1717, sixteen years after James and the year before his queen.

4

THE GLORIOUS COURT OF
THE PRINCE D'AMOUR

Unarm! Unarm! No more your fights
Must cause the virgins' tears,
But such as in the silent nights
Spring rather from their fears.

Such difference as when doves do bill
Must now be all your strife:
For all the blood that you shall spill
Shall usher in a life.

And when your ladies, falsely coy,
Shall timorous appear,
Believe, they then would fain enjoy
What they pretend to fear.

Sir William Davenant[2]

The chapter title here, from a satire by Buckingham, refers, of course, to the most important of the King's palaces: Whitehall. In the earlier poem by Davenant, 'blood' in the seventh line is ambivalent: bloodshed might imply warfare, but also, sex; at the time, semen was thought to be a product of blood – suggesting how courtiers might now expect to pass their time. The palace itself was an unimpressive jumble of relatively old buildings, some dating from early Tudor times, when Henry VIII appropriated York Place from Cardinal Wolsey (the Holbein Gate was designed by the artist, Hans Holbein); the most recent was Inigo Jones's Banqueting Hall, decorated by Rubens, built for James I and the site of Charles I's execution. (With the exception of the Banqueting Hall, almost the entire palace burned down in January, 1698, as the result of a kitchen maid's carelessness.[3])

With its gardens and courtyards; its great hall, set up in 1665 as a theatre, complete with proscenium arch and gallery; its council chamber; its chapel, set up in Laudian style with a raised altar and rail; its long galleries, side chambers and back stairs – all so convenient for gossip, flirtation and Charles's informal style of governing; its kitchens, stables and guardrooms; its battlements, chequered towers topped with ogival domes, spires and innumerable smoking chimney stacks, the whole conglomeration, rather like a seventeenth-century Gormenghast, sprawled over some twenty-three acres. The palace covered an area roughly bounded (in today's geography) by the Park to the west, Westminster Abbey and Hall to the south, the river to the east, with water-stairs and wharf, and with the royal mews near modern Trafalgar Square to the north.

There was a staff of about 1,500, from the Lord Chamberlain, Lord Steward and Master of Horse (all positions of high status and value), through the gentlemen, grooms and pages of the royal bedchambers, the Ladies of the Bedchambers and Maids of Honour (for the Queen, Queen Mother and the Duchess of York), down to innumerable minor officials, musicians, ostlers and kitchen maids. Some apartments were reserved for the King and his family, others allocated to senior courtiers, favourites, mistresses and elderly ladies-in-waiting who had waited too long.

Influenced by what he had seen in France, Charles had the Royal Bedchamber developed for formal, ceremonial use, with a great bed set in an alcove nineteen feet by twelve feet, with a parquet floor, a low, gilded screen and curtains held by carved cherubs with eagles overhead. Next to it were four rooms: the 'horn chamber', the 'royne room', the 'greene room' and a cabinet or 'stool room' (lavatory). Behind this were back stairs (useful for his page and pimp, Thomas Chiffinch, to bring in women) and a small sleeping chamber. Before it was a series of rooms and a 'matted gallery' (at the end of which a favoured mistress might be found). Grand apartments were also provided for the Duke and Duchess of York, Prince Rupert and, of course, the Queen, in 1662, overlooking the river with her own reception chamber and chapel. Also, at various times, places were found for the Duke of Monmouth; Louise de Kéroualle and her son, the Duke of Richmond; and Catherine Pegge, the King's earlier mistress and her son, known as Don Carlos. Barbara, Lady Castlemaine, was palatially installed with her offspring in a suite of upper-storey chambers near the Holbein Gate, which provided access to St James's Park and the Privy Garden. Apartments of varying degrees of comfort or discomfort could be found for courtiers' widows and other pensioners. It was a small town.

The King would be attended by twelve Gentlemen of the Bedchamber, all drawn from the nobility, paid – irregularly – £1,000 a year, with lodgings in the palace. The positions had great prestige and provided many opportunities; duties involved (shift work) attendance in the King's bedroom and accompanying him to various functions. There were also as many Grooms of the Bedchamber, of lesser degree – knights, esquires and their sons – on £500 a year and about half a dozen pages of the bedchamber (or of the backstairs) on £80 a year, who made beds and fires, ran errands and controlled access to the royal apartments. The Italian Count Magalotti remarked on a certain handsome, witty sixteen-year-old page named Booten, apparently 'furnished with certain parts more suitable to a giant than a boy'. Magalotti, knowing the court's fashion of pederasty, was concerned at the King's familiarity with the lad, but soon established that he was enjoyed only for his entertaining chatter and his stories. 'He now gives even more delight by recounting all the adventures that the special virtue of his great parts leads him into with the London ladies, in whose houses and at whose tables the King's favour makes him welcomed.'[4]

For all Charles's celebrated easiness and informality of manner (when he chose), the King's day was tightly organised and formalised, beginning with the *levée*. Always an early riser, he might rouse his Gentleman of the Bedchamber, sleeping on a collapsible bed in the royal bedchamber, soon after six. The Gentleman would then unlock the bedchamber door, bolted on the inside and guarded on the outside by yeomen of the guard. The pages of the bedchamber would light the fire, while gentlemen attended the King into the stool chamber; on shaving days, a barber trimmed him and a doctor would be in attendance. The captain of the guard would receive the watchword for the day.

When it was time to get dressed, the Grooms of the Bedchamber would warm the royal undergarments before handing them to the gentlemen, who would put them on the King. The King's outer garments were the responsibility of the Gentlemen of the Robes. Only the staff of the bedchamber and robes (and the Duke) had the right to enter the King's bedchamber; everyone else had to have the King's permission.

Business at council (attended by his spaniels) took up time from a brisk morning walk in the park or game of real tennis or pall mall (like a more vigorous form of croquet). The elderly poet Edmund Waller, eager to ingratiate himself, wrote in his poem *On St James's Park*:[5]

> His shape so lovely, and his limbs so strong,
> Confirm our hopes we shall enjoy him long.
> No sooner has he touched the flying ball,
> But 'tis already more than half the Mall;
> And such a fury from his arm has got,
> As from a smoking culverin 'twere shot.
> [Waller may not have been well informed as
>   to Charles's other activities:]
> No private passions do indulgence find;
> The pleasures of his youth suspended are,
> And made a sacrifice to public care.

Later, the King would dine in state – in public – in the mid-afternoon, seated on a platform under a red silk canopy; food was brought up by Yeomen of the Guard, tasted first and served on bended knee by sewers and a cupbearer.

Bedtime, or *couchée*, might be about 11 p.m., or later (at Christmas 1680, it went on until 1.30 a.m.), and was much less formal, with chat with favoured courtiers, or even rebukes for those who had displeased him. His wife or mistress would not be in evidence but visited in her own chambers; in later years, he would usually return to his own sleeping-room.[6]

The Queen, when she arrived in May 1662, also had a large entourage. She was served, principally, by the Mistress of the Robes, the Countess of Suffolk, who had, in addition, cornered the position of Groomess of the Stool and Keeper of the Privy Purse; this was a position very much worth having and when she retired in 1681, it was snapped up by the Countess of Arlington. Under her were ten Ladies of the Bedchamber, all peeresses. After the Popish Plot of 1678, the Test Act reduced the number of Catholic women attendants Catherine was allowed; Mary of Modena was allowed no English Catholics. As with the men, these positions gave great prestige and advantages such as influence and marriage opportunities for their children. Next down the hierarchy were the women of the bedchamber, drawn from the upper gentry. Least influential but probably the most visible were up to ten Maids of Honour who were young female attendants on the Queen (the Duchess of York had her own) at chapel, balls and other functions. With a modest salary of £10 a year, board and lodging at court and a promise of a dowry on their (approved) marriages, their official function was to 'adorn the court with grace and virtue' – i.e., to look pretty and charming. Milton might well – and not unreasonably – have had in mind such decorative young women when describing the 'daughters of men' of *Genesis* VI:

> — that fair female troop ...
> Bred only and completed to the taste
> Of lustful appetence, to sing, to dance,
> To dress and troll the tongue, and roll the eye ...
>   (*Paradise Lost*, XI, 614–20)

In practice, they were often the (not unwilling) prey of the Duke and the more amorous courtiers. Some were chaste and virtuous, such as Margaret Blagge, admired, platonically, by John Evelyn; nevertheless, the general manners and ethos of the court, as shaped by the King and Duke, were not conducive to chastity, and it is hardly surprising that several of these young blossoms were plucked prematurely.

Chief among their charming seducers were Pope's libertine 'mob of gentlemen who wrote with ease', mentioned earlier, their values lightly suggested by Sir Charles Sedley:

> Drink about till the day find us;
> These are pleasures that will last;
> Let no foolish passion blind us,
> Joys of love they fly too fast.
>
> Maids are long ere we can win 'em,
> And our passions waste the while,
> In a beer-glass we'll begin 'em,
> Let some beau take th' other toil.
>
> Yet we will have store of good wenches,
> Though we venture fluxing for't,
> Upon couches, chairs and benches,
> To out-do them at the sport ...[7]

The versifiers of the time frequently touch on transience, the instability and brevity of their life and its pleasures. In the second verse, the resisting young ladies are left to the attentions of dandies and beaux (despised by the wits), while in the third verse the speaker and his friends settle for the many prostitutes of the town, risking venereal disease and its treatment. (Several court ladies found themselves infected by their roving lovers – or husbands.)

The most entertaining, if not wholly reliable, account of court amours was provided by Philibert, Comte de Gramont, who had to leave the court of Louis XIV rather hurriedly after paying too much attention to one of Louis' mistresses; he arrived in time for the formal celebrations of the royal marriage, in May 1662, and soon got into the swing of things. He describes the atmosphere of the court as

> an entire scene of gallantry and amusements, with all the politeness and magnificence which the inclinations of a prince naturally addicted to tenderness and pleasure could suggest: the beauties were desirous of charming, and the men endeavoured to please: all studied to set themselves off to the best advantage: some distinguished themselves by dancing, others by show and magnificence; some by their wit, many by their amours, but few by their constancy.[8]

The business of government and politics never ruffled the fluff of his anecdotes, improved and refined years later to amuse ladies at the courts of Hanover and France, and which give a good sense of life and manners at 'the court of the Prince d'Amour'.

When Gramont first arrived at the English court he pursued several of the Maids of Honour, first, Miss Myddelton (or Middleton), 'fair and white skinned', but 'so much the coquette as to discourage no one; and so great was her desire of appearing magnificently, that she was ambitious to vie with those of the greatest fortunes',[9] eventually successfully becoming mistress to the Duke of York (and others). She had two weaknesses: pretentious speech and affected manners, with 'an ambition to pass for a wit [which] only gave her the reputation of being tiresome', and a reputation of very smelly feet, which pursued her through many lampoons:

> Middleton, where'er she goes,
> Confirms the scandal of her toes;
> Quelled by the fair one's funky hose,
> Even Lory's forced to hold his nose
> [Lawrence Hyde, Clarendon's son].[10]

After her, he tried Miss Warmestry, a beauty very different from the other: brunette, with 'a very lively complexion, very sparkling eyes, tempting looks, which spared nothing that might engage a lover and promised everything which could preserve him. In the end, it very plainly appeared that her consent went along with her eyes to the last degree of indiscretion'.[11] This habit of hers was to have predictable – but eventually surprisingly happy – consequences.

Lord Taaffe, eldest son of the Earl of Carlingford, former lover of Sarah Walter, drinking-friend of the Duke of Richmond, fell in love with Warmestry. One of the maids, Mlle de la Garde ('a little brunette who was continually meddling in the affairs of her companions'[12]), agreed to persuade the court duenna, the so-called 'Mother of the Maids', to allow Taaffe and Richmond into the maids' quarters, specifically into Miss Warmestry's room. She would stay with them, consuming her favourite green oysters and Spanish wine (supplied by the two men and Gramont) until she had had her fill, and then wander off to bed, leaving the others to do as they pleased. Soon after, a country gentleman, a relative of Henry Killigrew, came to London to contest a lawsuit and fell in love with Warmestry. Despite being warned that 'a girl educated at court was a terrible piece of furniture for the country', while, if he kept her up in town, the costs of her 'equipage, table, clothes and gambling-money' would be very great, he persisted. Modestly, he asked Killigrew to propose on his behalf, and was promptly rejected; he proposed again himself and was even more decisively rejected, and so returned to the country, even forsaking his dogs and horses, and renouncing all the delights and entertainments of a country gentleman.[13]

Meanwhile, the delightful Warmestry, 'who was certainly mistaken in her reckoning, took the liberty of being brought to bed in the face of the whole court [presumably this is not meant literally]. All the prudes of the court at once let loose upon it and those principally, whose age and persons secured them from any such scandal, were most inveterate, and cried most loudly for justice.' The Queen asked Taaffe if he recognised Warmestry as his wife; this he declined to do, and Miss Warmestry left court as soon as she could. Shortly after, Killigrew, on a journey, stopped by his cousin's house and told him of the scandal, only for the cousin, John Machell of Sussex, to leap at the chance: 'Who knows but the beauteous Warmestry will now accept of me for a husband, and that I may have the happiness of passing the remainder of my days with a woman I adore, and by whom I may expect to have heirs.' Killigrew assured him that he could count on that. Soon they were married, and 'the generous fair, first out of gratitude, and afterwards through inclination, never brought him a child of which he was not the father; and, though there have been many a happy couple in England, this certainly was the happiest.'[14]

Having failed with Myddelton and Warmestry (whose maid had kept the presents and love letters intended for her mistress), Gramont turned his attentions to Elizabeth Hamilton, Maid of Honour to the Duchess of York and impervious object of the Duke's attempts, and one of the so-called 'Windsor Beauties', whose portraits hung at Hampton Court Palace. Her portrait probably belongs to 1663, at the time of her wooing by the Count.[15] The courtship, when 'conversation completed what beauty began' and causing 'endless banter at court',[16] went well – so well that when Gramont heard that he was recalled to the French court and set off for Dover, he was intercepted by the lady's brothers, who inquired if there was anything he had forgotten: 'Ah yes, I have forgotten to marry your sister,' he replied. They all returned to London, the couple were married on 31 December and their child (which did not live long) was born in the following August.

During the time when Gramont was wooing her, they were among the livelier members of the court. In the autumn or winter of 1662–3, they attended a masquerade ball at court, at which Elizabeth set up some practical jokes of an unkind nature (which is usually the nature of such jokes). Her targets on this occasion were Henrietta Blague, Maid of Honour to the Duchess of York, and Lady Margaret de Burgh, wife of Lord Muskerry, whom her husband, according to Gramont, 'had most assuredly not married for her beauty, [being] made like the generality of rich heiresses, to whom just nature seems sparing of her gifts in proportion as they are loaded with those of fortune. She had the shape of a woman big with child, without being so: but had a very good reason for limping, for her legs were both uncommonly short, and one of them was much shorter than the other.' Miss Blague he described as 'another species of ridicule', but his description suggests an unremarkable appearance – very fair, with small eyes with very long, pale lashes. 'With these attractions, she placed herself in ambuscade to surprise unwary hearts; but she might have done so in vain had it not been for the arrival of the Marquis de Brisacier. Heaven seemed to have made them for each other ... He talked eternally, without saying anything, and in his dress exceeded the most extravagant fashions. Miss Blague believed that all this finery was on her account; and the Marquis believed that her long eyelashes had never taken aim at any but himself.'[17] So far, they had only made eyes at each other.

Lady Muskerry's ruling passions were dancing and dress. Elizabeth forged a note from the Queen, inviting her ladyship to attend, in 'Babylonian' dress. Her husband, a sober, serious man, forbade her to go, but the Queen's invitation settled the matter for her. As for Miss Blague, she received a note ostensibly from the Marquis praising her as the most charming blonde in the universe, and particularly her *'yeux marcassins'*; with the note came some very pale French gloves and four yards of yellow ribbon for her to wear at the masquerade, so that he might recognise her.

Just before the ball, Lady Muskerry paid a visit to Miss Hamilton, when she remarked on the oddness of men, particularly her husband in forbidding her to attend, and complaining that she had not been informed as to who her partner was to be; Elizabeth assured her that she would be told soon. Shortly after Lady Muskerry had bustled off to try to collect news of her partner, Lord Muskerry arrived, asking about the ball, for which he suspected his wife was making her preparations. Next, in came Miss Goditha Price, another Maid of Honour to the Duchess (and soon, another not especially lovely mistress to the Duke. Of her, Gramont remarked that, as 'her face was not calculated to attract many protestations ... when the occasion presented, she did not affect the slightest pretence at bargaining'). Previously she had been a successful rival of Blague for the affections of one Robert Dungan, a member of the Irish aristocracy and an early admirer of Nell Gwyn, who had recently died. (Among his possessions were found a casket of her love letters, and bracelets and lockets woven of 'hair of all descriptions'.[18]) 'Between these two divinities a long-standing hatred subsisted.' To Miss Price, therefore, Miss Hamilton gave another pair of the gloves she had sent to Miss Blague, together with some yellow ribbon. In addition, she urged her not to try to take away the marquis from Miss Blague: 'This was enough.'[19]

At the ball, Gramont remarked to the King that at the entrance to the hall he had been waylaid by 'the very devil of a phantom in a masquerade, who would by all means persuade me that the Queen had commanded me to dance with her'. He advised the King to see it, 'for she has placed herself in ambush in a coach to seize upon all those who pass through Whitehall. However, I must tell you, it is worth while to see her dress. She must have about her at least sixty ells [about seventy-five yards] of gauze and silver tissue, not to mention a sort of pyramid upon her head, adorned with a hundred thousand baubles.'

The Queen said that everyone she had invited was already there; the King wondered whether it might be the poetic Duchess of Newcastle, celebrated as an eccentric; Lord Muskerry thought it might be his wife. Out he went; his wife, despite 'all her glory', did not appear.

As for Miss Blague, she appeared looking 'more yellow than saffron: her hair was stuffed with the citron-coloured ribbon which she had put there out of complaisance [to the marquis]', while making great play with the aforementioned gloves.

> But if they were surprised to see her in a head-dress that made her look more wan than ever, she herself was very differently surprised to see Miss Price partake with her in every particular of Brisacier's presents: her surprise soon turned to jealousy; for her rival had not failed to join in conversation with him, on account of what had been insinuated to her the evening before; nor did Brisacier fail to return her first advances, without paying the least attention to the fair Blague.[20]

Miss Price, being 'short and thick', did not dance. 'The Duke of Buckingham, who brought Brisacier forward as often as he could,' urged him to dance with Miss Blague, but the marquis, claiming to dislike country dances (which the court enjoyed), declined. Miss Blague, thinking that it was she that he disliked, 'began dancing without knowing what she was doing. Though her indignation and jealousy were sufficiently remarkable to divert the court, none but Miss Hamilton and her accomplices understood the joke perfectly: their pleasure was quite complete.'²¹ It is hard to feel wholly endeared to the beautiful Miss Hamilton after this.

Later, Miss Blague, wanting to know what had gone wrong with the marquis and his compliments, asked what '*marcassins*' (eyes of a wild boar) meant; she was told it meant 'sucking-pig' (the marquis had probably been attempting a translation of the pet endearment, 'pigsneye'). Fortunately, next year, she married Sir Thomas Yarborough and went off to the country to bear him four sons and four daughters – which was more than Elizabeth Hamilton was to achieve.

Later that evening, Lord Muskerry came in to inform them that the vision at the gate had indeed been his wife, 'a thousand times more ridiculous than she had ever been before'; with great difficulty, he had persuaded her to go home, afterwards posting a sentinel at her bedroom door. (In 1665, Lord Muskerry was killed at the Battle of Southwold Bay; in 1676, Lady Muskerry married Robert Danvers, who was killed in a duel in 1684, and then, one Beau Feilding – of whom, more, later – who helped to dissipate what remained of her fortune, leaving her to later years of genteel poverty.)

Lady Muskerry's dancing passion featured in another of Gramont's stories, relating to the Queen's visit to Tunbridge Wells in July 1663. In the spring, Miss Hamilton had been away and now returned accompanied by a relative, a Mrs Wettenhall: 'A beauty entirely English, made up of lilies and roses, of snow and milk, as to colour; and of wax, with respect to the neck and feet; but all without animation or air; her face was uncommonly pretty, but there was no variety ... Nature had formed her a baby from her infancy; and a baby remained till death the fair Mrs Wettenhall.'²²

Her problem was that she was stuck in the country with a bookworm theologian husband, Thomas Wettenhall of East Peckham, who spent the day on his theology and went to bed early so as to get up early, 'so that his wife found him snoring when she came to bed and, when he arose, he left her there sound asleep.' Childless, she felt sure that, if she could get to London, someone would succeed in impregnating her. 'She was visibly pining away,' but Miss Hamilton, who had previously met her in Paris, 'whither Mr Wettenhall had taken her half a year after they were married, on a journey thither to buy books', brought her up to London.

There, George Hamilton (later to marry Frances Jennings) and Gramont met them; they took her to the royal court and Gramont arranged a variety of entertainments, such as balls and concerts, which greatly delighted her, 'except now and then at a play, when tragedy was acted, which she confessed she thought rather wearisome; she agreed, however, the show was very interesting when there were many people killed upon the stage, but thought the players were very fine handsome fellows, who were much better alive than dead.'[23] (In Wycherley's *The Country Wife*, of 1675, Mrs Pinchwife, also up from the country, declared, in Act II.i, 'Indeed I was aweary of the play – but I liked hugeously the actors; they are the goodliest, properest men.')

Meanwhile, Hamilton was for pressing on with her original idea, and, 'indeed, Mrs Wettenhall was much pleased with him ... but the more he pressed her to it, the more her resolution began to fail, and a regard for some scruples, which she had not well weighed, kept her in suspense.' Whether she was just timid, or a sexual tease, there is now no knowing, but the lewd author of *On the Ladies of the Court* (1663) noticed her:

> Wet'nall will not take a touch,
> But yet, to show her lust as much,
> She hath boys to grope her;
> For now and anon
> 'Tis Hamilton,
> But constantly Will Roper.[24]

(The need to rhyme may have determined the author's specific allegations.)

'Soon after being obliged to return to her turkeys and cabbages at Peckham, she had almost gone distracted ... As the Queen was to set out within a month for Tunbridge Wells [accompanied by her ladies and the Hamiltons], she was obliged to yield to necessity, and to return to the philosopher,' though making Miss Hamilton promise that when the court went to Tunbridge Wells she would stay at her house, not very far away, bringing Gramont who, in turn, promised he would bring George Hamilton too, 'which words overwhelmed her with blushes.'[25]

There was much gaiety and (very) informal socialising among the court at Tunbridge Wells, with dancing on the bowling green, to which Elizabeth managed to bring Mrs Wettenhall. Lady Muskerry wanted very much to join in the dancing, despite being six or seven months pregnant, and, carrying the baby on the left side, looking very odd. Lord Muskerry's chaplain tried to dissuade her, but with no success; so, Miss Hamilton and Mrs Wettenhall tried to help her dress. Finally, they put a small cushion under her skirt, to balance on the right side her bulge on the left. At the dance, it was at first thought she was wearing a farthingale, to honour the Portuguese fashion the Queen wore on her arrival in England, while some courtiers were sure she was carrying twins. When the time for country dances arrived, Hamilton had to lead her out. She was delighted, and

> trussed up as she was ... danced with uncommon briskness ... [but] in the midst of capering in this indiscreet manner, her cushion came loose without her perceiving it, and fell to the ground in the very middle of the first round. The Duke of Buckingham, who watched her, took it up instantly, wrapped it up in his coat and, mimicking the cries of a new-born infant, went about inquiring for a nurse for young Muskerry among the Maids of Honour.[26]

After everyone had recovered from their laughter, the Duke suggested that Lady Muskerry might benefit from a little exercise after her delivery; the cushion was replaced, securely, the Queen proposed a second round of country dances and Lady Muskerry happily took part, 'and entirely removed every remembrance of her late mishap.'[27] As to whether Mrs Wettenhall ever became pregnant, history does not relate.

Gramont devoted considerable attention to the various Maids of Honour, who included Frances Stuart (discussed separately below), Miss Bellenden, Mlle Bardon and Mlle de la Garde. Miss Bellenden he described as 'a good-natured girl, whose chief merit consisted in being plump and fresh-coloured; and who, not having a sufficient stock of wit to be a coquette in form, used all her endeavours to please every person by her complaisance.'[28] Unfortunately, not sufficiently alarmed by Miss Warmestry's example, she too had to leave the court before she was turned out; Mlle Bardon was given a pension and sent away, but de la Garde managed to get married. Miss Wells was taken up by the King, who probably also enjoyed Mary Bagot, Maid of Honour to the Duchess, which prevented her being considered as the second Duchess. As it was, in 1664 she was married for one year to Charles Berkeley, Duke of Falmouth (described by Clarendon as 'a fellow of great wickedness', and by Pepys simply as 'court pimp', on 21 October 1666), and then, in 1674, to Charles Sackville, Lord Buckhurst (probably Nell Gwyn's lover in 1667).

Worth more extended discussion were Miss Hobart and Miss Anne Temple, both Maids of Honour to the Duchess. Miss Temple he described as both 'simple and vain, credulous and suspicious, coquettish and prudish, very self-sufficient and very silly.'[29] She had the misfortune to attract the notice of the Earl of Rochester, who set out to seduce her, initially by reading her his latest poems, 'as if she alone had been a proper judge of them', declaring that he was more affected by her intelligence than her beauty, which 'so completely turned her head, that it was a pity to see her'. Seeking to protect her, the Duchess put her in the care of Miss Hobart. This woman, slightly older, had 'a good shape, rather a bold air, and a great deal of wit, which was well cultivated, without having much discretion ... She had a tender heart, whose sensibility some pretended was alone in favour of the fair sex.'[30] The writer of *An Heroic Poem* (1681) was in no doubt writing of her 'bulling round the town.'

She set about to warn Anne off men, while attempting to seduce her herself. According to Gramont, when Anne, after riding one day, went to Hobart for some sweets, she asked if she could undress to her chemise, to cool off. Hobart agreed, embraced and helped undress her, before inviting her into the adjoining bathroom, where they could relax and chat. Here, she warned Anne against men, especially the men of the court, such as the treacherous Earl of Oxford, all 'deficient in honesty', who looked on the maids 'only as amusements'. Particularly she warned against Anne's professed admirers: Sir Henry Sidney, Sir Charles Lyttelton and, above all, Rochester, a practiced seducer:

> the most witty man in all England, but then he is likewise the most unprincipled … No woman can escape him, for he has her in his writings, though his other attacks be ineffectual … had he even been so fortunate as to have gained your affections, he would not know what to do with the loveliest creature at Court; for it is a long time his debauches have brought him to order, with the assistance of all the common street walkers.[31]

She showed Anne verses by him mocking other maids, making 'hideous dissections' of their bodies – but changed the names to Temple. Anne was, naturally, outraged, and Hobart comforted her, advising her to have nothing to do with Rochester.

What she did not know was that the entire conversation had been overheard by the niece of the Mother of the Maids, who was fortuitously hidden behind the curtains screening the bath, where she had gone to do some washing. After they had gone, Miss Sarah, now thoroughly chilled, climbed out of the bath, and then went up to her little garret, where, at the appointed time, she told the whole story to her latest lover, the Earl of Rochester.

That evening, the ladies and Rochester met at the Duchess's; Anne was very embarrassed and uneasy, but he complimented her on her appearance 'after such a fatiguing day: to support a ride of three long hours, and Miss Hobart afterwards, without being tired.'[32] Anne had no idea of Hobart's reputation, so the innuendo was wasted on her. Sarah had told him that the two women were going to walk in The Mall that evening, wearing masks and each other's dresses (the frequent practice of young women looking for trivial flirtations). Rochester and his friend Killigrew went up to them there, Killigrew distracting Hobart while Rochester talked to Anne, pretending that he thought she was Hobart. He said that 'your passion and inclinations for Miss Temple are known to everyone but herself', and that Sir Charles Lyttelton, furious, said that it was 'most scandalous that all the Maids of Honour should get into your hands before they can look around them.'[33] Shocked beyond words, Miss Temple could not bring herself to speak to Miss Hobart.

When the women got home, Anne pulled off her borrowed dress; Miss Hobart came in and tried to give her a hug, whereupon Anne pulled free and screamed the house down. It was late at night; when the Mother of the Maids came in, she saw Anne in her shift fending off Hobart with expressions of horror, who was trying to get near to calm her down. In the end, everyone agreed in condemning Hobart, except the Duchess, who kept her on. Anne, who discovered that the verses she had been shown were not directed at her, wanted to make it up with Rochester; however, as so often was the case, he had been temporarily banished from the court, so she escaped the full recompense she might have found herself making. He carried off the Mother of the Maids and her niece to the country; here he encouraged Sarah in her acting ambitions and got her into the King's Theatre company, 'and the public was obliged to him for the prettiest but at the same time the worst actress in the Kingdom.'[34] As for Anne, she married Sir Charles Lyttelton, a much older man, in 1666, and bore him five sons and five daughters. Miss Hobart remained with the Duchess, did not marry, and died in about 1696 in her early sixties.

Among Gramont's earlier rivals for 'la belle Hamilton' had been Richard Talbot, a man of gigantic stature and absolute Stuart loyalty (which had led him to claim to have been one of Anne Hyde's lovers). After it was clear that he was out of the running there, Catherine Boynton, a Maid of Honour to the Queen, tried for him; 'her person was slender and delicate' with 'large, motionless eyes', and she affected to lisp, languish and to have fainting fits two or three times a day.[35] When she first encountered Talbot, she was overcome with one of these attacks of the vapours, and he was made to understand that this had been on his account. She made a fair effort to marry him but was cut out by the reigning court beauty and heiress, Frances Jennings, a beautiful blonde.[36] His offers to Frances were well received until he objected to her friendship with Goditha Price, who did not have a good reputation, when she broke off with him.

Now arrived on the scene Harry Jermyn, the small, large-headed, spindle-shanked nephew of, and heir to, the Earl of St Albans, (and reputed former lover and even husband, in 1660, of the Princess Royal, which gave him a certain cachet) and the most unlikely cock of the walk among the court ladies, now recently recovered from his brutal duel with Thomas Howard over Lady Shrewsbury's favours. He had been resting in the country for six months, but had heard of the charming Jennings. In turn, Price 'had heard Jermyn spoken of as a hero in affairs of love', and while telling Jennings about the sexual exploits of Barbara, Countess of Cleveland, had often mentioned him, though 'without in any respect diminishing the insignificancy with which fame insinuated he had conducted himself in those amorous encounters.'[37] So, on his return to court, Jennings made a play for him, infuriating Talbot, who stood aside. Cleveland made no objection at the time, and soon 'every person now complimented Miss Jennings upon having reduced to this situation [there was a suggestion of marriage – at some time] the terror of husbands and the plague of lovers.'[38]

Despite his unappealing appearance, Jermyn was a very fashionable trophy among the court huntresses. Gramont tells of Theodosia Hyde, wife of Henry Hyde, youngest son of the Earl of Clarendon, who

> was one of the first of the beauties who were prejudiced with a blind prepossession in favour of Jermyn. She had just married a man whom she loved; by this marriage, she became sister-in-law to the Duchess, brilliant by her own native lustre, and full of pleasantry and wit. However, she was of opinion that, as long as she was not talked of on account of Jermyn, all her other advantages would avail nothing for her glory; it was, therefore, to receive this finishing stroke, that she resolved to throw herself into his arms ...
>
> Jermyn accepted of her at first; but, being soon puzzled what to

do with her, he thought it best to sacrifice her to Lady Castlemaine. The sacrifice was far from displeasing to her; it was much to her glory to have carried off Jermyn from so many competitors; but this was of no consequence in the end.[39]

Meanwhile, Jennings and Price, waiting for Jermyn to take matters further with a definite marriage proposal, thought of visiting a fashionable soothsayer. On the way, they thought it might be fun to dress up, or rather, down, and join the orange-sellers at the entrance to one of the theatres (Pepys heard about it, on 21 February 1665). At the door, Henry Sidney, 'more handsome than the beautiful Adonis', brushed aside these importunate fruit-sellers. The more dangerous Killigrew paused at the door and told Price to bring him 'this young girl' the next day, when 'it would be worth all the oranges in London' to her, while fondling Jennings's breasts, which outraged her. He was surprised at 'a young whore who, the better to sell her goods, sets up for virtue, and pretends innocence.'[40] Price took her away.

They took a coach for the other theatre; they were nearly there when the unusual sight of two fruit-seller girls with expensive shoes and in a hackney coach intrigued the big, bad wolf Henry Brouncker, Gentleman of the Bedchamber to the Duke. Not considered attractive himself, he had 'a great deal of wit [and] a violent passion for women ... He had a little country house four or five miles from London [a ruined Carthusian priory at Sheen] always well stocked with girls; in other respects,' wrote Gramont, 'he was a very honest man [though John Evelyn thought him hard and vicious], and the best chess-player in England.'[41] He stopped the girls, thinking that Jennings was some young woman out to make money, with Price as her bawd or business manager, and pulled out his purse to begin negotiations. Recognising him, they turned away, which made him look more closely, when he realised who they were, remarking how 'the times were greatly changed since the Queen's and the Duchess's Maids of Honour forestalled the market, and were to be had cheaper than the town ladies.'[42] He felt sure that Price was indeed taking Jennings out to try her luck – and that Jermyn would be a cuckold before marrying.

After abandoning their oranges to some urchins, the two girls managed to get away, back to the gilded safety of St James's Palace. Brouncker, sure that Jennings had indeed tried the street, kept quiet about it at the time, resolving to tell 'the all-fortunate' Jermyn all about her, the day after they were married.

Miss Jennings's romantic feelings for Jermyn persisted, despite his dilatoriness. That summer, she had to accompany the Duke and Duchess on their progress north, which was very frustrating for her. 'Jermyn was not of the party; and in her opinion, every party was insipid in which he was not one of the company.'[43] (He was out of action, having over-taxed his not very great strength in losing a bet of 500 guineas against Gramont, to cover twenty miles in an hour on the one horse.) Jennings continually asked after his health. Meanwhile, Dick Talbot, who was in the party, thought he might try his luck again. He was about to declare himself, when into Miss Jennings's room came that bird of ill omen, Miss Hobart, with a comic verse by Rochester (now, alas, lost) about the doings (in every sense) at court, in which he wrote how the giant Talbot had caused consternation by his great size, but that Jermyn, like little David, had overcome the mighty Goliath. Both Talbot and Jennings laughed at this (he, less convincingly), but then Jennings sighed, 'Poor little David,' dropping a tear. Talbot, hurt, left the room, determined to try no more.

As it was, Jermyn had never intended to marry Miss Jennings, who instead married George Hamilton later that year (*faute de mieux?*). Catherine Boynton managed to marry Dick Talbot in 1669, who, after her early death, at last married his beloved Frances in 1679, before James made him Earl of Tyrconnel. Price spent some years as one of James's mistresses and never married.

It is doubtful that James made any provision for little Miss Price after his expulsion. Not all those who made themselves available to, and profited from, royal lovers did well; some got pensions, several got venereal diseases – Nell Gwyn and Louise de Kéroualle, for example, and Jane Roberts, a clergyman's daughter, who in her earlier years was mistress to the King and to Rochester. In a letter of 25 June 1678, Henry Savile reports meeting her suffering in a pox-doctor's establishment in Leather Lane, Hatton Garden, where, he wrote, 'what she has endured would make a damned soul fall a-laughing at his lesser pains, it is so far beyond description or belief.'[44] She did not recover. In November, as she lay dying, the Revd Gilbert Burnet was able to give her great spiritual comfort; in 1680, he was to bring Rochester to a terrified repentance and conversion.

Fortunately, very few young ladies suffered such a dreadful fate; a more comfortable fate and objective was an early marriage, many of them getting married off fairly soon after the age of puberty. For the upper classes, as Samuel Butler observed,

> — matrimony's but a bargain made
> To serve the turn of interest and trade;
> Not out of love or kindness, but designs,
> To settle lands and tenements like fines:
> Where husbands are but copy-books, and wives
> Mere messuages to have and t'hold for lives.[45]

With this in mind, heiresses were hotly pursued. On 22 February 1664, Pepys heard that 'a daughter of the Duchess of Lennox was by force going to be married the other day at Somerset House to Harry Jermyn, but she got away and ran to the King, and he says he will protect her.' A year later, on 26 May 1665, the eighteen-year-old Rochester kidnapped the even younger heiress Elizabeth Malet, carrying her off in a coach-and-six. It is not clear whether this was a serious attempt at abduction, rather than a romantic gesture to suggest unbridled desire. In any case, he had to spend three weeks in the Tower of London; later, they ran away, and got married on 29 January 1667, and his mother made sure Elizabeth's stepfather paid up the dowry. Young Bridget Hyde, an heiress and stepdaughter to Robert Vyner, Lord Mayor of London, was to marry Viscount Dunblane, second son of Lord Danby, when she was kidnapped by one George Emberton and forced into marriage. While the ecclesiastical courts looked into the matter, Bridget was returned home. Then, in 1678, a young officer, Cornet Henry Wroth (of good family in Essex), while dining with Sir Robert at his country house, also carried off Miss Hyde in a coach after dinner. When a wheel broke, Wroth, undeterred, put the girl across his horse and got as far as the Putney ferry, where another coach-and-six awaited, before the pursuers caught up and rescued her; he got away. In 1680, the courts decided that the Emberton marriage was valid – which pleased nobody, as Emberton merely wanted Dunblane to buy him off. Amazingly, Bridget was then abducted for a third time, in April 1682, this time by Dunblane, who married her and quickly got her pregnant. Danby now paid off Emberton, and the court decided that the Emberton marriage was not valid, after all. One would hope for a happy ending, after all this, but Dunblane simply spent all her money, leaving her almost destitute.[46]

What seems almost an upper-class fashion for abduction could also be used to outwit the marriage brokers. Henry Savile described to his brother, Viscount Halifax, in February 1673, how

> Mrs Colombine is married to one Mr Marberry [Marbury?], who has £1,200 per annum in Cheshire; but the method she took in it was something extraordinary; for she suffered herself to be lugged out of her coach at ten of clock at night, and thrust into a hackney which galloped towards Kensington with ten horsemen with swords drawn, she crying murder all the while; but before she came to Kensington she consented to return and marry quietly; so that an hour after her aunt [her guardian] had been with me the next morning, to get all the ports stopped to discover this ravisher, she sent for her [the aunt] to come and see her in bed with her dear husband, and is found to have been consenting from the beginning, and played this trick only to avoid further engaging her fortune, as she had already done something at the importunity of this aunt, who is now wholly defeated, and ready to hang herself.[47]

Henry Savile (a younger brother, and so *persona non grata* to mothers of marriageable heiresses) himself attempted a midnight seduction of the recently widowed Countess of Northumberland, Elizabeth Wriothesley (worth all of £10,000), in September 1671, when they were both guests at Althorp, in an episode worthy of an Edwardian country house weekend. A contemporary, John

Muddiman, wrote a humorous report, how 'the knight errant lodged in a convenient apartment, from whence in the dead night, tempted by his evil genius or the earthly part of his love ... made a sally into her bedchamber, having the day before stole away the bolt, so that there was nothing but a latch to lift.'[48] Kneeling by her bed, in only his shirt, he made eloquent protestations of love; in return, she rang her bell, cried out and roused her furious relatives. As he made a hasty retreat, pursued by her brother-in-law and Lord Sunderland, 'her family breathe nothing but battle, murder and sudden death'. Later, he said that he had seen a dildo under her pillow, as Rochester noted in his satires, *Timon* and *Signior Dildo*.[49] She might have done worse than settle for him, instead of marrying Ralph Montagu in 1673, who had affairs and neglected her.

Most heiresses were pursued by more orthodox means – steely-eyed prospective mothers-in-law – but even these could go wrong, even spectacularly so, as in the case of Lady Northumberland's own daughter, Elizabeth Percy, heiress to the vast estates of the last earl, which made her an especially valuable prize. While mother was away, not especially happily, in Paris, little Elizabeth (or Bette, as she was known) was brought up by her paternal grandmother, who had plans for her. The first match proposed, in 1678, when Elizabeth was twelve, was with the seven-year-old son of the King and Louise, Duchess of Portsmouth, but he was replaced by thirteen-year-old Henry Cavendish, Earl of Ogle, described as a puny youth and 'as ugly as anything young can be',[50] who died a few months after their unconsummated marriage in 1680. There is a fine portrait of her, displaying her red hair, by Henri Gascar, probably from about this time.[51] During the family disputes over money, her jointure and young Lord Ogle's debts, other suitors gathered, including the Duke of Somerset; there was also talk of a scheme by Henry Brouncker to abduct young Bette, to force her into marriage with George Fitzroy, son of Barbara, Duchess of Cleveland.

Next on grandmother's list was Thomas Thynne of Longleat, a rakish friend of Monmouth and the nasty Earl of Pembroke, and known as 'Tom of Ten Thousand', not generally thought of as sufficient quality for her, who had already made pregnant and abandoned a Miss Trevor, a former Maid of Honour. Lord Essex, Elizabeth's uncle, thought she had been 'betrayed for money', while a Colonel Richard Brett was rewarded by Thynne for helping to bring about the sale of young Lady Ogle.

As for her, it was said that 'the contract she lately signed rises in her stomach,' and she asked to defer the marriage for a year, but Thynne insisted. She had always disliked him as he was a notorious loose liver, and, as an intimate friend of Monmouth, almost certainly infected from frequent brothel-visiting. Almost immediately after the wedding in 1681, she ran away to The Hague, helped by 'handsome' Henry Sidney in a royal yacht (significantly named the *Cleveland*). Her friends claimed that the unconsummated marriage was void, and that Thynne had previously been contracted to Miss Trevor. Also on the scene was the handsome, long-haired Swedish mercenary Count Karl Königsmarck in hot (and possibly successful) pursuit. On Sunday 12 February, a group of men – a Captain Vratz, Boroski the Pole and Stern the Swede – waylaid Thynne in his coach in Pall Mall and mortally wounded him with five bullets from a musqueton (or blunderbuss). The three men were soon secured, while the Count was found in disguise in Gravesend, waiting to go aboard a Swedish ship. At the trial, the men were convicted and hanged, but he – a count, after all – was acquitted (possibly as a result of bribery), and sailed for the Netherlands, possibly still in hopes of Lady Bette – who, in fact, promptly returned to England. The count's responsibility was debated, as was that of the friends of Miss Trevor; a heartless mock epitaph appeared:

> Here lies Tom Thynne of Longleat Hall,
> Who never would have miscarried,
> Had he married the woman he laid withal,
> Or laid with the woman he married.[52]

There were rumours again that Lady Ogle (or Thynne) would be married to George Fitzroy, son of the King and Barbara, Duchess of Cleveland, who had in fact been granted the dormant title of

Northumberland, which had become extinct on the death of her father. Instead, she was persuaded to marry for the third time, on 30 May 1682, the nineteen-year old 6th Duke of Somerset, to whom she was to bear thirteen children. Known as 'the proud Duke of Somerset', he was absurdly haughty; in later years, his second wife once tapped him on the shoulder with her fan and was rebuked: 'My first wife was a Percy, and she never took such a liberty.'[53]

In her later years, Elizabeth, Duchess of Somerset, was very influential at the court of Queen Anne and was resented by Jonathan Swift, who believed he had failed to get a bishopric because of her (he called her 'an old red-pate, murdering hag'). In verses to Queen Anne, 'The Windsor Prophecy',[54] he wrote, bitterly,

> My dear England, if aught I understand,
> Beware of carrots from Northumberland;
> Carrots sown Thynne a deep rot may get,
> If so be they are in Somer set;
> Their conynges mark thou, for I have been told, [the Count]
> They assassinate when young, and poison when old.
> Root out these carrots, O thou whose name
> Is backwards and forwards always the same, [Anna]
> And keep close to thee always that name
> Which backwards and forwards is almost the same. [Masham]
> And England, wouldst thou be happy still,
> Bury those carrots under a Hill. [Masham's maiden name]

But that was much later, under a different monarch, in another century.

For some women, such as Barbara Villiers, most notably, or Lady Shrewsbury, marriage was only the starting point for affairs and a varied love life. One of the most spectacular was Lady Elizabeth 'Betty' Howard, daughter of the Earl of Suffolk, who, as Mme d'Aulnoy observed, 'had a beauty and youth that were almost dazzling, and won her the love of all who saw her' and who, 'being of a very gay disposition, seldom frightened her lovers away by her looks.'[55] Against her parents' wishes, she eloped with

Thomas Felton, Groom of the King's Bedchamber, 'a harmless little man and an excellent jockey'.[56] She then embarked on a hectic sex life, becoming mistress to the Duke of Monmouth and many others. *A Ballad* of 1680 celebrated her:

> Of all quality whores, modest Betty for me;
> He's an impudent rogue dares lay virtue to thee.
> Both of tongue and of tail, there's no female more free;
> She's always attended by ballocks and tarse,
> Sweet Ca[ven]dish in cunt and bold Frank [Newport] at her arse ...[57]

She gloried in her many conquests, made quarrels with other women and cried in bed when she could not get her way. In October 1681, she had a great, public row with Lady Arundel over who should have Lord Shrewsbury, which so annoyed the easy-going king that he sent to her father, to chain up his mad daughter and forbid her the court, which may have led to her death 'of an apoplexy' in December 1681, aged only twenty-five.

Others moved around and had easier lives. More sensible, and long-lasting, was Lady Mary Scrope (or Scroope), well known for her wit and the mother of faintly ridiculous courtier-versifier Sir Carr Scrope, widow of Sir Adrian Scrope and dresser to the Queen. In 1663 she was mistress to the Earl of Arlington. The author of *On the Ladies of the Court* sniped at her:

> Scrope, they say, hath no good breath,
> But yet she's well enough beneath,
> And hath a good figary;
> Or with such ease
> She could not please
> The King's great secretary.[58] [Arlington]

A 'figary' was a 'figuerie', or fig garden: go figure. Later, she transferred her affections to a younger, pleasanter man, plump Henry Savile, friend of her son's enemy, the Earl of Rochester, and had some happier years with him, while it lasted (he died in 1687, aged forty-five; venereal disease may have contributed).

For all its apparent gaiety, the court was a cruel world, of smiling betrayers and predators, of liaisons scandalous or condoned. Few escaped unscathed. Some court women, such as Barbara Villiers, most of all, and Louise de Kéroualle, sought wealth, power and influence; some were simply out for a good time; some – who tended not to figure largely in the memoirs of the time – achieved happy marriages. All looked for love, in one form or another. Aphra Behn, England's first female professional dramatist, may aptly conclude this chapter:

> *And forgive us our trespasses*
> How prone we are to Sin, how sweet were made
> The pleasures, our resistless hearts invade!
> Of all my crimes, the breach of all thy laws,
> Love, soft bewitching Love! has been the cause;
> Of all the paths that Vanity has trod,
> That sure will soonest be forgiv'n of God;
> If things on Earth may to Heaven be resembled,
> It must be love, pure, constant, undissembled:
> But if to Sin by chance the charmer press,
> Forgive, O Lord, forgive our trespasses.[59]

5

BUCKINGHAM:
THE WANTON HOURS

As the author of the so-called *Rochester's Farewell* (1680), reviewing notable and deplorable members of Charles's court, wrote:

> Buckingham's ... acts require a volume of their own:
> Where ranked in dreadful order shall appear
> All his exploits from *Shrews—y* to *Le Meer*.

As for the generally perceived character of George Villiers, 2nd Duke of Buckingham, the lines most likely to be remembered in modern times are by Dryden, in *Absalom and Achitophel*, writing in 1681 on behalf of the King and the Duke of York, against the anti-Yorkists:

> A man so various, that he seemed to be
> Not one, but all mankind's epitome.
> Stiff in opinions, always in the wrong;
> Was everything by starts, and nothing long:
> But in the course of one revolving moon,
> Was chemist, fiddler, statesman and buffoon;

> Then all for women, painting, rhyming, drinking;
> Besides ten thousand freaks that died in thinking.
> Blest madman, who could every hour employ
> With something new to wish, or to enjoy.[1]

Dryden's brilliant character assassination did much to wreck Buckingham's reputation, then and even more later. Many bitter lampoons were written against him, and many men hated him, but many in his own time also knew him as one of the most brilliant, glamorous and extravagant figures in the court and political worlds – and the most entertaining to scandalised observers.

'For his person,' wrote Brian Fairfax, his kinsman and agent, 'he was the glory of the age and any court where he came, of a most graceful and charming mien and behaviour, a strong, tall and active body, all which gave a lustre to the ornaments of his mind; of an admirable wit and excellent judgement.'[2] Even Clarendon, a lifelong opponent, had to praise 'the pleasantness of his humour and conversation, the extravagance and sharpness of his wit, unrestrained by any modesty or religion, [which] drew persons of all affections and inclinations to like his company.'[3] That there was something of the romantic – as well as the overambitious – in him is suggested by the great and embarrassing crush he got on Princess Henrietta, the King's younger sister, when she came over to England in November 1660. When she returned to France the next year, he went with her, arousing so much jealousy in her intended husband, the Duke of Orléans, that Charles had to order him to come back.[4] His restless energy led him to snap up mistresses, even from the Queen's unlovely Portuguese entourage, and to encourage the growth of science, becoming one of the earliest members of the Royal Society, and befriending a whole range of writers and the architect Christopher Wren. He set up a successful glassworks, researched into the philosopher's stone, played the violin, wrote verse and drama and engaged in politics. He was also Lord Lieutenant of Yorkshire, where he had large estates. 'The Restoration provided him with a vast annual income which he lost little time in squandering.'[5]

He had married little Maria Fairfax initially for their adjoining estates, but also in expectation of producing an heir, in which he was as unsuccessful as his king. After his death, a commonplace book, of notes, aphorisms and verses, was supposed to have been found by his secretary, Martin Clifford; it was assumed to be by Buckingham, and consequently an intriguing source for his private thoughts. Modern scholars doubt its entire authorship: it is written in Clifford's hand, so that the original authorship of individual passages is uncertain.[6] Citations here are, consequently, provisional. The commonplace book has some relevant observations: 'Wives we choose for our posterity, mistresses for ourselves', and, 'One mistress is too much, and yet twenty is not enough.'[7] He may well have had as many – though who kept score? – but one, Anna-Maria, Countess of Shrewsbury, was to prove, perhaps, one too many.

Brought up in France, she had been married at sixteen in 1659 to a thirty-five-year-old widower, Lord Shrewsbury, to whom she bore two children. In 1661 he was appointed Housekeeper of Hampton Court Palace, which brought them both to Whitehall, where her beauty and vivacity – to call it that – made an early impression. She 'placed her greatest merits in being more capricious than any other', and, as Gramont wrote, though 'no person could boast of being the only one in her favour, so no person could complain of having been ill received'. The court ladies' favourite, Harry Jermyn, 'was displeased that she had made no advances to him, without considering that she had no leisure for it.'[8] Apparently, at some stage she may have managed to fit him in, if a verse in the satire *On the Ladies of the Court* is to be believed:

> Shrewsbury hath sounding [swooning] fits,
> You'd think she'd almost lose her wits,
> She lies so on the ground, sir.
> But Jermyn's tarse
> Will claw her arse,
> And make her soon rebound, sir.[9]

Their relationship annoyed another admirer, the hot-tempered Thomas Howard, brother of the Earl of Carlisle. Howard invited

Anna-Maria to a party at Spring Gardens, which Jermyn decided to attend, where he flirted with her while ridiculing the entertainment that Howard had provided. Howard could barely contain his fury but sent Jermyn his challenge to a duel. The next day (as Pepys noted, on 18 August 1662) he and his second waylaid Jermyn and his friend, unprepared, at St James's Park; Jermyn's second, Giles Rawlins, was killed outright, and Jermyn was wounded in three places and had to be carried away to his uncle's house, while Howard and his second got away to France. As for Lady Shrewsbury, Gramont remarked with unusual asperity that he 'would take a wager she might have a man killed for her every day, and she would only hold her head the higher for it; one would suppose she imported from Rome plenary indulgences for her conduct.'[10]

Sometime later, in 1665, Henry Killigrew, one of the wilder men at the court, 'having nothing better to do, fell in love with Lady Shrewsbury; and, as Lady Shrewsbury, by a very extraordinary chance, had no engagement at the time [perhaps because she had only relatively recently given birth to her second son], their amour was soon established.' According to Gramont, Killigrew was 'amazed that he was not envied, and offended that his good fortune raised him no rivals'. He took to boasting drunkenly of his achievement and giving 'luxurious descriptions of Lady Shrewsbury's most secret charms and beauties, which above half the court were as well acquainted with as himself'. His salacious rhapsodies reached Buckingham's ears, who, according to Gramont, 'resolved at last to examine into the truth of the matter himself. As soon as he had made the experiment, he was satisfied.'[11]

It seems, however, that the affair took a little time to get going, as Buckingham was very much engaged with the outbreak of the Dutch War and his rivalry with the Duke of York. The onset of the plague and removal of the court, eventually to Oxford, also hindered their opportunities. It may have been a time of brief encounters and challenges. A couple of quotations from the commonplace book (which, admittedly, do not necessarily refer to this time) are suggestive: 'Love's like a game of chess, if both be cunning gamesters, they'll never make an end', and, 'Kisses – sharp-headed kisses that wound deep – are like bands of gold or silver found upon the ground, which are not worth much in themselves but as they promise a mine near to be digged'.[12]

With the Dutch War boiling up in 1666, Buckingham had to be up in Yorkshire, preparing defences. That summer, he encountered the Earls of Cardigan and Shrewsbury in Hull and invited them and their families to visit him at York. Sir John Reresby, Deputy Lieutenant of the West Riding of Yorkshire, was present, and recorded how 'the days were spent in visits and play, and all sorts of diversions that place could afford, and the nights in dancing sometimes till day the next morning ... The two Earls not being men for those sports, went to bed something early'. Buckingham and Anna-Maria did not. Her younger brother, Lord Brudenell, told Reresby one night that 'coming hastily through the dining room the evening before he saw two tall persons in a kind posture, and he thought they looked like the Duke and his sister, but he would not be too inquisitive for fear it should be so'. On another occasion he was sent for to reconcile her and her husband, 'they having a great quarrel of jealousy concerning the Duke'.[13] In August, the house party broke up, the families returning to their estates, before Buckingham had to rush down to London to help deal with the Great Fire.

By now, both of them were hooked, though not knowing how matters would develop. The commonplace book includes the following lyric (attributed to him in the Countess of Warwick's commonplace book in 1709, and performed publicly in 1669). Not serious in tone, it could provide an amusing comment on their respective amorous natures and careers, at the uncertain beginning of the affair.

> Since you will needs my heart possess
> 'Tis just to you, I must confess
> The fault to which it's given:
> It is to change much more inclined
> Than woman, or the sea, or wind,
> Or aught that's under heaven.

Nor will I hide from you the truth:
It has been from its very youth
A most egregious ranger,
And since from me it often fled,
With whom it has been born and bred,
'Twill scarce stay with a stranger ...

Nay often when I'm laid to rest,
It makes me act like one possessed,
For still it keeps a pother,
And though I only you esteem,
Yet it will make me in a dream,
Court and enjoy another.

And now if you are not afraid,
After all this that I have said,
To take this arrant rover,
Be not displeased, for I protest,
I think the heart within your breast
Will prove just such another.[14]

For all the teasing in such a lyric, the liaison proved a very serious one – 'no amour in England ever continued so long' according to Gramont – (and possibly the only real love affair in this book), and impossible to keep secret (supposing they had tried). In particular, jealous Henry Killigrew could not keep quiet, attacking her with bitter invective, drawing 'a frightful picture of her conduct, and turn[ing] all her personal charms which he used to extol, into defects.'[15] Anna-Maria complained to her family, but no one was keen to challenge Killigrew, who was a notorious duellist. Fortunately, at this time Killigrew was heard to say that Barbara Villiers had been 'a little lecherous girl when she was young', which got him temporarily dismissed from the court (Pepys, 4 October 1666).[16]

Meanwhile, Buckingham busied himself with politicking, encouraging criticism of the government by the cabal of the Dukes of York and Ormonde, Lords Clarendon and Southampton and Baron Arlington. A bill came before the House of Lords to prohibit the importation of Irish cattle, a bill naturally supported by English and Scottish cattle farmers and opposed by the Irish and the government, which was enough to make Buckingham support the bill. In the course of the debate, he declared that whoever was against the bill 'was there led to it by an Irish interest or an Irish understanding' – in other words, was either corrupt or a fool. An angry Irish lord, the Earl of Ossory, was outraged and challenged him to a duel – in despite of rules of Parliamentary privilege – which he felt he had to accept. Having named the ground as Chelsea Fields, he went home for his sword and then to the fields over the river, opposite to Chelsea, while Ossory waited in vain in the fields on the north side of the river. The story having got out, the next day Buckingham declared in the House that he had been improperly challenged for what he had said in Parliament, but had had to accept. Ossory was in a quandary: if he admitted having made the challenge, he was liable for severe penalties, and so tried to evade the charge of impropriety. The House debated what to do. Some thought Ossory should be sent to the Tower, some thought Buckingham equally to blame for accepting the challenge and some accused him of cowardice in deliberately going to the wrong place. In the end, Ossory was sent to the Tower and Buckingham put in the charge of the Gentleman Usher of the Black Rod.[17] Eventually the bill was passed, but Parliament held back some money from the King, for which he blamed Buckingham.

After this, he made a nuisance of himself in intervening in the scandalous divorce case between Lord Roos and his wife, the daughter of the Marquess of Dorchester. Both families wanted the case to proceed, but Buckingham objected on the grounds that Roos had used a title which belonged to him in the right of his mother. Roos had used it as a courtesy title, but Buckingham made him drop it. This was a tiresome nonsense, serving only to irritate everybody, including the King and his advisers, who were interested in the possibilities of divorce. Soon enough, Buckingham got into a stupid brawl in Whitehall with the Marquess, with Buckingham knocking off the Marquess's wig and the Marquess pulling out some of Buckingham's hair. Both men were sent to the Tower for three days. They were formally 'reconciled', but Buckingham carelessly or arrogantly broke protocol by returning to Whitehall without begging the King's pardon, for which he was banished from court for some weeks.[18]

For Buckingham, 1667 was dominated by the deadly machinations against him of Lord Arlington. Arlington got some agents to try to undermine him, which they did by seizing Doctor John Heydon, a naïve physician and astrologer, a client and admirer of the great Lord Buckingham, together with his papers. Among letters addressed to Buckingham, there was an unsigned letter, apparently by Buckingham, requesting Heydon to cast the King's horoscope; insofar as this involved reviewing his entire life, it would necessarily 'imagine the King's death', which was treasonous. Although loyal, Heydon would not confess to any such treasonous activity on Buckingham's part, Arlington went on, spoke to and shocked the King, and arranged for Buckingham to be arrested and sent to the Tower.

The Serjeant at Arms, John Barcroft, rode off, carrying his mace, to Buckingham's country residence, and by the evening of 28 February was only six miles away, when he was overtaken by Maria, the Duchess of Buckingham, in her six-horse coach, on her way back from visiting Lady Shrewsbury, who had been unwell. She, or one of her attendants, recognised the Serjeant and his mace, realised the danger, and drove off at full speed, outpacing Barcroft's tired horses and getting there before him. When Barcroft arrived, he found the gates barred and the servants unhelpful.[19]

The next morning, when Barcroft was at last admitted, the Duke was long gone – not out of guilt, but as a precaution – down to his friends in London; Barcroft returned, more slowly. On 8 March, the King issued a proclamation, requiring Buckingham to surrender himself, while also giving his position as Gentleman of the Bedchamber to his friend, the Earl of Rochester, and his lieutenancy in Yorkshire to the Earl of Burlington. Bravely, Heydon smuggled a letter out of the Tower, declaring, melodramatically,

> My lord duke is wronged, and with my life I will let the world
> know it. I pray, let not my Lady be afraid, for when his Majesty

hears the truth the Duke will be restored to more favour than ever
... the Duke is most unjustly abused and I am undeservedly a close
prisoner, tortured in the dungeon to speak their desires against him,
but death shall close up the scene before I will be found to damn my
soul for a witness to their wicked designs. My last word shall be, the
Duke is innocent, for I know nothing against him.[20]

While Arlington and Clarendon worked to increase the King's
suspicions, Buckingham amused himself by moving around
London from one 'safe house' to another. He tried, but failed, to
get an interview with Clarendon, and then wrote to the King for
an audience, which was refused. On 26 June he wrote a letter of
submission to the King, and then surrendered himself to Secretary
William Morice, as Pepys was told on 28 June 'that he has been
taken by the watch two or three times of late at unseasonable
hours, but so disguised that they could not know him ... the Duke
of Buckingham doth dine publicly this day at Wadlow's at the Sun
Tavern and is mighty merry, and sent word to the Lieutenant of
the Tower that he would come to him as soon as he had dined'.
Pepys commented, 'How sad a thing it is when we come to make
sport of proclaiming men to be traitors and banishing them, and
putting them out of their offices and Privy Council, and of sending
to and going to the Tower: God have mercy on us.' His comment
suggests how opinion was moving in favour of the Duke. A crowd
gathered outside the tavern, and after his dinner the Duke showed
himself from the balcony to receive their cheers, before he went off
to the Tower.

A commission headed by Arlington questioned him, as he firmly
denied everything and outwitted them, declaring that Heydon
was 'cracked in his brain', and that he had never written to him
and was prepared to bet Arlington £100 that he had never done
so; Arlington did not take up the offer.[21] On 12 July Pepys noted
that Buckingham was still being detained, and that Barbara, Lady
Castlemaine, a cousin but not normally a friend, was quarrelling
with the King on his behalf. On 28 July he was brought before
the Privy Council, when he was very submissive to the King but
sharp with Arlington. Accused of popularity-seeking, he retorted,

'Whoever was committed to prison by my Lord Chancellor or my Lord Arlington could not want being popular.'[22] He contemptuously dismissed accusations of having conspired with Heydon. When the letter, supposedly in his own hand, that was to have exposed him commissioning Heydon to cast the King's horoscope was shown him, he immediately denied that it was in his handwriting, and referred it to the King, who knew his hand. Asked whose handwriting it might be, he replied, 'Why, it is my sister of Richmond's hand, some frolic or other of hers of some certain person; and there is nothing of the King's name in it, but it is only said to be his by supposition.'[23] The King agreed that it was the Duchess's hand; the case collapsed. The order was made for Buckingham's prompt release from the Tower; Heydon, not being important, was released somewhat later.

Almost immediately, there was scandal again; his affair with Lady Shrewsbury was in full career (in the commonplace book, love is described as being 'like Moses' serpent, it devours all the rest'[24]). On Saturday 20 July 1667, he took Anna-Maria and his wife (who submissively put up with being a poor third) to the Duke's Theatre. In a nearby box was Harry Killigrew, still bitter. Seeing Lady Shrewsbury, he began abusing her loudly, and directed 'scurvy language' at Buckingham, who told him to behave himself. Killigrew then found Lord Vaughan and asked him to carry a challenge to the Duke, which he refused to do. Killigrew then went over and hit Buckingham twice on the head with his sheathed sword; Buckingham leapt up and chased him over the boxes and benches, and when he caught him, 'he did soundly beat Harry Killigrew', as Pepys reported two days later, 'and [did] take away his sword and made a fool of, till the fellow prayed him to spare his life'. The whole theatre was in uproar and the ladies were frightened; Killigrew had to run away. He borrowed thirty pounds and fled to France, where his reputation followed him. On 17 October, the King wrote to his sister, Minette:

> For Harry Killigrew, you may see him as you please, and though I cannot commend my Lady Shrewsbury's conduct in many things, yet Mr Killigrew's carriage towards her has been worse than I will

repeat; and for his *démêlé* with my Lord of Buckingham, he ought not to brag of [it], for it was in all sorts most abominable. I am glad the poor wretch has got a means of subsistence, but have one caution of him, that you believe not one word he says of us here, for he is a most notorious liar and does not want wit to set forth his stories pleasantly enough,[25]

as the Duke of York and his wife could have confirmed. Buckingham's conduct in the theatre was generally approved (as by Pepys, as that of a man of honour), with his wider reputation only slightly smeared, but Lady Shrewsbury, whose reputation was severely harmed, determined on revenge. Before she could carry that out, angry at the failure of her family to deal with Killigrew, she withdrew from public life, going for eight months to Pontoise convent in France.

It was at some time about now that Samuel Butler, author of the famous verse satire *Hudibras* (1662, 1663), who had been Buckingham's secretary, wrote one of his *Characters* (1667–9) about him:

Perpetual surfeits of pleasure have filled his mind with bad and vicious humours (as well as his body with a nursery of diseases) which makes him affect new and extravagant ways of being sick and tired with the old. Continual wine, women and music put false values on things, which by custom become habitual, and debauch his understanding so that he retains no right notion, no sense of things ... He rises, eats and goes to bed by the Julian account, long after all others that go by the new style, and keeps the same hours with ants and the antipodes ... He does not dwell in his house, but haunts it like an evil spirit, that walks all night to disturb the family, and never appears by day ... His mind entertains all things very freely that come and go; but like guests and strangers, they are not welcome if they stay long ... Thus with St Paul, though in a different sense, he dies daily, and only lives in the night.[26]

Without losing the wit, Butler might have written in rather less hostile fashion of his employer and patron, but friends, of whom he had plenty, wrote approvingly.

Anna-Maria's absence and Buckingham's rapprochement with cousin Barbara made it easier for him to deal with an old enemy, Clarendon, thought all-powerful, but consequently resented and subject to attack. In September 1667, Marvell's satire, *The Last Instructions to a Painter* (lines 355–8) invited:

> See how he reigns, in his new palace culminant,
> And sits in state divine like Jove fulminant.
> First Buckingham, that durst to him rebel,
> Blasted with lightning, struck with thunder, fell ...[27]

Like Milton's Satan, echoed here, Buckingham rose again, and, briefly allied with Arlington, campaigned to blame Clarendon for all that had gone wrong recently, notably the disaster of the Dutch raid up the Medway that summer. Responsive to Buckingham, Barbara and popular resentment, ungrateful Charles had soon broken and dismissed his great Chancellor. On 29 November, triumphant Buckingham was reconciled with the King and restored to his position of Gentleman of the Bedchamber and member of the Privy Council. He became very influential with the King, and gossip suggested 'how the King is now fallen in and become a slave to the Duke of Buckingham [who] will certainly ruin him' (Pepys, 27 November). He had hoped for successful involvement in international politics, arguing for an alliance with France against the increasingly important maritime trading rival Holland but was outmanoeuvred by his own rival, Arlington, who, in January 1668, brought about a Triple Alliance with Holland and Sweden against France.

Buckingham certainly had little respect for (and, come to that, little understanding of) the King; hoping, like others, to control him through his mistresses, he sought to supplant Barbara with little theatre wenches, Moll Davis of the Duke's Theatre and Nell Gwyn of the King's Theatre. Charles happily took them on and went on his own way. Now new – or old – troubles emerged, when, in the same month, the long- (and multiple) cuckolded Lord Shrewsbury, aged about forty-five and a quiet-living man, urged on by Buckingham's political enemies, at last stirred into action and issued a challenge, which he had to accept.

It was decided that the duel would be in the French style, with three men engaged on each side, almost guaranteed to produce a bloody result. Shrewsbury's seconds were Bernard Howard, brother of the Duke of Norfolk, and Sir John Talbot, an ally of Arlington and no friend of Buckingham; Buckingham chose fighting men, Sir Robert Holmes, a sailor, and Lieutenant William Jenkins. The King tried to prevent the duel, but there was a muddle, and the intervention, as Pepys wrote on 17 January, 'fell between two stools'. On the afternoon of 16 January, the six men met near Barn Elms, Holmes against Talbot, and Jenkins against Howard. Buckingham soon ran Shrewsbury through the body, 'from the right breast through the shoulder', but Howard quickly killed Jenkins. Talbot was wounded, and with Holmes and Buckingham against him, Howard gave up. Shrewsbury was carried to a coach, seriously wounded, though the physicians said that he was in no danger of his life.[28] Gossip said that Anna-Maria had been present, dressed as a page, but she was still away in France. As the law said that if one party to a duel was killed, then all involved were guilty, Howard and Talbot fled. Buckingham, however, on 27 January, was granted a pardon by the King, irrespective of any deaths arising from the duel (a pardon later granted to the others): the King needed him active in Parliament early in February, to help bring in votes for the King's money.

Despite public scandal about the duel and the pardons, all seemed to be going well, and on 6 February he was in Parliament and then at the theatre with his friends, but then, on 16 March, the Earl of Shrewsbury, thought to be convalescent, surprised everyone for the second time and died. The shock and condemnation of Buckingham was widespread; Buckingham's pardon was hastily renewed and the doctors and surgeons carried out a post-mortem and declared that the death was not caused by the wound – which persuaded few people. Afterwards, he was always known as the cuckold's killer, as lampoon and ballad after ballad were to insist:

> Now he so bravely and nobly begins,
> Must afterwards think (when such glory he wins)

Adult'ry and murder but trivial sins,
With a fa, la, la.

A New Ballad to an Old Tune (1673)[29]

Shortly after this, Anna-Maria returned to England only to find herself barred from court, disowned by her friends and relatives, control of her children taken from her and her jointure – her share in her husband's estate – taken from her; what caused great and immediate outrage was that Buckingham brought her back to his house, alongside his wife. Here, as Pepys was told on 15 May, 'His Duchess saying that it was not for her and the other to live together in a house, he answered, "Why, Madam, I did think so; and therefore ordered your coach to be ready to carry you to your father's", which was a devilish speech, but they say true; and my Lady Shrewsbury is there it seems.' It is a shocking moment, if true. Only a man besottedly in love, arrogant and indifferent to any other consideration or others' reaction, could have behaved like that.

Whatever he had in mind, Anna-Maria came to some kind of rapprochement with her family, got her jointure money and moved into King Street. The couple carried on openly, or even more openly than before, apparently taking part in court entertainments, theatre-visits and balls. Only the Queen, friend of the little Duchess, would not receive them.

Not that this greatly troubled the great Duke in his relationship with the King. On 18 July Pepys recorded that, in May, Buckingham had been with the King at Lord Cornwallis's house in Suffolk, after the races at Newmarket, and 'in the afternoon to please the King made a bawdy sermon to him out of Canticles' – he was always a skilful parodist and had endured many a moral sermon in his time. A modern biographer, J. H. Wilson, quotes one such parody, perhaps by Buckingham. The preacher's improbable text, perhaps derived very distantly from Proverbs, is, 'A lewd woman is a sinful temptation, her eyes are the snare of Satan, and her flesh is the mousetrap of iniquity.' He then explains:

I shall now explain at large what I mean by a lewd woman. I mean that unsanctified flesh which breaks through the confines of modesty and rambles through the brambles of impurity to graze on the loathsome commons of adultery and glut their insatiable appetites with the unsavoury fodder of fornication till they've fired their tails like Samson's foxes [heated their genitals], which trap, beloved, I fear you have all been caught in.

The conversation of a lewd woman is dangerous. She flatters with her tongue and charms with her tail till her pleasing dalliances, her languishing looks and lecherous kisses [have] roused up the devil in the flesh. Then arises a hurly-burly in nature. He embraces the temptation in his arms, and casting her on a couch full of crackling infirmities, she tussles, he bustles, the couch shrieks out to discover the baseness they are acting. But, alas, it being in the tents of the wicked, nobody will hear till they have glutted their souls with forbidden fruit and sowed their polluted seed amongst the thorns of abomination ...

I shall now proceed to the second part of my text, viz., her eyes are the snares of Satan. That is, friends, they are the deluding baits which first influence your frail natures by their pinking and winking, their rambling and rolling, their long and languishing motions ... [You become] so enamoured with this Satan's gimcrack that then 'tis 'oh! that I could,' and 'Aw, that she should,' 'Yes, that I would!' ... Therefore I say unto you, the eyes of a lewd woman are the snares of Satan. They are the very allurements with which he baits his mouse-trap of iniquity, this is the *ignis fatuus* that leads you into dark pits, stinking bottomless pools and filthy water-gaps of destruction ...

So much for the first and second part of my text. I come now to the third and last part, wherein I shall endeavour to handle the mouse-trap of iniquity, which I fear, beloved, you have all been handling before me ... This trap of Satan lies hid like a coney burrow in the warren of wickedness between the supporters of human frailty, covered over with the fuzzes of iniquity which grow in the very cleft of abomination. A lewd woman, beloved, I say is this warren of wickedness; therefore let not her eyes entice you to be fingering the fuzzes which grow in the cleft of abomination, lest Satan thrust you headlong into the mousetrap of iniquity. Let not Satan with his cloven foot tread upon your tender consciences,

but erect your actions upon the pedestal of piety, that Providence
may put you in a posture of defence against the devil and all his
accomplices ... May Providence hedge you and ditch you with His
mercy and send His dung-carts to fetch away the filthiness from
among you.[30]

It would have been amusing enough on a dull afternoon ('We
made our own entertainment in those days'). Not only unofficial
court jester, Buckingham now paid a lot of money to become the
King's Master of Horse, a position grander than it might seem,
with automatic membership of the Privy Council and a variety of
perquisites and privileges. Throughout that summer, the two great
stags of the court butted against each other to gain advantage and
dominance.

He attempted to initiate another scheme for a French alliance,
only to find his French contacts not overly enthusiastic. What he
did not know was that Charles, with the Duke of York, Arlington,
Arundell and Sir Thomas Clifford were in secret negotiations –
the so-called 'Grand Design' – with Louis XIV, whereby Charles
would allow Louis a free hand on the Continent, with a fleet
against the Dutch and a promise eventually to convert England to
Catholicism, in return for huge subventions of money, well over
a million pounds, for his own purposes. As a committed (if by no
means very principled) Protestant, Buckingham had to be kept
ignorant of the whole scheme. While this – arguably treacherous
– scheme proceeded over his head, he went on with his own
campaigns against Yorkist opponents, first ousting Ormonde as
Lord Lieutenant of Ireland, and then Sir William Coventry, an
earnest, conscientious Commissioner of the Treasury.

In the previous year, 1668, Buckingham, in collaboration with
Sir Robert Howard, had written a play, *The Country Gentleman*,
mocking Coventry in the character of Sir Cautious Trouble-all,
who was to be shown working in the centre of a round table, with
drawers labelled 'Affairs of Spain', 'Affairs of Holland', and so on –
an exact imitation of Sir William's circular table, which he himself
had proudly shown to Pepys (4 July 1668). Coventry heard of this
and complained to the King, who sent for the script and found

nothing offensive in it (the desk scene having been removed). Not deceived, Coventry then threatened the actors that he would have their noses cut and then sent Buckingham a challenge, only for the King to forbid the duel. The next consequence was that Sir William was dismissed and sent to the Tower in March 1669 – a severe punishment for a minor offence, except that he was a Protestant and so one whom Charles would want out of the way should the Grand Design ever come to anything. On 7 March Charles wrote to his sister Minette that he was pleased that Coventry had provided the excuse to get rid of him out of the Council and Treasury: 'The truth of it is, he has been a troublesome man in both places, and I am well rid of him.'[31]

The Grand Design moved on its secret way. Meanwhile, Buckingham did one good thing of permanent significance: he arranged for Christopher Wren to take over from Sir John Denham as Surveyor of the King's Works and so be responsible for rebuilding London (as Pepys noted, 21 March). Even then, when Wren and Robert Hooke put up a high, oversized monument to the Great Fire, he mocked it in a little verse:

> Here stand I,
> The Lord knows why,
> But if I fall,
> Have at you all.[32]

Something else to distract him that summer was the wretched Harry Killigrew. While in semi-retreat in France, Killigrew had got into serious trouble, accused of having drugged a young woman and her mother, before raping the daughter. He was convicted and sentenced to hang, but got off through the mediation of the Queen mother and the Duchess of Orléans. He had then returned to London and his bad old ways, joining a drink and sex club of rakes, known as 'the Ballers', whom Pepys fell in with one evening – 'Harry Killigrew, a rogue, newly come back out of France but still in disgrace at our court ... as very rogues as any in the town, who were ready to take hold of every woman that came by them ... mad bawdy talk ... loose, cursed company.'[33]

Killigrew's 'mad, bawdy talk' apparently included more salacious boasting about Lady Shrewsbury, who by now had had enough of him and was determined on revenge. On the night of 30 May 1669, as his coach returned to Turnham Green, near Hammersmith, a six-horse black coach drew up alongside, and several men dragged him out and stabbed him nine times; one story said that a woman's voice cried out to kill him. It was obvious to everyone who was responsible.[34] Buckingham rushed to the Queen's bedchamber and told the King and Harry Killigrew's father, who was there, that Lady Shrewsbury was not responsible, and that the attackers had meant only to beat him – hardly a convincing story. Fortunately for all concerned, Killigrew recovered from his injuries, apologised to both Lady Shrewsbury and the Duke, and was, sometime later, even allowed to return to court. (If something did not concern him directly, Charles was never much bothered.)

The incident had not done the Lady and Buckingham's reputations any good, who nevertheless carried on their high life, drinking and dining and partying into the early hours. The elderly poet Edmund Waller, a favourite of the Rochester-Buckingham clique, wrote once to his wife how 'The Duke of Buckingham with the Lady Shrewsbury came hither last night at this time and carried me to the usual place to supper, from whence I returned home at four o'clock this morning, having been earnestly entreated to sup with them again tonight, but such hours cannot always be kept.'[35] He was sixty-two and out of practice.

The early part of the year provided entertainment for the court with the progress through the House of Lords of the Roos divorce case, when Lord Roos, having divorced his wife from 'bed and board' and illegitimised her children, now needed a bill enabling him to remarry and produce a legitimate heir. The Yorkists opposed this bill, which might set a precedent for the King to divorce and remarry, while Buckingham supported it, arguing that 'he knew not why a woman might not be divorced for barrenness, as a man for impotency'.[36] Both he and Charles had barren wives.

The Grand Design was approaching completion. Parliament had not provided the King with the money he wanted, so that he was more than ever well disposed to the scheme: he was to get from

Louis £225,000 a year towards the cost of the war with Holland and £150,000 for his commitment to Roman Catholicism when the time seemed right (though the money was to come within six months, in any event). On 16 May 1670, Henrietta, Duchess of Orléans, came over to Dover, ostensibly to see her dear brothers, but in reality to complete the deal; after three weeks of public junketing and secret bargaining, the treaty was signed. On 2 June she sailed for France; within three weeks she was dead, from peritonitis from a perforated ulcer.

Protocol required that an envoy be sent to France for the funeral. It was also quietly agreed that Buckingham, who knew nothing of the secret Treaty of Dover, should now negotiate a double of the treaty – but without the Catholic part – which was signed on 21 December. He was treated magnificently, with banquets, concerts and dances. Shortly before his departure, there was a grand dinner, when three masked dancers (Louis and two ladies) disarmed him of his sword and presented him with another, set with diamonds, valued at 20,000 crowns. So impressed were other French courtiers when they visited him to admire it, that several of the diamonds were picked off, which he had to replace at his own cost. Louis also arranged for an annual pension of 10,000 livres for Lady Shrewsbury.

During Minette's stay in Dover, Charles had greatly admired one of her Maids of Honour, Louise de Kéroualle, and it was now agreed that Buckingham should bring her back with him, as a Maid of Honour for the Queen and a present for the King (and agent for Louis). On 6 September, he and Louise set off in separate parties, Louise heading for Dieppe while he made for Calais, where he was expecting to be reunited with Anna-Maria, who was now pregnant, and his wife, who had come to welcome him. Unfortunately, rough winds and seas had prevented their crossing, and they had gone to Dover to meet him there. Not finding them at Calais, he found a ship ready to sail and joined them there. He forgot about Louise, waiting, with increasing fury, for some ten days in Dieppe. Eventually, the English ambassador, Ralph Montagu, got in touch with Arlington, who was only too pleased to send a yacht for her. She never forgave Buckingham.

In February 1671, Lady Shrewsbury gave birth to a son, whom Buckingham had christened George Villiers, and, to whom, quite improperly, he gave the title of Earl of Coventry (a spare title of his); the King was godfather. A few days later, the little boy was dead. On 12 March the child was buried in the family vault in Westminster Abbey; the shocked and grieving parents withdrew to the country. An entry in the commonplace book could refer to this event: 'My happiness is like a winter's sun, that rises late and sets, alas, betimes.'[37]

Despite his grief, he had to return to life and public engagement, bickering with Arlington, whom he pipped to the post of Chancellor of Cambridge University, an unpaid but prestigious position which cost him considerable sums both before and after the election. These were trivial compared with all his other debts and expenses, which ran into thousands, causing even him some difficulties. About this time, he put his financial affairs into the hands of sympathetic trustees and bankers, who eventually cleared his debts and ensured him an annual income of £5,000.[38] They also persuaded him to sell various lands and especially his palace in the Strand, York House. The builders knocked down most of the structure, leaving only the water gate, a grey stone structure on the Embankment, near Charing Cross. The streets they built were named George Street, Villiers Street, Duke Street, Of Alley and Buckingham Street. Land sales enabled him to start building his own expensive palace at Cliveden, by the Thames, intended to become, in Pope's words, 'the bower of wanton Shrewsbury and love', but never completed.[39]

December 1671 saw his play *The Rehearsal* performed at the King's Theatre. Some years earlier, he had collaborated in a burlesque of the newly fashionable 'heroic' dramas that paraded highfaluting professions of love and honour in inflated rhetoric, rhyming couplets and exaggerated gestures. Now he and some friends revised it, echoing and parodying at least seventeen popular dramas of the time, including, particularly, six by John Dryden (though everyone got mocked, even such friends as Aphra Behn). The ostensible author of the play-within-the-play, *The Two Kings of Brentford*, Bayes, is mocked for his pretentiousness and absurd stories and situations – 'What a devil is the plot good for, but to bring in fine things?' – and habit of echoing other writers. This served partly as a cover for the real writers' quotations and allusions, though not everyone got the point of or appreciated the use of other writers' lines:

> With transferring of that, and transversing of those,
> With transmuting of rhyme, and transfusing of prose,
> He has dressed up his farce with other men's clothes,
> With a fa, la, la.[40]

The play was seen as a parody of Dryden but it seems was also a criticism of Arlington.[41] It was a great success, performed again and again for many years, even into the next century by David Garrick and influenced Sheridan's *The Critic*. To it we owe the phrase, 'The plot thickens.'

The next year, 1672, brought new problems, both public and personal. With a war against Holland to pay for, Sir Thomas Clifford proposed that repayments by the Exchequer for bankers' loans should be stopped for a year – which caused a financial panic; a version of the Treaty of London was published; and Clifford proposed a Declaration of Indulgence, suspending laws against Nonconformists (Bunyan was released from jail) and Catholics, ostensibly to keep the country quiet during the war, but with an eye on promises made to Louis XIV in the Grand Design. War was declared and Buckingham was eager – desperate – to sail with the Duke of York, which the Duke refused. London had cause to be grateful, when a serious fire broke out on 25 May and Buckingham energetically took the lead in putting it out.

There was considerable opposition in the country, both to the Declaration of Indulgence for the Catholics, and to the war, both of which he approved. In his *Letter to Sir Thomas Osborne* he argued that

> the undoubted interest of England is trade, since it is that only which can make us either rich or safe; for without a powerful navy, we should be a prey to our neighbours, and without trade, we could

neither have seamen nor ships. From hence it does follow, that we ought not to suffer any other nations to be our equals at sea, because when they are once our equals, it is but an even lay, whether they or we shall be the superiors. And it would not be a stranger thing that the Dutch should come to be so.[42]

Seeking, however, to come to terms, he and Arlington were sent to Holland to bargain with King Charles's nephew, William of Orange, now Stadtholder. There, he told the Dowager Princess of Orange that they loved Holland like a wife. 'Indeed,' she pointedly replied, 'I believe you love us like you love your own wife.'[43] William impressed them, not only by his determined resistance but by his emphasis on the difficult situation for England if Holland were badly reduced, so strengthening France's position. The ambassadors retired to Utrecht and Louis' ministers and settled for a treaty whereby the English and French promised not to make separate peaces with William.

Things had not gone well for Buckingham, while, on 15 June Arlington was made Knight of the Garter; that August, Arlington's four-year-old daughter, Isabella, was formally married to the nine-year-old son of Barbara and the King. It could well have been about now that the exasperated Buckingham wrote his

Advice to a Painter to draw Lord Arlington, Grand Minister of State
> First draw an arrant fop, from top to toe,
> Whose very looks at first dash show him so,
> Give him a mean, proud garb, a dapper face,
> A pert, dull grin, a black patch 'cross his face;
> Two goggle eyes, so clear, though very dead,
> That we may see, through them, quite through his head.
> Let every nod of his and subtle wink
> Declare the fool would talk, but cannot think.
> Let him all other fools so far surpass
> That fools themselves point at him for an ass.[44]

Despite what Buckingham thought, Arlington was shrewd and gained money, power and influence, while Buckingham lost them.

He was still in financial difficulties, having to rent out Wallingford House (to Clifford) and move into Whitehall apartments, while protecting his glassworks from creditors by giving it to Lady Shrewsbury. A witness to the deed of gift was the sturdy young dramatist William Wycherley, whose first play, *Love in a Wood*, had gained the attention of Barbara, Lady Cleveland, who promptly took him on as her latest lover. Initially, Buckingham was hostile to him, but his friends Rochester and Sedley brought them together. 'After supper, Mr Wycherley, who was then in the height of his vigour both of mind and body, thought himself obliged to exert himself, and the Duke was charmed to that degree that he cried out in a transport, "By God, my cousin was in the right of it," and from that very moment made a friend of a man whom he believed to be his happy rival.' So reported a contemporary writer, John Dennis;[45] a modern writer, noting Dennis's suggestion that Buckingham was sexually jealous of Wycherley and remembering that Buckingham was on a couple of occasions accused of sodomy, wonders what exertion of Wycherley's body and/or mind helped to bring Buckingham to a 'transport', confirming Cleveland's response to Wycherley's charms.[46]

Politically, he was in difficulties for supporting a French alliance and the Declaration of Indulgence. When Charles summoned Parliament in February 1673 for money for the war, it demanded the withdrawal of the Declaration to be replaced by a Test Act, requiring holders of public office, and others, generally, to accept Church of England doctrines. Buckingham spoke against this, with ineffective wit, suggesting that press-ganged sailors would declare themselves Catholics to obtain their release. Parliament having voted the King the money he needed for the war, the Duke of York was named as supreme commander and Buckingham was made a lieutenant-general and sent up to Yorkshire to obtain recruits. The Test Act now began to bite (Bunyan went back to jail), bringing about the resignation of Clifford (replaced as Lord Treasurer by Sir Thomas Osborne, Buckingham's protégé) and the Duke of York, who was replaced as army commander by a French Huguenot soldier, much to Buckingham's disgust, and bringing about his resignation.

In July, the Lady Shrewsbury connection briefly flared up again, when two gentlemen of the Horse Guards quarrelled violently near the court gate; Lady Shrewsbury's coachman intervened and lashed one in the face with his whip. The gentleman immediately killed him with his sword; he was brought before Buckingham, who beat him and threatened to have him hanged, but the court acquitted him of manslaughter.

By now, he was aware that he was in serious trouble with Parliament, whose members wanted him dismissed from his offices and the royal presence and so asked to address the Commons to defend himself. He blamed Arlington for the fumbling in the war and insisted that he had opposed the stoppage by the Treasury of payments to bankers. He defended the Declaration of Indulgence, as good for the peace of the country. Arlington's counter-attack, shifting blame back on Buckingham, was more effective, and the Commons voted against Buckingham, removing him from his posts. Despite this, he continued his efforts to demonstrate that he had not improperly worked for French interests, even getting authorisation from Charles to show Parliament that the his Treaty of London was purely political and not a scheme against the political and religious liberties of England. It was all too late: his enemies – Arlington, the old Clarendon gang, Ormonde – were ready.

In January 1674 the King again asked the two Houses for money, declaring – lying – that there was no other treaty with France. No sooner had he left the Lords, than Lady Shrewsbury's brother-in-law, the Earl of Westmorland, rose to present a petition to the House from the late Earl of Shrewsbury's young son, complaining how he had become

> every day more sensible of the deplorable death of his father, and of
> the dishonour caused to his family by the wicked and scandalous life
> led by George, Duke of Buckingham, with Anna-Maria, Countess
> of Shrewsbury, relict of the late Earl, multiplying every day new
> provocations to two noble families [the Talbots and the Brudenells]
> by the insolent and shameless manner of their cohabiting together
> since the death of the said Earl.[47]

The petitioners said that they would not have complained had the offenders been normally discreet, but had persisted ostentatiously in their 'shameless course of life', going so far as to have their 'base son' buried in Westminster Abbey, under the title of Earl of Coventry. There was also a suggestion of 'conduct even more unnatural than that already ascribed to Lady Shrewsbury', hinting at sodomitical practices. Such an attack was unprecedented and a terrible shock. Buckingham rose to say that he was astounded that the petitioners had been prepared to dishonour their kinswoman, declared his innocence and that the lady had left England (not yet true), and he would never see her again.

It was not clear what punishments that Parliament, or the bishops, might impose, or for what exact offence, but he and Anna-Maria were given until 15 January to prepare a defence. By the time messengers arrived at Lady Shrewsbury's house with a summons, she had fled, but his loyal wife was reported to be 'crying and tearing herself' and rushing about town attempting to gain support from other nobles and friends.[48]

In his written defence he admitted 'faults committed against temperance and the strict rules of morality', but insisted that there had been no open living together before the death of the Earl, who had been 'exasperated by others', and that Lady Shrewsbury had gone to Paris because she thought her honour had not been vindicated upon Killigrew's 'barbarous and public affront'. He himself had been as grieved by the Earl's death as any of the petitioners, and after her return, when she was disowned by her family and had had her jointure taken from her, he had helped her as any 'man of honour' would have. He concluded by asking God's and their lordships' forgiveness.

He then chose to go before the House of Commons, who were already extremely bitter and hostile towards him, accusing him of, among other offences, being an encourager of Popery, a breaker of the Triple Alliance, endangering the King's life and having 'attempted the sin of buggery'. His defence was uncertain; he abandoned his prepared speech but defended his political activities, having 'spent an estate in the King's service, when others have got thousands'. After a further debate in the House, feverishly denouncing his immorality, he appeared before them again, arguing that Arlington was to blame for what had gone wrong.[49] He denied any responsibility for shutting up the Exchequer or making any treaty against the Triple Alliance and defended the Declaration of Indulgence. As for charges of sodomy, he declared, 'I have much to answer for in the plain way, but I never was so great a virtuoso in my lusts.' The House then debated, and at last voted to ask the King to remove him from his employments and from the royal presence. His friends then counter-attacked Arlington, who in turn appeared before the House, blamed Buckingham, and, by a close vote, was acquitted of the various accusations; after all, he was not a notorious adulterer.

Buckingham worked desperately to try to save his career, but could not even get through to the King, who did not stand by him, and at last sent him word dismissing him from all his posts.[50] The grisly procedural business dragged on, and then, at last, the Lords required that Buckingham and Anna-Maria, under penalty of £10,000 each, were forbidden to 'converse or cohabit for the future'. After nearly eight years, they were ripped apart, the long love affair brought to an end, as was Buckingham's public career. In the commonplace book was written,

> In love the blessing of my life I closed,
> And in her custody that love disposed.
> In one dear freight all's lost! Of her bereft,
> I have no hope, no second comfort left.
>
> If such another beauty I could find,
> A beauty too that bore a constant mind,
> Even that could bring no med'cine for my pain;
> I loved not at a rate to love again.[51]

A popular verse, picking up on his political, religious and sexual reputation, appeared:

> When great men fall, their fall makes weeping eyes
> In two or three or four great families,

> But at this great man's fall, four cities sorrow,
> Rome and Geneva, Sodom and Gomorrah.[52]

He was ruined; his court places had provided money, but they were gone. He wrote a long, impassioned letter to the King, asking permission to sell the position of Master of the Horse, worth £20,000. He reproached the King:

> I wonder very much that you can find in your heart to use me with so much cruelty who have ever loved you better than myself ... I hope at least you will not be harder to me than the House of Commons were ... I hope you remember that I had the honour to be bred up with your Majesty from a child ... I have been so far from getting that I have wasted the best part of my estate in following and waiting upon your Majesty.[53]

Every (heart)string was pulled; permission was granted – the King himself buying the mastership for his son, Monmouth. As for public opinion, that was hardly swayed when, on Sunday 25 January, he went to St Martin in the Fields church with his wife.

After a year or two, Anna-Maria was permitted to return to England, and in 1677 she married George Rodney Bridges, getting him a position of Groom of the Bedchamber and bearing him a son. As for Buckingham, his court titles gone, he retired to Yorkshire, where he spent time riding to hounds, becoming familiar with all and sundry and drinking with friends.

In April 1675 he returned to London, and to Parliament, where his former protégé, Thomas Osborne, now Earl of Danby, was Lord High Treasurer and ruler of the roost. Danby introduced a Non-resistance Bill, known as the Test Oath, an extension of the Test Act, which Buckingham of course opposed. In October he proposed a bill in favour of religious toleration for dissenters: 'I conceive it's a mistake in religion ... an inexcusable conception, that men ought to be deprived of their inheritance, and all their certain conveniences and advantages of life, because they will not agree with us in our uncertain conceptions of religion.'[54] Unfortunately Parliament was prorogued before this could get any further – not that Parliament was in a tolerant state of mind, anyway.

In February 1677, when Parliament was reassembled, he was in trouble again, when he argued that under two statutes of Edward III, Parliament ought to meet at least once every year, and since the recent prorogation had lasted fifteen months, Parliament was in effect dissolved, and a new one should be elected. 'The ground of this opinion of mine is taken from the ancient and unquestionable statutes of this realm, and, give me leave to tell your Lordships by the way, that statutes are not like women, for they are not one jot the worse for being old.'[55]

Charles was furious, and Danby had Buckingham and his allies sent to the Tower until they apologised. For some time he refused to do so, while his (and the King's) friends, including Nell Gwyn, worked on his behalf. In June, Nelly got him a two-day break to inspect work going on at Cliveden, and then again in July. At last he was released, and went to stay, first with Rochester in Whitehall, 'leading the usual life' (as Marvell phrased it) and then with Nelly, in Pall Mall, before he made his formal apology to the House of Lords in January 1678. Again he wrote a long, impassioned letter to the King, his sometime friend:

> I was so surprised with what Mrs Nelly has told me, that I know not what in the world to say. The more sensible grief I had in being put away from Your Majesty, was not the losing my place, but the being shut out of Your Majesty's kindness ... You that have been a lover yourself, know what it is to think oneself ill-used by a mistress that one loves extremely and it is that only I can truly compare my great misfortune to ... Oh Christ sir for heaven's sake know that I would as willingly die tomorrow to do Your Majesty's service, as any of those about you would have me dead, to satisfy their envy and their ill nature.[56]

It seemed that he was not wholly cast out; he was even put onto a committee to investigate the claims of Titus Oates, in the so-called 'Popish Plot' scandal that year. In 1680 he had the satisfaction of observing the imprisonment and downfall of the Earl of Danby, after his exposure by the scheming Ralph Montagu, the English ambassador to France, for his negotiations on Charles's behalf for money from Louis XIV. He, and some friends, gloated in *A Song on Thomas, Earl of Danby*:

> What a devil ails the Parliament
> Since they were drunk with brandy,
> When they did think to circumvent
> Thomas Earl of Danby.
> Then Commons trust him not a whit,
> If you do, you will trepanned be, [tricked]
> There's not as false a Jesuit
> As Thomas Earl of Danby ...
> [Jesuits were popularly thought to be behind the Popish Plot.
>   The poem goes on to review the remarkable sex histories
>   of the Danby family – with, it appears, some truth.]
> His creator Bucks he'd hang for fees
> And bribes that he may trepanned be,
> Who gave him clothes when out of hose
> For Thomas Earl of Danby.
> His preserver King, he has made a thing,
> The poorest thing that can be,
> Condemned, betrayed and odious made
> By owning Tom of Danby.
> God bless the King, and save his life,
> And grant he still may stand free
> From fools, French whores, from Popish knife,
> And rogues like Tom of Danby.[57]

Another dangerous personal scandal blew up, or was contrived, possibly by Danby, that February: the charge that Buckingham had committed sodomy with a woman named Sarah Harwood and a young man called Philip Le Mar. Two men made a statement declaring that she had confessed to them 'that the Lord Duke of Buckingham was with his privy members as far in both her privy parts as he could go with forcible entrance, stopping her breath', and went on that he had sent her abroad out of the way, and committed sodomy with several others.[58] Faced with conflicting evidence, the jury cleared him with a noncommittal verdict of Ignoramus; Buckingham's verse included:

> Lamarr that bawdy nasty whore
> That was made drunk with brandy,
> She blabbed out all that ere she swore
> For Thomas Earl of Danby.

The Lamarr here is probably Philip's mother, Frances Loveland, who was also a witness at the trial. Buckingham counter-prosecuted, and both Philip and Frances were found guilty; he died in prison, and she was pilloried.[59]

The following year, Dryden brought out his major satire on behalf of the King, *Absalom and Achitophel*, with its destructive description of Buckingham; in 1679, another, not unkind, if mocking, character sketch was provided by a friend of Dryden, John Sheffield, Earl of Mulgrave, in *An Essay Upon Satire*:

> First, let's behold the merriest man alive
> Against his careless genius vainly strive,
> Quit his dear ease some deep design to lay
> 'Gainst a set time, and then forget the day.
> Yet he will laugh at his best friends and be
> Just as good company as Nokes or Lee [comic actors].
> But when he aims at reason or at rule,
> He turns himself the best in ridicule;
> Let him at bus'ness ne'er so earnest sit,
> Show him but mirth, and bait that mirth with wit,
> That shadow of a jest shall be enjoyed
> Though he left all mankind to be destroyed ...[60]

In 1685, his erstwhile friend and king died, succeeded by James. Charles's son, the Duke of Monmouth, rebelled and was clumsily executed on Tower Hill on 15 July, a few days before Arlington died at home. In November, Buckingham's sister, Dowager Duchess of Richmond, died. Buckingham went back again to Yorkshire, hunting, drinking with friends and tending his greatly reduced estates.

On 14 April 1687, he went out hunting, and caught, instead, a severe chill, and decided to rest at the farmhouse of one of his tenants. It became clear to his friends and his cousin, James Douglas, Earl of Arran, that he was dying. An Anglican clergyman was sent for, but was rejected, as were offers of a Catholic priest or a Presbyterian. When the village parson asked what his religion was, he replied, 'It is an insignificant question. I have been a shame and a disgrace to all religions. If you can do me any good, do.'[61] He received the last sacraments of the Church of England and died on 16 April 1687. (His widow, Maria, died in 1705, not very well off.)

As was so often the case with him, he was maligned even in his death, as in the famous lines by Alexander Pope in his *Moral Essay: Of the Use of Riches*. His description is simply not true: no inn, but the best bed in a tenant's farmhouse:

> In the worst inn's worst room, with mats half-hung,
> The floors of plaster, and the walls of dung ...
> Great Villiers lies – alas! How changed from him,
> That life of pleasure, and that soul of whim! ...
> There, victor of his health, of fortune, friends,
> And fame, this lord of useless thousands ends.[62]

It was indeed a comedown from his glory days, but there was more to be said of him: brought up with royalty, with a great title and wealth; hopelessly spoiled; talented, impatient, arrogant, careless; in love with another man's wife; advanced and liberal in his thinking; and, often, fun. The commonplace book contains one poignant couplet (unlikely to have been by his secretary), that looks back on a rackety, gaudy, unsatisfied life:

> Methinks I see the wanton hours flee,
> And as they pass, look back and laugh at me.[63]

6

THE KING AND THE LADY OF PLEASURE

On 10 September 1667, Pepys heard gossip about a proposed pension to pay off Lady Castlemaine, though she was resisting, and seemed 'as high as ever she was', while the King was reported to be 'as weary as is possible, and would give anything to remove her; but he is so weak in his passion that he dare not do it' – a sufficient testimony to the effect of her rages.

Meanwhile, despite her brief support of his cause against the King, Buckingham had renewed his efforts to replace Barbara's influence over the King with the actresses Nell Gwyn and Moll Davis, whom the King quickly enjoyed. Mrs Pearse described Moll at the theatre as 'the most impertinent slut ... the King gazing on her and my Lady Castlemaine melancholy and out of humour all the play, not smiling once'. When Moll came to dance her jig, 'the Queen would not stay to see it; which people do think it was out of displeasure at her being the King's whore ... My Lady Castlemaine is, it seems, now mighty out of request, the King coming little to her, and she mighty melancholy and discontented.'[1] In response, she took up with a leading actor, Charles Hart (Nelly's former lover), 'and by this means she is even with the King's love for Mistress Davis' (Pepys, 7 April). The affair drew widespread comment, as in *A Ballad*, that year:

> Next comes Castlemaine,
> That prerogative quean;
> If I had such a bitch I would spay her,
> She swives like a stoat,
> Goes to't leg and foot,
> Level coil with a prince and a player.[2]

('Prerogative' suggests that she is privileged above the law; the *OED* derives 'level coil' from the French *lever le cul*, or 'hitch-buttock', as it puts it.)

Private entertainment following public entertainment was then provided by Jacob Hall, gymnast and rope-dancer at Bartholomew Fair. Gramont remarked,

> His strength and agility charmed in public, even to a wish to know what he was in private; for he appeared, dressed in his tumbling-dress, to be quite of a different make, and to have limbs very different from the fortunate Jermyn. This tumbler did not deceive Lady Castlemaine's expectations, if report may be believed; and as was intimated in many a song, much more to the honour of the rope-dancer than of the Countess; but she despised all these rumours, and only appeared still more handsome.[3]

The cuckold King was irritated by her continuing involvement with Harry Jermyn, that she 'who was still obliged to his budget for extremely large sums, should be seen hauled along at the chariot-wheels of one of the most ridiculous conquerors who ever made his appearance'. He advised her 'to bestow her favours upon Jacob Hall, the rope-dancer, who was able to return them, than lavish away her money upon Jermyn, to no purpose.' Predictably, this aroused her fury: 'It very ill became him to throw out such reproaches against one who, of all the women in England, deserved them the least; that he had never ceased quarrelling thus unjustly with her, ever since he had betrayed his own mean, low inclinations; that to gratify such a depraved taste as his, he wanted only such silly things as [Frances] Stuart, [Winifred] Wells, and that pitiful strolling actress, whom he had lately introduced into their society.'[4] She concluded by threatening to massacre her children and set fire to the palace.

Having calmed down (and presumably silenced Charles), she appeared at a court celebration on Shrove Tuesday, 1668, where 'the excessive gallantry [display of jewels] of the ladies was infinite,' remarked John Evelyn, 'those especially on Castlemaine esteemed at 40,000 pounds and more, and far outshining the Queen.'[5] It transpired that he was not the only one there to notice her flamboyant display of wealth.

It was an almost annual custom on Shrove Tuesdays for the London apprentices to run riot, in varying degrees, usually wrecking the brothels (sexual jealousy masked as moralism). This year they appeared to be in larger numbers and more violent than usual; this time their frenzy had political overtones, as they seemed ready to go further: 'It was said how these idle fellows have had the confidence to say that they did ill in contenting themselves in pulling down the little bawdy houses and did not go and pull down the great bawdy house at Whitehall.'[6]

The rioting, which caused a brief panic, was quickly and fiercely suppressed, but, within a few hours, a court wit took the opportunity to have printed what purported to be a petition from the prostitutes of London '(a trade wherein Your Ladyship hath great experience)' to their great patron, Lady Castlemaine. *The Poor Whores' Petition* was addressed 'To the most splendid, illustrious, serene and eminent Lady of Pleasure, the Countess of Castlemaine.' It complained of the loss of 'habitations, trades and employments' caused by the riots and having the cures for their venereal diseases 'retarded through this barbarous and un-Venus-like usage', and asked for financial assistance and for action to deal with these

> evil disposed persons, that a stop may be put to them before they come to your Honour's palace and bring contempt upon your worshipping of Venus, the great goddess whom we all adore ... So your Ladyship may escape our present calamity, else we know not how soon it may be your Honour's own case. For, should your Eminence but once fall into these rough hands, you may expect no more favour than they have shown to us poor inferior whores.[7]

It was purportedly signed by two celebrated brothel-keepers whose houses had been attacked, Madam Cresswell and Damaris Page, 'the great bawd of the seamen', according to Pepys. (Cresswell was particularly notorious. When she died, she left £100 for a clergyman to speak well of her. He said, 'She was born well, she lived well, and she died well; for she was born with the name Cresswell, she lived in Clerkenwell and Camberwell, and she died in Bridewell.' [*DNB*]) He heard that Castlemaine was 'horribly vexed', but the Duke of York joked that he had lost two tenants whose houses were pulled down and who had paid £15 a year for their wine licences. Soon enough (on 24 April), however, more satiric entertainment started up, with a broadsheet titled *The Gracious Answer of the most illustrious Lady of Pleasure, the Countess of Castlem ... to the Poor Whore's Petition*. According to this, she considered that the titles accorded her in the petition were her due,

> for on Shrove Tuesday last splendidly did we appear upon the theatre at W[hite] H[all] being to amazement wonderfully decked with jewels and diamonds which the (abhorred and to be undone) subjects of this Kingdom have paid for.
>
> We have also been serene and illustrious ever since the day that Mars [the King] was so instrumental to restore our goddess Venus to her temple and worship; where by special grant we quickly became a famous lady; and as a reward of our devotion soon created Right Honourable the Countess of Castlemaine ... we have *cum privilegio* always (without our husband) satisfied ourself with the delights of Venus; and in our husband's absence have had a numerous offspring (who are bountifully and nobly provided for). Which practice hath episcopal allowance also, according to the principles of [Archbishop] Seer Seldon [who had, as noted before, a reputation for being, in Pepys's words, 'as very a wencher as can be'].[8]

The satire took a more obviously political turn, as the fictive Castlemaine mocked the Church of England, 'which is but like a brazen basin tied to a barber's wooden pole, protestant doctrine and order tied by Parliamentary power to Roman Catholic foundation', and promised financial aid and the protection of 'Holy Mother Church', with the

> setting up as many playhouses as his holiness the pope hath holidays in his calendar, that the civil youth of the City may be debauched and trained up in looseness and ignorance, whereby the Roman religion may with ease be established in court, church, city and nation ... Venereal pleasures accompanied with looseness, debauchery and profaneness are not such heinous crimes and crying sins ... [for] eight years' experience in court hath made us both know and understand that pimping and procuring are the most principal qualifications requisite in privy Councillors ...[9]

The attack was powerful and embarrassing, directed not only at Barbara's profitable profligacy, but also at the King, his court and his policies. Though their relationship had been deteriorating for some time, he had to stand by her in the short term – while also to prepare for later cutting her adrift. Not long after, he borrowed £8,000 to buy her Berkshire House, the former home of Lord Clarendon (a nice touch), and in January 1669 she secured £4,700 a year from Post Office funds in the names of her uncles. She soon demolished the building, sold the materials, sold off the land for development and had herself built a new mansion, to be called (after she was raised to the dignity of Duchess of Cleveland), Cleveland House.

Her former lover, the Earl of Chesterfield, now remarried and interested in gardening at Bretby, gave her a statue for the fountain in her new estate, 'which is a Cupid kneeling on a rock and shooting from his bow a stream of water up towards heaven. ... my meaning in it is, that your Ladyship, not being content with the conquest of one world, doth now by your devotion attack the other'.[10] The author of the *Petition* might have queried to which deity she was devoted. Charles also gave her Henry VIII's old palace and park of Nonsuch, in Surrey, now neglected; this also was turned to profit, the grounds and park let out as farmland, the building's contents sold off for £7,000 and the empty shell left to decay. One biographer details her annual income in 1676 from Customs, the Post Office, excises on beer and wine licences, Sir Henry Wood's estate, with grants for her sons, as £58,200, while not including other rents, estates and separate payments.[11] Of course, she had heavy outgoings: money for her various lovers – she could afford to be quite generous – household expenses and thousands of pounds in gambling debts (though the King was very helpful).

Roger Palmer, now formally separated, had no claim on Barbara; he had made somewhat of a career in Catholic apologetics and diplomacy in the Levant and was now sent off to Constantinople with the new ambassador, Sir Daniel Harvey, to whose house Barbara had retreated in her last quarrel with the King. Harvey's wife, Anne, and he did not get on – she was reputed to have lesbian inclinations and to be pleased to see him go.[12] Charles was supposed to have rallied her by saying, 'I hope, Lady Harvey, that I have pleased you by sending your husband far enough from you.' She countered, 'I acknowledge your goodness, and only wish it were in my power to return it by sending the Queen as far from Your Majesty.' ''Odsfish,' cried the King, 'I had better have left my compliments alone.'[13]

Lady Harvey was busy in court politics – she got her brother, Ralph Montagu, made Ambassador to France. She was an ally of Arlington, Buckingham's old foe. Buckingham persuaded an actress with the King's Company, Mrs Corey, to take the part of Sempronia in Ben Jonson's *Catiline*, an ageing former courtesan with political ambitions: Mrs Corey obligingly, and very pointedly, imitated Lady Harvey, who in turn got her cousin, Edward Montagu, the Lord Chamberlain, to imprison her. Unfortunately, Barbara, who must have cooled towards Lady Harvey, had so enjoyed the impersonation that she told the King to have the actress released, and then to order the play to be performed again. Mrs Corey played up to the full, but Lady Harvey had paid people to hiss her and throw oranges, and the performance ended in a near riot, so 'making the King cheap and ridiculous' in revealing his involvement in 'this woman's business', thought Pepys in January 1669. He thought there was real trouble at court about it. There was another tiff when Barbara discovered that Charles had made one of her maids, named Wilson, pregnant (whom Pepys had previously chatted up in the theatre in 1668); the maid was immediately thrown out into the street and Charles was in disgrace. As Pepys wrote on 16 January, 'My Lady Castlemaine is now in a higher command over the King than ever, not as a mistress, for she scorns him, but as a tyrant, to command him.'

Meanwhile, the King had more important matters to deal with, less openly, with a view to getting greater financial independence from Parliament, with Louis XIV's help. However quietly he tried to proceed, alert minds around the court had a shrewd idea of what he might be up to. Even Pepys had heard, by April, about a proposed

> league with the King of France; wherein ... my Lord Chancellor is also concerned ... and that this sum of money will so help the King as that he will not need the Parliament ... My Lady Castlemaine is instrumental in this matter and ... never more great with the King than she is now. But this is a thing that will make the Parliament and Kingdom mad, and will turn to our ruin – for with this money the King shall wanton away his time in pleasures, and think nothing of the main till it be too late.[14]

In the negotiations that were to produce the secret treaty, emissaries went to and fro, while the French ambassador bribed Barbara to the very limit of his funds. To help matters along, Louis sent over an astrologer, an Italian monk, the Abbé Pregnani, with instructions to find enough astrological omens to persuade Charles of the advisability, even the necessity, of the French alliance. Unfortunately, Charles took him along to the Newmarket races, when, as he wrote to his sister, 'he lost his money upon confidence that the stars could tell which horse would win, for he had the ill luck to foretell three times wrong together, and James believed him so much as he lost his money upon the same score.'[15] The Abbé was recalled.

At home, in 1669, Catherine had had her last miscarriage, and there was no hope of a child from her. Mistresses lay in wait in hopes of replacing her if she could be got out of the way. According to Gilbert Burnet, Buckingham even came up with a suggestion that she be abducted and carried off in secret to a plantation in one of the West Indian territories, where she could live quietly, with it being given out that she had deserted her husband and consequently been divorced. It is hard to believe that Buckingham was serious; Burnet had no sense of humour.

The poor woman had attempted to fit in with court life, attending functions, joining in the dancing that the King and the court generally enjoyed, having card-gambling in her apartments and trying to be pleasant with everyone: 'She is always showing [her teeth] because she never stops smiling,' wrote Magalotti.[16] Kindly Edmund Waller wrote nice things about her, as 'the choice of the whole nation …' whose example 'chases vice away … [and] though louder fame attend the martial rage, / 'Tis greater glory to reform the age'. Her Portuguese background gave her connections with the Far East, and a taste for tea, which she was instrumental in introducing to the country, as he praised 'The best of queens, and best of herbs … The Muse's friend, tea does our fancy aid'.[17]

Foreign, Catholic, futile in her barrenness, she was the focus of lampoons from various factions. In 1670 a mean little jibe appeared:

> Poor private balls content the Faery Queen;
> You must dance, and dance damnably, to be seen.
> Ill-natured little goblin, and designed
> For nothing but to dance and vex mankind,
> What wiser thing could our great monarch do
> Than root out ambition by showing you?
> You can the most aspiring thought pull down,
> For who would have his wife to have his crown? …[18]

She did try to have a little fun, joining in the court craze for going into town in plain hackney coaches, in masquerade, and calling on people, unrecognised. Once, in October 1670, she, the Duchess of Buckingham (a friend, another neglected wife) and Richmond went to a country fair at Audley End in Essex, dressed in what they thought was rustic clothing. Their dresses, and their three gentleman escorts, gave them away, and they had to hurry away from an excited and not very friendly crowd.

Although the King frequently said he would not have her put away for something that was not her fault, divorce was up for discreet discussion at court, particularly in view of a scandalous case that intrigued everybody: the Roos divorce, mentioned earlier, but worth reviewing here. John Manners, third son of the Earl of Rutland, on 21 July 1658, married Anne Pierrepont, daughter of the Earl of Kingston, later Marquess of Dorchester. A daughter was born early the next year, but died young. Lady Anne, 'not finding the satisfaction she expected where she ought to have received it, looked for it abroad where she ought not to find it, while Lord Roos did not concern himself overmuch how she behaved herself', as Clarendon phrased it.[19] There was a tacit separation, then an attempted reconciliation, 'the lady having the ascendant over the lord who was very desirous to live quietly upon any conditions, that he might enjoy himself though he could not enjoy her'. Lady Anne went off to London, and then returned very pregnant. When asked, 'Who got it?' she replied, rather tactlessly, 'Whoever got it, if it proved a boy as she believed it would, he should be Earl of Rutland.' On this, Lord Roos told his mother, who confined Anne to her chamber, to be sure of the birth; it was indeed a boy, baptised Ignoto and put out to foster.[20]

Lady Anne turned to her father, who challenged Roos to a duel, which was declined. Dorchester appealed to the King, who, despite witnesses providing 'so many indecent and uncleanly particulars', as Clarendon noted, made no decision, with Ignoto's status as putative heir not settled. The Rutlands refused to surrender the child or return Lady Anne's bridal portion, and legal proceedings ensued. Lady Anne got custody of Ignoto, left her father and led a scandalous life, producing another boy, and her exasperated father now joined forces with the Rutlands. Divorce 'from bed and board' was secured in the ecclesiastical courts. The next step was the illegitimisation of her children (now known as John and Charles Manners), which required an Act of Parliament, which was given its first reading in October 1666 and received the royal assent in February 1667. Now there was still a need for divorce *a vinculo matrimonii*, to enable him to remarry and produce legitimate heirs (a subject of interest at court).

Charles attended the debates in the Lords, declaring, the whole thing was 'as good as a play'. Biblical texts on the legitimacy of divorce for fornication and remarriage were compared; even John Milton, the author of *The Doctrine and Discipline of Divorce* (1643), was consulted. At last, in April 1670, the final bill received the royal assent.

In 1671, Roos married Lady Diana Bruce, who died in childbirth. In 1673, he married Catherine, daughter of Viscount Campden, who successfully produced a son and heir in 1676. Lady Anne remarried and died in 1696. What Charles made of it all and the implications for his own situation and possible remarriage, there is no knowing.

In 1670, the diplomatic manoeuvres over the secret treaty were completed, and Henrietta, the King's sister, came over to Dover to help complete the deal; within weeks of her return to France, she was dead. Buckingham was sent over for the funeral and to complete a double of the original deal, but without Charles's promises to make England Catholic, of which he was ignorant. He returned with a treaty and a new mistress for the King, Louise de Kéroualle, intended by him to be Barbara's replacement. By then, the King had made a public announcement in the Queen's drawing room (what a choice of venue!) that he had created Lady Castlemaine the Duchess of Cleveland, Countess of Southampton and Baroness Nonsuch, in consideration, according to the Letters Patent, 'of her noble descent, her father's death in the service of the Crown, and by reason of her own personal virtues'. The last clause must have provoked a few quiet smiles.

While Charles amused himself with Moll Davis and the gentlemanly pursuit of Louise, Barbara busied herself. Most in the public eye was the thrusting young dramatist William Wycherley, 'manly Wycherley' as he was known, who had had a success with his play *Love in a Wood*. John Dennis reported in a letter how, when Wycherley was passing through St James's Park in his coach, he was pursued by the foresaid lady in hers, who, thrusting half her body out of the chariot, cried aloud to him, You, Wycherley, are a son of a whore, at the same time laughing aloud and heartily – Mr Wycherley was certainly very much surprised at it, yet not so much but he soon apprehended it was spoke with allusion to the latter end of a song in the forementioned play:

> When Parents are slaves
> Their brats cannot be any other,
> Great wits and great braves
> Have always a punk to their mother.

Wycherley went after her, arranged to meet her in the theatre that night and very soon became her lover; in his dedication to her of the printed version of the play, he ambiguously acknowledged the 'favours' he had received from her. The story – and lampoons – went, that, at the time, Wycherley was lodging at the Inner Temple, where she would visit him in disguise, dressed as a country girl, in a straw hat with pattens on her feet. They also met at the lodgings of the singer (and procuress) Mall Knight (of whom, more anon) in Pall Mall; the King got wind of this and went there, passing a cloaked figure on the stairs. Barbara told him she was there in retreat, to pray, to which he replied, 'Very likely, and that was your confessor I met on the stairs.'[21]

At the same time, or even a little earlier, there was handsome young John Churchill, who at sixteen became a page to the Duke of York, and was now an ensign in the Foot Guards; he was regularly sent with his regiment to Tangier but equally regularly every winter came back to London and to her. Her daughter Barbara, not acknowledged by the King, was born in July 1672, so was conceived at some time in November 1671. She was extremely generous to him, which he exploited to the full: she even gave him £5,000 in cash. Others might have spent it, but he invested it, to purchase an annuity, the basis of his future fortune. Once, Buckingham arranged that the King should visit her, unannounced, while she and Churchill were together; he entered the room unexpectedly and abruptly, causing young Churchill to jump out of the window. The King looked down, and said, sourly, 'I forgive you, for you do it for your bread.'[22]

It is thought that, in order to get the £5,000 in ready money, it was about now that she engaged in direct prostitution (her whole career had been one of indirect prostitution). This was with the elderly Sir Edward Hungerford, who was willing to pay the enormous sum of £10,000 for a night with her. Somehow, in a darkened room, she managed – like something in Chaucer or *Measure for Measure* – to trick him and then let him know that he had been fooled, and offered him a second chance for the same fee. The incident was celebrated later by Pope, writing of one

> Who of ten thousand gulled her knight,
> Then asked ten thousand for a second night.
> The gallant too, to whom she paid it down,
> Lived to refuse that mistress half a crown.[23]

(The second two lines refer to an incident, years later, when John Churchill was rich and successful, and Barbara was elderly and not so well off. At a gambling table, when he held the bank, she lost her money and asked for a loan of twenty guineas, which he refused, as the bank never lent money. 'As to the Duchess's part, her resentment burst out into a bleeding at her nose, and breaking of her lace; without which aid, it is believed, her vexation had killed her on the spot.'[24])

Apart from her vigorous sex life, with the arrival of Louise de Kéroualle, and Nelly's latest pregnancy, she needed to look to her children's futures, which she did with her accustomed ruthlessness and rapacity. Her campaign over the next few years is not without interest.[25]

The sons were, of course, the most important, particularly Charles, the first son, born in June 1662, eight years old and simple-minded (and from 1670, Earl of Southampton). John Aubrey thought him good-looking, while accounting for the simple-mindedness: 'A most lovely youth, had two foreteeth that grew out, very unhandsome. His cruel mother caused him to be bound fast in a chair and had them drawn out; which has caused the want of his understanding.'[26] The lucky young lady chosen to be his bride was the seven-year-old Mary, daughter of Sir Henry Wood, a miser of great wealth and estates in Suffolk. He had been Clerk to the Spicery for Charles I, a mean-minded treasurer for Henrietta Maria and finally Comptroller of the Board of Green Cloth under Charles II, responsible for provisions in Whitehall. In his *Last Instructions*, Marvell described his odd, hunchback appearance in Parliament, how

> Still his hook-shoulder seems the blow to dread,
> And under's armpit he defends his head.
> The posture strange men laughed at, of his poll
> Hid with his elbow, like the spice he stole.
> Headless St Denis so his head does bear,
> And both of them alike French martyrs were.[27]

(St Denis was beheaded, and was pictured with his head in his hands; Wood's French martyrdom implies venereal infection.)

At the age of sixty-seven he fathered his only child, Mary, and now, at seventy-four, he surrendered her and his estates to the King's mistress. By the contract, the marriage was not to take place until Mary was sixteen, when she would have the right to refuse. If young Charles had died by then, his marital rights would transfer to his brother George; if the marriage went ahead, the happy couple would get a dowry of £2,000 a year plus the profits of Sir Henry's estates. If, however, she refused the match, £20,000 from the estate would be paid over, while the estate itself would go to Sir Henry's brother Dr Thomas Wood, Dean of Lichfield and Coventry (who, thanks to Barbara, speedily became Bishop of Lichfield and Coventry).

As soon as the contract was signed, Sir Henry made his will and loyally died in May 1671; by the will, Mary was sent to his sister, Lady Chester, widow of Sir Henry Chester. Barbara would not allow that and demanded Mary be sent to her, before kidnapping her. When Lady Chester wrote, requiring she be returned, the Duchess replied, 'I have her and I will keep her. I wonder that so inconsiderable a person as you will contend with a lady of my quality.'[28] She then had the two children married, to block any attempts to marry the girl elsewhere, before claiming the whole of Sir Henry's estate on the grounds that it had been willed to revert to Mary and her husband on the day of her marriage – which had now taken place. Legal action was now attempted by the Wood family, but in vain, not only because of the connection with the King, but because Barbara was a peer, giving her legal immunity, and a 'feme covert', whose husband, presumed to have authority (like Dickens's Mr Bumble), was overseas and out of reach.

Next son in succession was Henry (Palmer, later Fitzroy and Duke of Grafton), who, also at the age of eight was to be married to five-year-old Isabella, daughter and sole heir of the Earl of Arlington, acquiring rights to Euston Hall and the titles of Earl of Euston, Viscount Norwich and Baron of Sudbury. The wedding was slightly delayed while the groom's mother gave birth to another child, also named Barbara (presumed the daughter of John Churchill). When, the year after, Henry was to be sent to Paris to further his education, Arlington objected, wanting some oversight of the training of the heir to his estates. The Duchess would not release the boy: 'I care for no education other than what nature and I can give him, which will be sufficient accomplishment for a married man.'[29] He grew up to be a soldier and was killed fighting for King William at the siege of Cork in 1690. George, born in Merton College on 28 December 1665, was made Earl of Northumberland (with other titles) at the age of eight and sent to Oxford University, to be under the undelighted eye of the celebrated Dr Fell, Dean of Christchurch.

As for her daughters, Anne, her firstborn in 1661, had been kept in a French nunnery until 1672 and married in 1674 to a Gentleman of the King's Bedchamber, Thomas Lennard, Lord Dacre, who was given the title Earl of Sussex, £20,000 dowry and a pension of £2,000 a year. Within a few years, she embarked on a scandalous affair in Paris with the ambassador there, her mother's lover, Ralph Montagu, and then, equally scandalously, with her father's latest foreign mistress, Hortense Mancini, Duchesse Mazarin (discussed later). Charlotte, born in 1664, was married in 1674 to Edward Henry Lee, made Earl of Lichfield, with a dowry of £18,000 and a £2,000 annual pension; the wedding was a formality and Charlotte stayed with her mother until 'remarried' in 1677.

With Parliament's passing of the anti-Catholic Test Act in 1673, Barbara had to give up her hard-won position as Lady of the Bedchamber to the Queen. By this time, that did not matter very much, especially as the Queen had by now largely withdrawn to a quiet life in a separate establishment in Somerset House (demolished and replaced by the present building in 1775).

The Queen was not entirely out of court life, however. In that year, the Duke of York married young Mary of Modena, to whom Catherine, no doubt remembering her own early days in a new marriage in a foreign country, was kind and generous, in her way. In February 1675, she set up a court entertainment for the Duchess, a rather unusual one: a masque, of a kind that had long gone out of fashion. By John Crowne, the story was of *Calisto, or the Chaste Nymph*, a chaste young woman transformed by jealous Juno (played by Anne Fitzroy, one of Charles's bastards) into a bear: it had parts for seven ladies, two of whom were to dress as men (Jupiter was played by Lady Henrietta Wentworth, one of Monmouth's mistresses); other players included the new Duchess's stepdaughters, Mary (who played Calisto) and Anne, with the notorious Lady Jane Mordaunt and the professionals – and royal mistresses – Moll Davies and Mall Knight. Crowne himself later described it as 'a weak, lean, rickety, deformed piece', but the ladies were pleased.[30]

It is thought that it was about this time that Barbara performed her most bizarre exploit, as recorded by Henry, Lord Coleraine, in her dealings with Bishop Braybrooke. The Bishop had died in 1404 and been buried in St Paul's Cathedral. After the Great Fire of London, his mummified body, 'tough and dry, like a spongy dry leather', fell out of his tomb in the crypt and became one of the sights of London; 'a great man in his time, and Lord Chancellor – and now exposed to be handled and derided ... Many flocking to see it', as Pepys reflected, on 12 November 1666. Barbara also went to see it, according to Coleraine, accompanied with a few attendants, but asked to view it in private, alone. The keeper withdrew, before noticing 'Her Ladyship addressing herself towards the carcase with many crossings and great tokens of superstition' (an anti-Catholic note by Coleraine). When the keeper returned 'to shut up the carcase [he] unexpectedly found it served like a Turkish eunuch and dismembered of as much of the privity as the lady could get into her mouth to bite (for want of a circumcising penknife to cut).' His Lordship concluded his account with the observation, 'Though some ladies of late have got Bishopricks for others [Barbara got her mother's uncle, Dr Henry Glemham, 'a drunken swearing rascal and a scandal to the Church', consecrated Bishop of St Asaph, wrote Pepys in July 1667], yet I have not heard of any but this that got one for herself.'[31] The story was not widely known at the time – fortunately for Barbara, of whom anything might be believed.

Young Charles Southampton was made a duke and sent up to Oxford in the autumn of 1675; Churchill came back from Tangier for the winter and all that Barbara could provide by way of money and services. 'He has pillaged the Duchess of Cleveland,' reported the French ambassador, Honoré Courtin. 'She has given him the value of more than £100,000. In one way or another he has got so much money out of her that in desperation she is obliged to go to France to live quietly for some time.'[32] Whether this was the cause – she was still very wealthy – or the effective end of her sexual relationship with Charles, coupled with the successes of the Duchess of Portsmouth and the dramatic arrival of Duchess Mazarin, is not clear. Escorted by the Comte de Gramont and Henry Savile, and taking with her four of her children – Henry, Duke of Grafton, George, Earl of Northumberland, Charlotte and Barbara – she crossed to France and installed herself in the Convent of the Immaculate Conception of our Blessed Lady, in Paris, in hopes of a new adventure – after all, she was still only thirty-five.

Her daughters were soon in the care of the English abbess at Pontoise, in Normandy;[33] Churchill was in England; and Barbara herself was not one for retired meditation, and was soon active again. Edward Bernard, a scholar of St John's College, Oxford, had mistakenly agreed to be a tutor to her boys, but was so abused by her that he left, but reported that 'She driveth a cunning trade, and followeth her old employment very hard there, especially with the Archbishop of Paris, who is her principal gallant.'[34] In successful competition with the archbishop was the first Gentleman of the Bedchamber to Louis XIV, Alexis, Marquis de Châtillon.[35] And then there was another lover: the English Ambassador, Ralph Montagu.

Thirty-eight years old in 1676, ambitious and cunning, with a reputation for sexual proficiency, Montagu had secured his financial position by marrying the extremely wealthy widow Elizabeth Percy, Countess of Northumberland. Despite this, he had had a liaison with, and a daughter by, the English court beauty Jane Middleton, and also had a fancy for Mazarin. Mazarin, however, was away in England, having an extraordinary affair with Barbara's daughter, Anne, until her husband took her away into the country. Here, her rages and quarrels with her husband persuaded the King to send her to France in 1677, where she stayed in the nunnery in Conflans (which proved no great confinement, and a useful *poste restante* for Barbara's letters to Châtillon). Charles wanted to keep an eye on Charlotte and had her brought back to England and remarried to the Earl of Lichfield.

Both Montagu and Barbara had marriages on their minds. He wanted his stepdaughter, little Lady Bette Percy (born in 1667), to marry Charles's son by Catherine Pegge, 'Don Carlos', or Charles Fitzherbert, Earl of Plymouth; Barbara, on the other hand, wanted Lady Bette for her son, George Fitzroy, Duke of Northumberland. Nevertheless, by the terms of her father's will, Lady Bette was now theoretically in the control of her grandmother, who proposed to marry her to Lord Ogle.

While this marital manoeuvring went on, Montagu had other fish to fry as well. In March 1677, he wrote to Lord Treasurer Danby how French foreign policy required England's abstention from French wars and assistance to France's enemies and that Charles's neutrality could be bought for something between 9 and 12 million *livres* (up to £110,000) a year, which would relieve him from financial dependence on Parliament. The proposal would have its consequences later.

Charles's financial difficulties, partly caused by his expensive tastes in duchess-whores, were well known, and widely commented on. He seemed to have little power of resistance against the demands of the Duchess of Cleveland and her offspring, Louise, now the Duchess of Portsmouth, and even Nelly, who got £20,000, presumably in lieu of a title. One ballad had him complain how

> This making of bastards great,
> And duchessing of every whore,
> The surplus and Treasury cheat,
> Have made me damnable poor,
> Quoth Old Rowley the King,
> Quoth Old Rowley the King.[36]

Lampoons generally picked up on the moral laxity and political misrule of the King's conduct; it was for printing this one, that Julian was pilloried.

In France, in 1677, things had moved on: Anne had arrived in Conflans; Barbara now wanted Lady Bette for her son Henry, Duke of Grafton; and George was to be switched to four-year-old Anne Montagu, daughter of Ralph and Elizabeth Montagu. There was a problem, in that George, now twelve, was already technically married to Isabella Bennet, Arlington's daughter; however, Isabella was not yet twelve, when marriage vows became binding, and the marriage had not been consummated, so Barbara decided to come back to England to push through the marriage (re-)arrangements and collect some rents. Now Montagu became fully aware and jealous of the extent of her relationship with Châtillon – with unexpected consequences.

His political machinations had also moved on: he now had in his possession letters from Danby, proposing the setting-up of a peace deal, with France on one side and Holland and Spain on the other, with Charles as chief negotiator, receiving an annual pension of about £500,000 for three years, which would enable him to do without Parliament. Montagu himself wanted the post of Secretary of State in London and even offered the incumbent £10,000 for it, but Danby would not approve this. Montagu, unwisely, had told

Barbara of his grand scheme, which was to get rid of unhelpful Danby, obtain the Secretary of State post, then become Lord High Treasurer himself and so rule the King, when, as Barbara quoted him in a letter, 'I will find a way to furnish [the King] so easily with money for his pocket and his wenches that we will quickly out Bab May and lead the King by the nose.' In his heart, she wrote, he despised the King and the Duke of York, for Charles was 'a dull governable fool and the Duke a wilful fool. So that it was yet better to have [Charles] than him, but that [Charles] always chose a greater beast ... to govern him.'[37]

Having discovered Barbara's affair, he got hold of her notably indiscreet letters to Châtillon, probably from Anne at Conflans, and sent them to Charles, which angered him and caused considerable coolness on his part when she showed up. Worse, while Barbara was away, Montagu seduced seventeen-year-old Anne (not a hard task), moving her to a different, even less strict nunnery (more like an easy-going hotel); here, as Henry Savile (another of Barbara's former lovers) reported to Rochester, he 'lived with her in a most open scandal to the wonder of the French court and the high displeasure of this, the King being very angry with the Ambassador and his friends and enemies now struggling at court to support or ruin him.'[38]

When Barbara got back and found out, she was furious, and vengeful, and promptly wrote to Charles, telling him what Montagu's plans were and what he had done with Anne. Her next letter recounted Anne's defiance of her parents' express wishes in Montagu's presence. As for herself, she admitted to 'a kindness' with Châtillon and 'a foolish letter'. She went on, rather touchingly, 'Now all I have to say for myself is that as you know, as to love, one is not mistress of oneself, and that you ought not to be offended with me, since all things of this nature is at an end with you and I; so that I could do you no prejudice.' She went on, surprisingly apprehensively, to hope that he would not be too severe with her, as she knew he did not 'have it in [his] nature ever to do no cruel thing to anything living', and concluded:

I promise you that, for my conduct, it shall be such as that you nor nobody shall have occasion to blame me; and I hope you will be just to what you said to me, which was at my house, when you told me you had letters of mine. You said, 'Madam, all that I ask of you, for your own sake, is to live so for the future as to make the least noise that you can, and I care not who you love.' Oh, this noise that is had never been had it not been for the Ambassador's malice. I cannot forbear once again saying I hope you will not gratify his malice in my ruin.[39]

It had been a tempestuous relationship, extreme in its heights and depths, and now it was all over, in Charles's flat, sad words.

Charles got Anne sent to a stricter convent (though she later came back to court, becoming a Lady of the Bedchamber to Mary of Modena, and marrying twice more).[40] He then turned his attention to Montagu, who came hurrying back to London in an attempt to retrieve his position but was deprived of his ambassadorship, his membership of the Privy Council and even the Mastership of the Royal Wardrobe, which had cost him £14,000. Montagu then counter-attacked vigorously. First, he made a deal with the French ambassador, Paul Barillon, to get rid of anti-French Danby in return for £25,000 (*DNB*). Then he got himself elected to Parliament, in order to secure Parliamentary immunity. He then threatened to reveal Danby's letters negotiating with Louis for large subsidies for Charles in return for promising to prorogue Parliament if it attempted to press for anti-French policies. Danby tried to have his papers seized, but Parliament blocked this and demanded that the evidence be produced. Danby had tried to protect himself by having on each letter the words, 'I approve of this letter. Charles R.', so that he could claim that he was acting under orders, but Parliament impeached him for treason on 21 December. The King promptly prorogued Parliament, and then, on 24 January 1679, dissolved it, so bringing to an end the long-lived 'Cavalier Parliament.' The new Parliament of 6 March continued to demand Danby's impeachment; Danby resigned his post, and Charles made him a marquis but could not prevent him being sent to the Tower, where he remained until 1684.

1679 also saw, notably, the horrible, stupid, anti-Catholic,

'Popish Plot', maliciously invented for his own profit by Titus Oates, with disastrous effect:

> The Nation's curse,
> Bad in itself, but represented worse.
> Raised in extremes, and in extremes decried;
> With oaths affirmed, with dying vows denied.
> Not weighed, or winnowed by the multitude;
> But swallowed in the mass, unchewed and crude.
>
> Dryden, *Absalom and Achitophel*, 1681[41]

This horror got tangled up with the so-called 'Exclusion Crisis', the Protestant attempt to exclude James from the throne; possible rival claimants included James's daughter Mary with her husband, William of Orange, and a popular candidate was the bastard Duke of Monmouth. In July, there was a revolt in Scotland and Charles sent Monmouth to deal with it, which he did, so increasing his popularity. This in turn led to Charles dismissing him from his offices and sending him off to Holland, where he tried to get support from William. He then returned without permission, to talk to his allies, notably Buckingham and Shaftesbury, in London, and sheltered in Nell Gwyn's house in Pall Mall.

In August, after a strenuous session of tennis, Charles fell ill with a fever; his death seemed imminent, causing fears of possible civil war and a coup by Monmouth. Prayers were offered up, and the Duke of York was quietly brought back from Brussels, just in case. However, Charles quickly recovered and was tucking in to mutton and partridge when James, disguised in a black wig, arrived breathlessly at his bedside. For the time being, the King sorted out matters: James was sent back to cool his heels in Brussels, and Monmouth was deprived of his military commands.

In 1680, Barbara was back again, partly for the marriage of her son, Henry, to Isabella Bennet, but also to squeeze £25,000 from Charles and the Treasury. In general, Charles was now living a quieter life with the Duchess of Portsmouth, as well as sailing and fishing. A new verse now appeared, *Flatfoot the Gudgeon Taker*,[42] apropos of an attempt by a cabal of Buckingham and his sister, Nelly, and Lady Mary Howard, to insert a new mistress for Charles, a young kinswoman of Buckingham's, Jane Lawson. The idea was to displace Louise and reconcile the King with Buckingham.

> Methinks I see our mighty monarch stand,
> His pliant angle trembling in his hand,
> Pleased with the sport, good man, nor does he know
> His easy sceptre bends and trembles so.
> Fine representative, indeed, of God,
> Whose sceptre's dwindled to a fishing rod.
> [Sceptre, fishing rod and phallus are all too pliant,
>   as fisherman and fish elide together.]
> ... greedily he swallows every bait,
> A prey to every kingfisher of state.
> For how he gudgeons takes you have been taught;
> Then listen how he himself is caught.
> Too well, alas, the fatal bait is known,
> Which Rowley does so easily take down;
> And howe'er weak and slender be the string,
> Bait it with whore and it will hold a king.
> [The writer concludes with a warning, and showing
>   how the gang will profit by the girl's whoredom.]
> Old Richmond, making thee a punk,
> Shall twice a day with brandy now be drunk.
> Her brother Buckingham shall be restored,
> Nelly a countess. Lory be a lord [Laurence Hyde,
>   Clarendon's son].

In the event, none of that came to pass.

In 1682, Charles spent much of the summer sailing. Buckingham mocked this – not very publicly – in a verse, *The Cabbin-Boy*,[43] how

> He could sail a yacht both nigh and large,
> Knew how to trim a boat, and steer a barge,
> Could say his compass, to the nation's joy,
> And swear as well as any cabin boy.

> But not one lesson of the ruling art
> Could this dull blockhead ever get by heart.
> Look over all the universal frame,
> There's nothing the will of man can name
> In which this ugly, perjured rogue delights,
> But ducks, and loit'ring, buttered buns, and whites.

The King enjoyed a duck pond in St James's Park (where, as one ditty had it, 'the ducks and the drakes may their freedoms enjoy, / And quack in their language still, Vive le Roy'[44]) and chatting up women, who had been had by other men; 'whites' were menstrual flux. He was rather better at politics than Buckingham.

In 1684, the winter was very severe: in London, the slow-flowing Thames above London Bridge froze solid, several feet deep. A fair was set up on it, with booths selling roast beef, and people riding and driving carts across. The King ordered a royal pavilion to be set up, and Nelly presided over the various entertainments provided for courtiers and the general public.[45] In that year, Barbara returned to London and set herself up in Arlington Street, off Piccadilly, and now, aged about forty-five, took up with an actor again, handsome thirty-five-year-old Cardonell Goodman, by whom she had a child. Expelled from Cambridge for defacing the Duke of Monmouth's portrait and dismissed as a Page of the Back Stairs, he had turned to acting with the King's Company, admired by the actresses and acquiring the nickname, 'Scum'. In October he was charged with attempting to poison the Dukes of Grafton and Northumberland, found guilty, not hanged but fined £1,000 which he paid for with the profits from highway robbery. Perhaps in sheer arrogance, parading the relationship, he refused to let any performance begin until Barbara had arrived. On one occasion, Queen Catherine attended; when the curtain rose, he stepped forward and demanded, 'Is my duchess come?' Told she had not, he swore and declared, 'The play does not start until my lady is come.' Fortunately, Barbara arrived at that moment, so saving the situation – while providing her with another little triumph.[46] In about 1696, he had to leave England rather hurriedly, suspected of being involved in a Jacobite conspiracy.

6 February 1685 marked the death of Barbara's former lover, King Charles II, which will be discussed separately.

In 1705, Barbara heard of the death in Wales of her wronged and multiply cuckolded husband, Roger Palmer, Earl of Castlemaine, aged seventy-one, who bequeathed most of his property to Anne, Countess of Sussex, whom he had always regarded as his daughter. Now Barbara could marry again – and did, almost immediately. Once again she was drawn to a good-looking rogue: Robert Feilding, known as Beau Feilding, now aged fifty-four. He had already married two heiresses: Mary, daughter of Lord Carlingford; and Lady Muskerry, whose first husband had been killed in the Battle of Southwold in 1665, and whose second husband, Robert Danvers, had died in 1684. A Catholic, Feilding had been an army officer under James II and was now looking for a new source of income. He first thought of a young widow he had heard of, named Anne Deleau, who had been left £60,000; his tactic was not to approach her himself, but to promise a hairdresser called Charlotte Villars £500 to introduce him and bring about the marriage. Villars accordingly brought to his lodgings a lady in widow's dress, introduced as Mistress Deleau.

After a third meeting, they were married by a Catholic priest on 9 November; the marriage was consummated that night, but the bride went away in the morning, saying that the marriage had to be kept secret until she had won her father round. She came back to sleep with him and receive the presents and money that he was investing in her. Unfortunately for Feilding, his new wife was actually Mary Wadsworth, recently released from Bridewell Prison.

Meanwhile, Feilding had realised that that the Duchess of Cleveland was now newly on the market, and engaged in a brisk courtship of the ever-game sixty-four-year-old, who soon consented, and on 25 November they also were married. As soon as they were married, Feilding moved in and began to seize all she had – as her husband, her property was his. He would have had everything had she not complained to her grandson, the Duke of Grafton, who discovered that Feilding was already married. Barbara flew into one of her rages, but she had met her match: Feilding threatened to kill her, broke open her closet, took her money and beat her, until she screamed 'Murder!' from the window, when he began firing a blunderbuss at random.

After this low comedy, Barbara was in a state of collapse; Grafton got a warrant and brought Feilding before the Lord Chief Justice, who committed him to Newgate. At the trial on 4 December at the Old Bailey it became clear that Feilding himself had been tricked by Villars and Wadsworth. He was convicted of bigamy – though he was pardoned by Queen Mary (perhaps out of spite?), and later apparently lived well enough with Wadsworth. Eventually a decree of nullity of marriage between Feilding and Barbara was declared, and at last, aged sixty-seven, Barbara was single again.[47]

With this dreadful shock to her self-esteem, Barbara declined. She moved out of London to Chiswick Mall, looked after by her grandson, Charles Hamilton, Barbara Fitzroy's son. In her last years she developed a dropsy (oedema), which bloated her enormously – in her portrait by Godfrey Kneller she is hardly recognisable – and on 9 October 1709, she died.[48] A beauty for most of her life, domineering, ruthless, sexually and financially rapacious, she had risen to the rank of duchess in her own right by her own efforts (if not merits). One of her satirists phrased it well:

> Cleveland, I say, was much to be admired,
> For she was never satisfied or tired.[49]

'Admiration' did not then necessarily imply approval, rather, wondering or marvelling, as at some extraordinary natural phenomenon.

7

LA BELLE STUART: THE ONE
WHO GOT AWAY

In 1662 a new beauty arrived in court, destined to wreak
unprecedented havoc in the King's heart. This was Frances Teresa
Stuart, born in 1647 or 1648, the daughter of Walter Stuart,
physician to the Queen Mother, and his wife Sophia. A Scottish
family and loyal Royalists, in 1650 they had gone over to the
court of Queen Henrietta Maria, where young Frances became
a favourite of both Louis XIV and Henrietta Maria, who later
described her in a letter to Charles as 'the prettiest girl in the world
and the most fitted to adorn a court'.[1] Her mother thought she
would stand a better chance at the court of Charles II, and by 1663
she had attracted attention there generally, where she was referred
to as 'La Belle Stuart', and particularly from Charles.

Gramont's description of the blue-eyed, golden-haired fifteen
year old was a distinctly cool celebration:

> Her figure was more showy than engaging. It was hardly possible
> for a woman to have less wit, or more beauty; all her features were
> fine and regular; but her shape was not good: yet she was slender,
> straight enough and taller than the generality of women; she was
> very graceful, danced well, and spoke French better than her mother

tongue; she was well bred and possessed, in perfection, that air of dress which is so much admired, and which cannot be attained, unless it be taken, when young, in France.[2]

So wrote the Frenchman. He also remarked that

the Countess of Castlemaine perceived that the King paid attention to her; but, instead of being alarmed at it, she favoured, as far as she was able, this new inclination, whether from an indiscretion common to all those who think themselves to be superior to the rest of mankind, or whether she designed, by this pastime, to the King's attention from the commerce which she held with [Harry] Jermyn. She was not satisfied with appearing without any degree of uneasiness at a preference which all the Court had begun to remark; she even affected to make Miss Stuart her favourite, and invited her to all the entertainments she made for the King; and, in confidence of her own charms, with the greatest indiscretion she often kept her to sleep. The King, who seldom neglected to visit the Countess before she rose, seldom failed to find Miss Stuart in bed with her.[3]

Castlemaine's calculated fun went further, and quickly: on 8 February 1663, Pepys recorded a court story (mentioned earlier) of how

my Lady Castlemaine, a few days since, had Mrs Stuart to an entertainment, and at night began a frolic that they two must be married; and married they were, with ring and all other ceremonies of church service, and ribbands and a sack-posset [spiced drink] in bed and flinging the [bride's] stocking. But in the close it was said that Mrs Castlemaine, who was the bridegroom, rose, and the King came and took her place with pretty Mrs Stuart. This is said to be very true.

Frances must have had a difficult time, one way and another, and with Charles in bed with her. This remarkable episode was widely reported; a contemporary writer of *On the Ladies of the Court* confidently reported what he thought had happened:

Strangely pleasant were their chats
When Mayne and Steward played at flats, [lesbian sex-play]
Their marriage night so taught them,
Till Charles came there,
And with his ware
Taught them how their fathers got them.[4]

Despite what this writer assumed, Barbara and Charles must have been frustrated in their attempt to overcome young Frances's defence of her virginity; Barbara's plan, presumably, was that once Charles had had Frances, his interest would diminish, and he would return to his previous and more experienced bedmate. On the other hand, it is not clear whether Frances's determined rearguard action was principled virtue or part of a long-term campaign, directed by her ambitious mother.

That summer, in fact, the King and Queen were on better terms; on 13 July, Pepys saw them riding together, hand in hand, in St James's Park, when the King seemed to take no notice of Barbara. In Whitehall, he saw the Queen and her ladies laughing and playing together, and now even the devotee of Castlemaine wavered: 'Above all, Mrs Stuart in this dress, with her hat cocked and a red plume, with her sweet eye, little Roman nose, and excellent *Taille*, is now the greatest beauty I ever saw I think in my life; and if ever woman can, doth exceed my Lady Castlemaine; at least, in this dress.'

In August, the Queen was to take the waters at Bath; the French ambassador, the Comte de Cominges, reported that 'every method of getting a successor to the English throne is to be tried, and the King in his part contributes all that could be asked of true affection and regular assiduity.'[5] Dr Pierce, Pepys's regular provider of court gossip, thought Frances 'only an innocent, young, raw girl', and not considered very important as yet. Later that year, however, he was complaining

how loose the Court is, nobody looking after business but every man his lust and gain; and how the King is now become besotted upon Mrs Stuart, that he gets into corners and will be with her half an hour together, kissing her to the observation of all the world; and she now stays by herself and expects it, as my Lady Castlemaine did use to do; to whom the King, he says, is still kind ... Yet it is thought that this wench is so subtle, that she lets him not do anything more than is safe to her.[6]

It does not seem very subtle in a young girl to play her only card – a trump card – her virginity, which kept her lover keen; that gone, she might become no more than another of the Maid of Honour trulls, 'soiled doves' fluttering about the court.

Others were thinking how to exploit her, and on 6 November, Lord Sandwich, Pepys's kinsman and employer, told him that there was a committee including Ralph Montagu and the Duke and Duchess of Buckingham 'for the getting of Mrs Stuart for the King. But that she proves a cunning slut and is advised at Somerset House and by her mother, and so all the plot is spoilt and the whole committee broke'. Buckingham and his sister set up a party for her with Charles there to take his chance. However, word had leaked out, and the Queen and Barbara both turned up to join in the dancing until 3 a.m., when Frances was able to leave in the same condition as when she came.

Gramont remarked how at this time she came so openly into favour with the King 'that every person perceived that, if she was but possessed of art, she might have become as absolute mistress over his conduct as she was of his affections.'[7] It seems unlikely that Charles would have been swayed by a fifteen-year-old's opinions, whose only 'art' was limited to saying 'no' charmingly but persistently. As it was, young Frances was not really up to it. Gramont observed,

She was childish in her behaviour, and laughed at everything; and her taste for frivolous amusements, though unaffected, was only allowable in a girl about twelve or thirteen [She was fifteen, or sixteen at the most]. A child, however, she was in every other respect, except playing with a doll; blind man's buff was her favourite amusement [like many other girls at courts throughout Europe at that time]; she was building castles of cards, while the deepest card-play was going on in her apartments, where you saw her surrounded by eager courtiers, who handed her the cards, or young architects, who endeavoured to imitate her.

She had, however, a passion for music, and had some taste in singing. The Duke of Buckingham, who built the finest towers of cards imaginable, had an agreeable voice. She had no aversion to scandal, and the Duke was both the father and the mother of scandal; he made songs, and invented old wives' stories, with which she was delighted. But his particular talent consisted in turning into ridicule whatever was ridiculous in other people, and in taking them off even in their presence, without their perceiving it.[8]

This mimicry-mockery talent had earlier endeared him to the youthful Prince Charles. Led on by his success in charming and amusing Frances, he went on to make a pass at her, but 'met with so severe a repulse that he abandoned at once all his designs'.[9]

He was not the only one to try his luck: along came Lord Arlington, aged about forty-five, with his black plaster over his nose (a perpetual in-your-face reminder of his wound in the Civil War) and a pompous speech of proposal on the benefits of

the situation to which it had pleased God and her virtue to raise her. But he was only in the preface of his speech, when she recollected that he was at the head of those whom the Duke of Buckingham used to mimic; and, as his presence and his language exactly revived the ridiculous ideas that had been given her of him, she could not forbear bursting out into a fit of laughter in his face, so much the more violent in that she had for a long time struggled to suppress it.[10]

Arlington, naturally, was furious; he left her abruptly and went off to Holland to get a Dutch wife (the very wealthy daughter of the head of the Dutch embassy and cousin of William of Orange), 'in order to complete his felicity'.

Another admirer was George Hamilton, who became infatuated with her that autumn until Gramont warned him of the danger of pursuing the King's beloved – chiefly, of being sent away from

King Charles II. Resting between various engagements, sceptre in hand. (Bridgeman)

George Villiers, Duke
of Buckingham. Rash,
energetic, here showing the
effects of years of high living.
(Bridgeman)

Lady Anna-Maria Brudenell,
Countess of Shrewsbury.
Widely active in court life,
then Buckingham's long-term
mistress. (Bridgeman)

John Wilmot, Earl of Rochester. Notorious seducer, wit and poet. (Dillington House, Somerset C.C.)

Diana Kirke, Countess of Oxford. Court beauty, reputed affairs with Henry Jermyn and Henry Sidney. (Yale Centre for British Art)

Aphra Behn. First
English woman
professional writer,
friend of Rochester
and Nell Gwyn. (Yale
Centre for British Art)

Frances Stuart,
Duchess of Richmond
and Lennox. 'La
Belle Stuart', pursued
by Charles almost
to distraction.
(Bridgeman)

Above: Eleanor 'Nell' Gwyn. Actress, the King's most popular mistress, 'the Protestant whore'. (Bridgeman)

Right: Louise de Keroualle. Unpopular, greedy, Charles's last, best beloved. (Bridgeman)

Ortance Manchini Duchesse of Mazarin &c.

Left: Hortense Mancini, Duchesse de Mazarin. Flamboyant, extravagant, sexual adventuress. (Rijksmuseum)

Below: A feast at the Duke of Buckingham's, by Augustus Egg, 1853. (Yale Centre for British Art)

court. He told of her little amusements – she was delighted with his trick of holding the lit end of a candle in his mouth – and enjoyed her naïve pride in her beauty, displayed on request – as when, on one occasion in 1662, the King having declared that there were no legs finer than hers, she lifted her skirts above the knee, in confirmation.[11] He even declared that, given enough skilful flattery, 'one could induce her to strip naked, without ever reflecting upon what she was doing'.[12] He also claimed to have seen further than most when, out riding together, she fell off,

> so that I alone was the witness of a disorder in her clothes, which displayed a thousand new beauties to my view. I had the good fortune to make such gallant and flattering exclamations upon that charming disorder as to prevent her being concerned or out of countenance upon it.[13]

Frances did not need to fall over to attract eyes; on 26 August 1664, Pepys saw her being painted, 'in a most lovely form, with her hair all about her ears ... There was the King and twenty more, I think, standing by the while, and a lovely creature she in the dress seems to be'. This incident would be about the time that Anne Hyde, Duchess of York, commissioned the series of paintings by Peter Lely known as 'The Windsor Beauties'. One writer, however, thinks that the portrait that Pepys saw was an unappealing one attributed to Jacob Huysmans (but perhaps by Samuel Cooper).[14]

Meanwhile, Charles's pursuit was getting ever closer, while Gramont felt that she had done 'all that was necessary to inflame the King's passion, without exposing her virtue by granting the last favours; but the eagerness of a passionate lover, blessed with favourable opportunities, is difficult to withstand, and still more difficult to vanquish' (is he imagining some struggles?). He thought that 'Mrs Stuart's virtue [was] almost exhausted, when the Queen was attacked [in October 1663] with a violent fever which soon reduced her to extreme danger'.[15] There was every expectation of Catherine's death and her possible replacement, but then, partly encouraged by Charles's kindness, the Queen recovered.

With this recovery, things went back to how they had been, if not more so. On 20 January 1664, Pierce told Pepys that the King was now exclusively interested in Frances,

> and that to the leaving off all business in the world, and to the open slighting of the Queen. That he values not who sees him or stands by him while he dallies with her openly, and then privately in her chamber below, where the very sentries observe his going in and out – and that so commonly that the Duke or any of the nobles, when they would ask where the King is, say, 'Is the King above or below?', meaning with Mrs Stuart.

On 8 February, he told Pepys that 'the good Queen will of herself stop before she goes sometimes into her dressing-room, till she knew whether the King be there, for fear he should be, as she hath sometimes taken him, with Mrs Stuart'.

Gramont was himself indirectly responsible for one absurd incident involving the rival women. He often laid on expensive, spectacular contributions to the court entertainments, such as banquets and riverside concerts; the King granted him a pension of 1,500 'jacobuses, which is not a great deal' (about £1,775). He once arranged for a very stylish calash (or *calèche*, a light, low-wheeled, open carriage) to be brought over from France for the King. The ladies were all charmed with it: the Queen wanted to be the first to show herself in it; Lady Castlemaine demanded that she should first appear in it; 'la belle Stuart' also wanted this, for the same day. The poor Queen, of course, did not stand a chance. Gramont reported that Castlemaine, pregnant at the time, threatened to bring on a miscarriage if her rival were favoured; however, 'Mrs Stuart threatened she never would be with child, if her request was not granted. This menace prevailed, and Lady Castlemaine's rage was so great, that she almost kept her word; and it was believed that this triumph cost her rival some of her innocence'.[16]

The squabbles went on. On 17 November 1665, Lord Sandwich told Pepys,

> factions are high between the King and the Duke of York, and all the Court are in an uproar with their loose amours – the Duke

of York being in love desperately with Mrs Stuart. Nay, that the Duchess herself is in love with her new Master of Horse, one Harry Sidney ... that his amours to Mrs Stuart are told the King – so that all is like to be naught among them.

The Duke soon got over it, and moved on to his new mistress, the recently married – and doomed – young Lady Denham. By 9 January 1666, Pepys noted that the King visited Castlemaine and Frances together every morning before breakfast. On 15 April, Pierce was saying that 'for certain, Mrs Stuart doth do everything now with the King that a mistress should do' – but, almost certainly, not everything.

On 15 November, Pepys managed to see the great ball in Whitehall for the Queen's birthday, 'The gloriousest assembly everybody said that has been in England since the King's return, except the Coronation ... It was indeed a glorious sight to see Mrs Stuart in black and white lace – and her head and shoulders dressed with diamonds ... Mrs Stuart danced mighty finely ...'.

For all the glamour of the court, which was very great, the stress on Frances was becoming more and more intense, as Charles increased his efforts to possess her by any means. He even went on to ask Archbishop Sheldon about divorce and received an evasive answer; Gilbert Burnet, ever helpful, went on to write a treatise, *A Solution of Two Cases of Conscience*, on polygamy and divorce, and 'what the Scripture allows in these cases', writing that he could 'see nothing so strong against polygamy as to balance the great and visible imminent hazards that hang over so many thousands, if it be not allowed'.[17] The King offered Frances the title of duchess in her own right, extensive estates, the promise that he would forsake all others and keep only unto her (in the words of the marriage service) – but she would still be unmarried, still only a mistress. He did try, briefly, when 'he discarded, without any exception, all the other mistresses which he had in the various parts of the town. The Nell Gwyns, the Miss Davises and the joyous train of singers and dancers in His Majesty's theatre, were all dismissed. All these sacrifices were ineffectual'.[18] Then the court was shaken by the sudden death of the Duke of York's mistress, Lady Denham, about the same age as Frances, some said poisoned at the instigation of his wife; it could have caused her to think very seriously.

Occasionally, the great world of international politics impinged on the little world of court romancing: the Dutch War had gone badly and was concluded with peace negotiations at Breda, on 31 July 1667. Gold medals were prepared to mark British naval victories and then to mark the peace. On the obverse was the King's profile, and on the reverse, at his fond command, the object of his obsession, Frances Stuart as Britannia. Pepys was at the studio of Jan Roettier, the goldsmith, on 25 February, where he saw 'the King's new medal, where in little is Mrs Stuart's face, as well done as ever I saw anything in my whole life I think – and a pretty thing it is that he should choose her face to represent Britannia by'. 'Pretty' was not always used by Pepys to express commendation.

With a court readership in mind, Waller wrote 'Upon the Golden Medal', interestingly drawing an analogy between Frances's resistance to Charles's attempted seduction and Britannia's resistance to Dutch naval attacks. The poem begins with a description of the medal:

> Our guard upon the royal side!
> On the reverse our beauty's pride!

The figure is Frances before it is Britannia. The poem concludes ambiguously, with an allusion to Danaë being seduced by Jove in a shower of gold:

> Britannia there the fort in vain
> Had battered been with golden rain;
> Thunder itself had failed to pass;
> Virtue's a stronger guard than brass.[19]

'Thunder' is Jove, Dutch cannon and Charles; as the Dutch assail Britain, so Charles/Jove assails Frances/Danaë; insofar as Frances is Britannia, Charles (in his womanising and misrule) is debauching Britain. Frances, as Britannia, was to figure on British coinage well into the twentieth century – though the current Britannia on the bit of tinsel now offered as a 50-pence coin is not her.

Now, at this critical time, Charles Stuart (a name to conjure with), a distant cousin of the King, 4th Duke of Richmond, 6th Duke of Lennox and Lord High Admiral of Scotland, twice a widower, not very bright and rather too keen on drink, took a particular interest in Frances. Rather run of the mill at court, where the King took less notice of him even than the courtiers, he now, according to Gramont, 'took it into his head either to marry her, or to die in the attempt'.[20] Certainly, he would now be noticed by the King and there was no telling what might ensue.

For all her celebrated beauty, it was not obvious why one would want to marry a young woman already well earmarked as the King's next mistress-in-waiting. Indeed, Pepys felt that only the Duke's high social status might stop people ridiculing the match, whereas 'had a meaner person married her, he would for certain have been reckoned a cuckold at the first dash'.[21] However, it has been suggested that in this case it was the King's rank that was the deciding factor. 'By marrying a royal mistress, and by implication inviting the King to make him a cuckold, Richmond might be viewed as seeking "honour" and royal favour by his own horning. At the highest levels of society, rank seemed to rewrite normal codes of sexual reputation.'[22] As Samuel Butler observed,

> For to be known a cuckold can be no
> Dishonour, but to him that thinks it so,
> For, if he feel no chagrin, or remorse,
> His forehead's shot free, and he's ne'er the worse.[23]

As what would have been called a 'pimping cuckold', Richmond was very willing to marry Frances, but insisted that he would have to receive a marriage portion, which Charles indicated he might provide (Frances had been a Maid of Honour to the Queen since 1663), supposing that matters got that far, though Frances was offended that he was not willing to have her only for her own sweet sake.

At this point, Barbara intervened, to stir up trouble. One night, she went to Charles's bedroom through the apartment of his page-pimp William Chiffinch and told him that, though Frances had only just sent him away on some pretext, his rival, Richmond, would soon be with her. The King hurried through the corridors to her apartment; entering, he found Frances in bed and Richmond seated at her bedhead. The King was in extreme fury, and the Duke made a hasty retreat. Attack being the best form of defence, Frances was on her high horse, declaring that if a lady could not receive a gentleman of the Duke's quality and honourable intentions – unlike Charles – it was not a free country, that – in tears – she could always go back to France, to a nunnery. The King was overwhelmed with this verbal onslaught, until she told him to leave her in peace for the night, as otherwise he might offend the person at whose suggestion he had come – which infuriated him again, all the more.[24]

Richmond was banished from the court, and Frances went to the Queen, tearfully begging her assistance; after a while, it seemed that the King would give his approval. On 18 March, Sir William Penn told Pepys, 'For certain the Duke of Richmond is to marry Mrs Stuart, he having this day brought an account of his estate and debts to the King on that account.' Actually, it was the Chancellor, Clarendon, who was instructed to examine Richmond's affairs, chiefly in hope of finding him discreditable or financially insufficient. Sexually, Richmond had a bad reputation, as Magalotti heard: he and his friend the Duke of Monmouth were 'the two most intrepid patrons of bawdy-houses in London', where Monmouth was seriously infected 'five or six times'.[25] Perhaps this did not weigh heavily with Clarendon, who apparently reported that, although Richmond's financial position was not strong, yet 'a family so nearly related to the King could never be left in distress, and such a match would not come Mistress Stuart's way every day; so she had best consider well before she rejected it'.[26] This greatly annoyed Charles, suspecting that Clarendon was trying to prevent him remarrying and producing legitimate offspring, so blocking the way to the Crown for his own grandchildren.

It was decision time. One night at the end of March, Richmond (as recorded by Pepys on 3 April), 'by a wilde [dodge] did fetch her to the Bear [Inn] at the Bridge foot, where a coach was ready, and they stole away into Kent [to Cobham Hill, near Gravesend], without the King's leave' – as required for the marriage of a Maid of Honour. He went on, saying that he heard that 'the King is not so well pleased of this marriage [on 30 March] ... as is talked ... and that the King hath said he will never see her more'. He was able to go on to give a fuller account, from John Evelyn, who considered her to be 'as virtuous as any woman in the world'. She had told a friend of Evelyn's, 'a Lord ... and a sober man ... that when the Duke of Richmond did make love to her' they both got the King's consent. She also told this lord, as Evelyn in turn told Pepys,

> that she had come to that pass as to have resolved to marry any gentleman of £1,500 a year that would have had her in honour – for it was come to that pass, that she could no longer continue at Court without prostituting herself to the King, whom she had so long kept off, though he had liberty more than any other had, or he ought to have, as to dalliance.

Consequently, she had decided that she had to marry and leave the court, so that everyone could see her concern for her honour, but hoped to be able to reconcile the King and her husband, so as to live agreeably on his estate. She also told this friend about all that she had been given: £700 a year from the Privy Purse for her clothes, a pearl necklace of about £1,100 from the King and

> about seven months since, when the King had hopes to have obtained some courtesy [sic] of her ... some jewels ... and ... a pair of pendants. The Duke of York, being once her Valentine, did give her a jewel of about £800; and my Lord Mandville, her Valentine this year, a ring of about £300 ... so that Mr Evelyn believes she may be worth in jewels about £6,000, and that is all she has in the world – and a worthy woman, and in this hath done as great an act of honour as ever was done by woman.[27]

Well, these things are relative. Her return of Charles's jewels was honourable but tactless.

The morning after the elopement, the King went to her apartment, and in the doorway met Lord Cornbury, Clarendon's son, who knew nothing of what had happened and had gone to see her on some unrelated matter. The King, in a jealous fury, suspected him and 'spoke to him as one in a rage, that forgot all decency, and for some time would not hear Lord Cornbury speak in his own defence'.[28] Furthermore, he suspected Clarendon of being party to this betrayal, as he saw it, despite Clarendon's protestations of innocence.

Another of the King's hopes and plans went horribly wrong, with the mishandled peace treaty with the Dutch at Breda and the Dutch Admiral De Ruyter's raid up the Medway, which outraged public opinion. Andrew Marvell joined in the criticism: in his *Last Instructions to a Painter*, Frances, now the Duchess of Richmond, also figured on coins as well as the medal:

> The court in farthing yet itself does please,
> (And female Stuart there rules the four seas),
> But fate does still accumulate our woes,
> And Richmond here commands, as Ruyter those.

Both the Duke of Richmond and De Ruyter had outdone Charles, and she still ruled him. The poem continues with Charles having a vision of a bound, naked virgin, reminiscent of Frances when he first pursued her, which he attempts to possess, before it escapes his hold (as did Frances):

> In his deep thoughts the wonder did increase,
> And he divined 'twas England or the Peace.[29]

Someone else would have to pay the price for all this – the military disaster and loss of Frances – and by 30 August the great Lord Clarendon had been ruthlessly dismissed from office and fled to France. When Charles's sister, the Duchess of Orléans, heard of Charles's angry reaction to the elopement, she wrote to plead for a reconciliation. On 26 August, he replied:

I do assure you I am very much troubled that I cannot in everything give you that satisfaction I could wish, especially in the business of the Duchess of Richmond, wherein you may think me ill-natured. But if you consider how hard a thing 'tis to swallow an injury done by a person I had so much l['love', deleted] tenderness for, you will in some degree excuse the resentment I use towards her. You know my good nature enough to believe that I could not be so severe if I had not had great provocation, and I assure you her carriage towards me has been as bad as breach of friendship and faith can make it. Therefore, I hope you will pardon me if I cannot so soon forget an injury which went so near my heart.[30]

In June that year, and then later, there was gossip that Frances was expecting; if so, she must have miscarried. Later, in 1679, when the Duchess of Portsmouth was rumoured to be considering fleeing to France to avoid the 'Popish Plot' frenzy, a ribald satire, *Colin*, facetiously reviewed possible claimants to succeed her as *maîtresse en titre*:

> Up stepped fair Richmond once so famed.
> She offered much but was refused,
> And of miscarriages accused.
> They said a cunt so used to puke
> Could never bear a booby duke.[31]

She remained childless; divorcing the barren queen in hopes of this fresh womb could well have proved fruitless.

Otherwise, the Richmonds' marriage seems to have been not unsuccessful by the court standards of the time; despite Gramont's disparaging remarks about her youthful lack of intelligence, her letters to her husband during his absence on military duty (raising troops in Devon amid fears of invasion) show common sense in dealing with estate matters, as well as affection. The couple considered moving to France where Richmond, as Duc d'Aubigny, had estates, but she wanted to regain a place at court and started holding receptions for courtiers at Cobham. Again there were rumours of a reconciliation; when Charles's sister wrote, inquiring, he replied,

> You were misinformed in your intelligence concerning the Duchess of Richmond; if you were as well acquainted with a little fantastical gentleman called Cupid as I am, you would neither wonder nor take ill any sudden changes which do happen in the affairs of his conducting, but in this matter there is nothing in it.[32]

Then, that winter, Frances was struck with smallpox; she survived, but with her face somewhat marked. Pepys was provoked to moralising: 'All do conclude she will be wholly spoiled, which is the greatest instance of the incertainty of beauty that could be in this age; but, then, she hath had the benefit of it to be first married and to have kept it so long under the greatest temptations in the world from a king, and yet without the least imputation.'[33] Charles wrote to Minette, 'I cannot tell whether the Duchess of Richmond will be much marked with the small pox. She has many and I fear they will at least do her no good.'[34] Although one eye was affected, on 7 May Charles wrote that 'she is not much marked with the small pox, and I must confess this last affliction made me pardon all that is past'.

This return of affection was soon demonstrated. Frances returned to her mother at Somerset House, and on 19 May Pepys reported that, though the King supped every night with great pleasure with the Queen,

> yet it seems he is mighty hot upon the Duchess of Richmond; insomuch that upon Sunday was sennight, at night, after he had ordered his guards and coach to take him to the Park, he did on a sudden take a pair of oars or sculler, and all alone, or but one with him, go to Somerset House and there, the garden door not being open, himself clamber over the walls to make a visit to her where she is; which is a horrid shame.

These frequent visits were widely known. Magalotti reported that 'some people say that she serves as a pretext, and that in reality his present inclination is towards Mistress Stuart, her sister', but dismissed this, chiefly on the grounds of Frances's 'angelic and wonderful beauty'.[35] The Queen was on good terms with her and made her a Lady of the Bedchamber, with lodgings in Whitehall. On 30 August, Pepys saw her in the park, 'her face worse than it was considerably by the small pox'. (Magalotti had not seen her before her illness.) Nevertheless, the ineffable John Sheffield, Earl of Mulgrave, thought, against all reason, that she might fancy an affair with him, and wrote an *Elegy to the Duchess of Richmond*, urging her,

> Thou lovely slave to a rude husband's will,
> By nature used so well, by him so ill:
> For all that grief we see your mind endure,
> Your glass presents you with a pleasing cure;
> Those maids you envy for their happier state,
> To have your form, would gladly have your fate ...
> Then from so dull a care your thoughts remove,
> And waste not sighs you only owe to love.[36]

There is no evidence that her husband was particularly 'rude' or 'used' her badly, though they may not have spent much time together; he applied to Louis XIV for the fiefdom of Aubigny, and Charles interceded on his behalf. She and the Queen were now friends. The Richmonds attended the royal progress to Norfolk in the autumn of 1671, when Charles, though now more engaged in the pursuit of Louise de Kéroualle, was reported to have drunkenly boasted to Richmond that he had indeed 'triumphed over his wife's virtue'.[37] Her consent, or yielding, seems understandable, and very likely – though it would have been unkind of Charles to crow openly over the cuckolded husband, who could do nothing about it.

Perhaps as a compensation, Richmond was appointed Ambassador Extraordinary to Denmark (the kind of post for which he had long been angling), to persuade the Danish King to join an Anglo-French alliance against the Dutch; not surprisingly, people thought he had been got out of the way. The French ambassador, Colbert de Croissy, reported on 24 December 1671: 'The Duke of Richmond is getting ready to leave as ambassador extraordinary to Denmark, and the King his master has been caressing his wife in her husband's presence, at least one can quite well see indications that she is very attractive to the King.'[38] This kind of improper public behaviour that she had permitted and enjoyed as a young girl seems a different matter now that she was married and permitting in her husband's presence. It is to be hoped that the cuckold Duke got some pleasure from his new title; in December 1672, he rowed out for an evening's drinking with an English frigate captain moored off Elsinore, fell into the water and died soon after. As there was no heir, his title and estates reverted to the King (as did his widow); Cobham Hall and estate were left to her as a life interest.

As it was, her time was over: Mazarin and Louise de Kéroualle were now the new contestants for place and favour. After a while, Frances sold the life interest in Cobham Hall and the rights to the fiefdom of Aubigny, so that she was well off. Mulgrave had another try and failed. John Grubham Howe, a low-life courtier and would-be wit, claimed to have enjoyed her favours (she would be a trophy, after all), and showed a letter, which Charles inspected and said was a fake (of course). Howe was a good example of Samuel Butler's *Amorist*, 'a sworn servant to all ladies ... His passion is as easily set fire as a fart, and as soon out again. He is charged and primed with love-powder like a gun, and the least sparkle of an eye gives fire to him, and off he goes, but seldom, or never, hits the mark'.[39]

Howe wrote libels, which he thought were satires, and promoted himself as a lover of celebrated beauties; a contemporary verse described him:

> His person too he much admires, and strove
> Once to be thought renowned for feats of love.
> But of his constancy and trust in those,
> Churchill repents and Richmond too well knows. [Sarah]
> These in their lusts happy might still have been
> Had they not loved, believed, and trusted him.

A face he had much like a skeleton,
Two inches broad and fifteen inches long,
His two cheeks sunk, a visage pale as death,
Adorned with pimples and a stinking breath ...[40]

The writer despises him, but, like some other court satirists, seems to think that these affairs might have happened. It does seem improbable, especially with such an unprepossessing lover, but in the Restoration court anything seems possible.

Frances was on the fringes of the court for a while but withdrew to a retired life; on 15 October 1702, she died, aged fifty-four. In her will, she made provision for the care of her cats.

8

PORTSMOUTH BUT NOT PLYMOUTH: NELL AND LOUISE

At some time early in 1671, Lord Arlington observed to the French ambassador that it would be better for everybody if the King had to do with Mlle Kéroualle, who was polite and a lady, rather than with a 'termagant' of an 'evil disposition' (obviously Castlemaine) or with 'lewd and bouncing orange-girls and actresses, of whom no man could take the measure'.[1] The orange-girl/actress was to be the King's most popular mistress, celebrated through the centuries, Nell Gwyn; Mlle Kéroualle was to be the one for whom he declared the most fondness. From opposite ends of the social scale, opposite personalities, even opponents, they outlasted other rivals and were the women he thought of on his deathbed. They are most conveniently discussed together.

Nell (Helen, Eleanor) Gwyn (Gwynne) was there first. Her birth date is as uncertain as her name; generally it is thought to be in 1650, though some writers push for earlier, even 1642. Her parentage and birth place are also disputed. Some think of her father as having served in the Royalist army and Welsh (Gwyn being a Welsh name); he is thought to have died in a debtors' prison, possibly in Oxford (in her will, Nell left money for the release of poor debtors – 'So pious a remembrance still she bore

/ Ev'n to the fetters her father wore' (*A Panegyric*, 1681).[2] The preferred location is Coal Yard Alley, off Drury Lane. Her mother, fat, boozy Helena or Eleanor, probably ran a bawdy house nearby. A lampoon of 1677 asserted that Nell's 'first employment was, with open throat / To cry fresh herrings even at ten a groat'.[3] Other writers, joining in her denigration, called her a 'cinder-wench' or 'Cinder Nell' (which fits well with the Cinderella element in her life story); later, Nell said that she had been employed in serving brandy to customers in her mother's bawdy house. The panegyric notes how 'This first step raised, to th' wond'ring pit she sold / The lovely fruit, smiling with streaks of gold',[4] suggesting her hair colour; she went on to sell oranges in the new theatre, probably supervised by Mrs Mary Meggs, 'Orange Moll'.

One of the first things that Charles did after his coronation was to license two theatre companies: the King's Company, eventually set up in the Theatre Royal, off Drury Lane, owned by the witty immoralist and Charles's friend Sir Thomas Killigrew; and the Duke's Company at the Playhouse in Lincoln's Inn Fields, owned by loyal, long-serving Royalist Sir William Davenant, who had, despite Parliamentary disapproval, managed to put on theatrical entertainments since 1655, including *The Siege of Rhodes* (thought the first English opera), and been happy to sacrifice his mother's reputation, to be thought the natural son of William Shakespeare. (John Aubrey reported how, in the early 1630s, Davenant unfortunately 'got a terrible clap of a black handsome wench that lay in Axe Yard [back of Drury Street] ... which cost him his nose, with which unlucky mischance many wits were too cruelly bold'.[5] Here, 'black' may simply mean that she was dark-haired; Charles II was also referred to as black. Aubrey himself was infected, in similar fashion – but not disastrously – in 1656.) In 1671, the Duke's Company was established in the Dorset Gardens Theatre, built by Wren, and in 1682 took over the King's Company.

The theatres had proscenium arches with a thrust or fore stage, lit by candles and chandeliers. Davenant introduced movable and changeable scenery, with flats sliding in and out, together with 'machines' for gods to descend in chariots and trapdoors from the underworld. In the auditorium, there were side boxes, close to the stage, for royalty and 'the quality'; round and above were upper galleries for the lower classes and middle galleries for citizens, their wives and daughters (to be ogled by the aristocracy or royalty, as was Pepys's wife[6]); in front in the pit, seated on benches were the raucous squires, wits and whores – as Wycherley's Mrs Pinchwife observed, 'none but naughty women sat there, whom [the men] toused and moused'.[7] As for the loutish rakes, Shadwell describes in *The Virtuoso* (1676) how they 'come drunk and screaming into a playhouse and stand upon the benches, and toss their full periwigs and empty heads, and cry "Damme, Jack, this is a damned play, prithee, let's to a whore, Jack".'[8] The performers had to deliver their lines, not in attentive quiet, but through a barrage of backchat, badinage and occasional brawls. The women of all classes contributed to the general distracting clatter of chatter, as a satire *Utile Dulce* (1681), by Grubham Howe and Viscount Falkland, remarked:

> The orange wench that prostrates at the door
> Would be thought chaste, and frowns at the name of whore,
> While ladies in the boxes seem at strife,
> Whose reputation shall have the shortest life ...
> Now all the ladies' pride and chiefest joy
> Is to be ogled at the next new play,
> Fleering about, with softest looks they sit
> And give encouragement to all the pit.
> Then, filled with hopes, to the box the coxcombs crowd,
> Grin and speak powerful nonsense very loud.[9]

Behind the stage were the storage rooms and dressing rooms for the actors and actresses – the latter frequently visited by gentlemen. The actresses themselves constituted the major change, instituted by royal command in the patent to prevent the scandal of men dressing as women and provide 'not only harmless delight, but useful and instructive representations of human life'. Nothing could seem more moral or sensible. Predictably, the introduction of actresses provided more 'delights', as Thomas Killigrew pointed out in the epilogue to his *The Parson's Wedding* of 1672:

> When boys played women's parts, you'd think the stage
> Was innocent, in that untempting age –
> No: for your amorous fathers then, like you,
> Amongst those boys had playhouse misses too;
> They set their bearded beauties on their laps,
> Men gave 'em kisses, and the ladies claps.
> But they, poor hearts, could not supply our room:
> They went but females to the tiring room,
> While we, in kindness to ourselves, and you,
> Can hold out women to our lodgings too.[10]

At first, there were not enough women to act, and several men continued in cross-dressing parts, notably Edward Kynaston, whom Pepys admired in several drag parts, as in Jonson's *Epicoene*, on 7 January 1661: 'And in them was clearly the prettiest woman in the whole house.' Once, when the King attended a performance of *Hamlet*, there was a delay: on being told that the Queen, Kynaston, was not yet shaved, he replied, 'Ods fish, I beg her majesty's pardon. We'll wait till her barber has done with her.'[11] It would have been interesting to see Hamlet dressed as a Restoration courtier, in his broad-brimmed hat, long periwig, lace-trimmed shirt, loose surcoat, full breeches and shoes with ribbon bows.

The women came from a variety of backgrounds: a few were from 'good' families come down in the world, victims of the Civil War; some were gentlemen's bastards, some daughters of tradesmen from the servant classes. They worked hard enough, with rehearsals in the morning, performances in the late afternoon – and evenings to make the most of. Not considered respectable, and not well paid, they were surrounded by temptations. The writer Tom Brown observed, ''Tis as hard a matter for a pretty woman to keep herself honest in a theatre, as 'tis for an apothecary to keep his treacle from the flies in hot weather, for every libertine in the audience will be buzzing about her honey-pot.'[12]

Mistress Squeamish, in *The Country Wife*, jealously complained 'that men of parts, great acquaintance, and quality should take up with, and spend themselves and fortunes in keeping little playhouse creatures'. Many were kept women, and did well out of it (for as long as they were kept). As Robert Gould remarked, 'For with good rigging, though they have no skill, / They'll find out keepers, be they ne'er so ill.'[13] Jane Long, small, dark and no great beauty, who left the Duke's Company in 1673 to become mistress to George Porter, caught the attention of versifiers, notably Rochester, imagining the King saying

> When on Portsmouth's lap I lay my head
> And Knight does sing her bawdy song,
> I envy not George Porter's bed,
> Nor the delights of Madam Long.[14]

(Portsmouth is of course Louise de Kéroualle; Knight was Mary Birkhead, mistress and singer, whose brother founded the Oxford Chair of Poetry; George Porter was Gentleman of the Privy Chamber to the Queen, who left his wife and children in 1675 for Jane, and of whom Henry Savile wrote in 1677 that 'the rogue is grown so ravenous that he now surfeits of everything he sees but Mrs Long and his son Nobbs which he can never have enough on'.[15] Jane, former mistress of the Duke of Richmond – later husband of Frances Stuart – left the Duke's Company for Porter in 1673.) Among others, Mrs Uphill was kept by Sir Robert Howard and Mrs Betty Hall by Sir Philip Howard; the Earl of Peterborough looked after Mrs Johnson. Peg Hughes did very well, snapping up Charles I's gallant cavalry leader, Prince Rupert (unfortunately poxed, as Pepys noted on 15 January 1665), who installed her in a house in Hammersmith. The finest actress of them all, Elizabeth Barry, was during her teens the mistress of the Earl of Rochester, by whom she had a daughter (taken away by the father because of her poor mothering) and who trained her as an actress, when she went on to perform a hundred roles, particularly as a tragedy queen (in 1681, she starred in Nahum Tate's notorious 'happy ending' *King Lear*, in the love story of Cordelia and Edgar).

We must include here the story of one would-be virtuous young actress, Hester Davenport. A good actress, she starred as Roxalana in *The Siege of Rhodes* in 1661, and was unfortunate enough to catch the fancy of the Earl of Oxford, who pursued her passionately for eight months. At last he offered her marriage and arranged a wedding. An early account reports:

> The first night was scarcely past, when Roxalana, being still asleep, the Earl pushed her very roughly. 'Awake,' said he, 'awake, Roxalana, 'tis time to be gone.' She turning her eyes upon him, 'Why, my lord,' said she, 'do you call me Roxalana? Why must not I have the honour of being Countess of Oxford?' 'No,' he replied, 'you are not so, you are not married to me; and, to unfold the whole mystery, know, that it was my steward disguised who performed the ceremony of marriage betwixt us.' 'Oh! traitor!' cried she, taking hold of his throat, and endeavouring in that first fury to strangle him, 'thou shalt die by my hands.'[16]

She then chased him round the room with his sword, before attempting to turn it on herself. In spite of her complaints even to the King, it proved impossible to make the Earl marry her. Having been thus betrayed, she nevertheless made the best of it, continued as his mistress, and a couple of years later bore him a son, known as Aubrey de Vere, and received an annual pension of 1,000 crowns; she was always known as Roxalana. In 1673 the Earl married the very pretty Diana Kirke, who in 1682 became the mistress of Henry Sidney; her daughter Diana married Nell Gwyn's son by the King, Charles, 1st Duke of St Albans, in 1694.[17]

So much for context, the milieu from which Nell emerged. The theatres were of considerable cultural importance at this time; here all levels of society, from Royalty and members of the court, to the middle and lower classes, were together in a shared experience, able to observe each other. The plays themselves, exploring indirectly the assumptions and behaviour of their audiences, not only in the social comedies but in some tragedies (such as Rochester's *Valentinian*), mirrored, with exaggerations and distortions, their audiences' images of themselves, reflecting, questioning and serving to create a new urban society coming into being.

If she was indeed born in 1650, little Nell began her stage career at the age of thirteen. In 1663, her older sister Rose got off a charge of theft with the assistance of Harry Killigrew, Groom of the Bedchamber to the Duke of York and son of theatre owner Sir Thomas. This might be the connection that got Nelly onto the stage. Small, pert and pretty, a 'Cockney sparrow', she was 'taken in hand', as the phrase has it, and trained in dancing by John Lacy and in acting by the very successful Charles Hart.

In November 1664, Killigrew cast her in his play *Tomaso* as 'Paulina, a courtesan of the first rank'. She must have made an impression very quickly; on 3 April, Pepys referred to 'pretty witty Nell'; in March, she was in Dryden's *The Indian Emperor*. Then came the terrible plague in June 1665, devastating London life and killing some 70,000 people. The theatres had to close, causing considerable hardship to the performers. Then there was the Great Fire, in September 1666.

At last, the theatres reopened. On 23 January 1667, Mrs Knipp (or Knepp), an actress and what one might call a bosom friend of Pepys, took him and his wife backstage to the King's House, 'and brought us to Nelly, a most pretty woman, who acted the great part, Celia, today very fine, and did it pretty well; I kissed her and so did my wife, and a mighty pretty soul she is ... and so away thence, pleased with this sight also, and especially kissing of Nell'. In March, she scored a great success in Dryden's *Secret Love, or The Maiden Queen*, at the King's Theatre; the part of Florimel was written for her. One scene, where the philandering Celadon (Charles Hart) flirts with the masked Florimel, describes her:

Florimel: What kind of beauty do you like?

Celadon: Just such a one as yours.

Florimel: What's that?

Celadon (peering): Such an oval face, clear skin, hazel eyes, thick brown eyebrows, and hair as you have, for all the world. Then you have – let me see (snatches at mask).

Florimel: I'll swear you shall not see.

Celadon (after a quick look): A turned up nose that gives an air to your face. – oh, I find I am more and more in love with you! – A full nether lip, an out-mouth that makes mine water at it, the bottoms of your cheeks a little blub, and two dimples when you smile. For your stature, 'tis well; and for your wit, 'twas given

to you by one that knew it had been thrown away upon an ill
face. – Come, you're handsome, there's no denying it.

Florimel was a comic part (at which Nelly always excelled), and a
'breeches' or cross-dressing role – these were always very popular
with audiences, as it gave the opportunity of seeing the women's
legs. (The women also sought to profit – literally – from this
exposure: Elizabeth Boutell hinted, ''Tis worth money that such
legs appear, / These are not to be seen so cheap elsewhere.'[18]) On
2 March, Pepys was delighted with Nell: 'I never can hope ever to
see the like done again by man or woman. The King and Duke of
York was at the play; but so great a performance of a comical part
was never, I believe, in the world before …'

On May Morning, a day of traditional festivities, Pepys walked
through Westminster, 'on the way meeting many milkmaids with their
garlands upon their pails, dancing with a fiddler before them, and
saw pretty Nelly standing at her lodgings door in Drury Lane in her
smock-sleeves and bodice, looking upon one – she seemed a mighty
pretty creature.' She soon became a popular star. In Buckingham's
epilogue to Fletcher's *The Chances*, in which she performed,

> … the author dreads the strut and mien
> Of new-praised poets, having often seen
> Some of his fellows who have writ before,
> When Nell has danced her jig, steal to the door,
> Hear the pit clap, and with conceit of that
> Swell, and believe themselves the Lord knows what.[19]

About this time, Buckingham, seeking to replace Barbara, Lady
Castlemaine, with more manageable mistresses for the King, and
his friends, Colonel Thomas and Sir Robert Howard, came up
with a couple of theatre wenches, Nell Gwyn and Moll Davis.
Moll (Mary) Davis was reputedly an illegitimate daughter of
Colonel Howard and an actress in Davenant's company at the
Duke's Theatre. In March 1668 she appeared in Davenant's play
The Rivals, and Pepys praised her dancing as better than Nell's.
She had a song in the play that was a great success:

My lodging it is on the cold ground,
And very hard is my fare,
But that which troubles me most is
The unkindness of my dear;
Yet still I cry, O turn, love,
And I prithee love turn to me,
For thou art the man that I long for,
And alack what remedy ...[20]

It was found very affecting, especially by the King; she could sing, dance and play the guitar (and was painted with one, by Lely[21]). Soon (as Pepys heard on 11 January 1668), the King had raised her from the cold ground to a royal bed, given her an expensive ring, a pension of £1,000 and put her in a house in Suffolk Street. Nelly marked her early rivalry with a song in James Howard's comedy *The Mad Couple*, lamenting a fat lover:

My lodging is on the cold boards,
And wonderful hard is my fare,
But that which troubles me most is
The fatness of my dear.
Yet still I cry, oh melt love,
And I prithee now melt apace,
For thou art the man I should long for
If 'twere not for thy grease.[22]

The parody and minor theatre-war aroused great amusement. Nelly had a significant success in the play with another cross-dressing part, this time wearing 'rhinegraves', loose, very full-cut breeches, open at the bottom, very likely to flap up and show the thighs as she had to roll about the stage to get away from her fat suitor rolling after her. Charles Sackville, Lord Buckhurst, was a delighted spectator and decided to take her away from Hart, who, as Etherege noted,

More manners had than not to tender,
When noble Buckhurst begged him to surrender.
He saw her roll the stage from side to side,

> And through her drawers the powerful charm descried.
> 'Take her, my Lord,' quoth Hart, 'since you're so mean
> To take a player's leavings for your queen.
> For though I love her well, yet as she's poor,
> I'm well contented to prefer [promote] the whore.'[23]

On 12 June, the Dutch raided up the Medway, causing a general panic and the temporary closure of the theatres, and Buckhurst took her away to Epsom with his friend the notorious Lord Sedley. To what extent it was a true *ménage à trois* is unknown; on 13 July Pepys was told that 'my Lord Buckhurst hath got Nell away from the King's House, lies with her, and gives her £100 a year, so as she hath sent her parts to the House and will act no more'. As to what went on at Epsom, a lampoon written in 1687 speculated pruriently,

> To Buckhurst thus resigned in friendly wise,
> He takes her swinge and sometimes lends her thighs
> To bestial Buckingham's transcendent prick,
> And sometimes witty Wilmot had a lick. [Rochester]
> And thus she traded in a noble ware,
> Serving the rest with what her Lord could spare;
> For Buckhurst was Lord of the Hairy Manor,
> The rest were only tenants to his honour.[24]

While it seems just possible that young Nelly was so used by Buckhurst and his friends, and Buckingham and Rochester later became her friends, she herself, in a quarrel that October with another actress, Beck Marshall, who called her 'my Lord Buckhurst's whore', retorted, 'I was but one man's whore, though I was brought up in a bawdyhouse to fill strong waters to the guests; and you are a whore to three or four, though a Presbyter's praying daughter.'[25]

Whatever went on there, it did not last long, and Nell was soon back at the theatre. On 26 August Orange Moll confided in Pepys that 'Nell is already left by my Lord Buckhurst, and that he makes sport of her, and swears that she hath had all she could get of him; and Hart, her great admirer, now hates her; and that she is very poor, and hath lost my Lady Castlemaine, who was her great friend also; but she is come to the House, but is neglected by them all'. Perhaps she would not oblige all of Buckhurst's friends, or he would not pay her enough, while her former colleagues resented her assumption that she could just come back again. On 5 October Mary Knipp took Pepys and his wife backstage again

> into the tiring-room and to the women's shift, where Nell was dressing herself and was all unready; and is very pretty, prettier than I thought ... and then below into the scene-room, and there set down and she gave us fruit; and here I read the cues to Knipp and she answered me ... but lord, to see how they were both painted would make a man mad – and did make me loathe them – and what base company of men comes amongst them, and how lewdly they talk ...

Nelly was starting to get noticed by the King; that year, he and the Duke of York sat in a box next to hers, where she was the guest of another Mr Villiers. The story ran that they went on to supper at a tavern, but when it was time to pay, neither Charles nor the Duke, in true royal fashion, had money on him, so the luckless Villiers had to pay for all; Nell was reputed to have commented, using the King's favourite oath, "Ods fish! But this is the poorest company that ever I was in before at a tavern.'[26]

Moll Davis had been brought in, in accordance with Buckingham's scheme. Now Nelly was acquired, after a little difficulty about how much she was to be paid, and Pepys was told that 'the King did send several times for Nelly, and she was with him ... The King first spoiled Mrs Weaver [another actress]'. At the time, Charles was very actively cutting a swathe through the actresses – Nelly, Moll, Elizabeth Weaver, Mrs Knight and many more. As for Nell, she remarked cheerfully that, after Charles Hart and Charles Sackville, the King was, for her, Charles III – which rather put him in his place. Buckingham's involvement, no great secret, was noted in *The Lady of Pleasure*, in characteristic fashion:

> Damn me, quoth Buckingham, in duty bound
> Am I to give your kingship counsel sound.
> I wonder you should dote so, like a fop,

On Cleveland's cunt which all her footmen grope:
D'you think you don't your parliament offend
That all you give, you on a baggage spend;
Permit me, Sir, to help you to a whore,
Fuck her but once, you'll ne'er fuck Cleveland more;
She'll fit you to a hair, all wit, all fire,
And impudence to your heart's desire;
And more than this, Sir, you'll save money by her ...
    [As it was, she did not come entirely free: the King
    in effect bought her from her previous owner]
'Soft, quoth Lord Buckhurst, then first pay my score,
She cost me many a pound, then take the whore.'
Old Rowley knew his meaning, and to lay his itch
Gave him an earldom to resign the bitch.[27]

The King made Buckhurst a Gentleman of the Bedchamber, worth £1,000 a year, and granted several lands with good rents; later Buckhurst became Earl of Dorset. Moll was now set up on the north side of Pall Mall, while Nelly, after a brief residence in Lincoln's Inn Fields, moved into No. 79, on the south side, overlooking the park. The competition between them could be fierce. Alexander Smith, in 1716, recorded a story of how, at one time,

Nell Gwyn having notice that Miss Davis was to be entertained at night [by the King] in his bedchamber, she invited the lady to a collation of sweetmeats, which being made up with physic ingredients, the effects thereof had such an operation upon the harlot, when the King was caressing her in bed with the amorous sports of Venus, that a violent and sudden looseness obliging her ladyship to discharge her artillery, she made the King, as well as herself, in a most lamentable pickle, which caused her royal master to turn her off ...[28]

J. G. Turner suggests that a similar story is to be found in Boccaccio and the sixteenth-century *Tariffa delle puttane di Venegia*,[29] but there seems to be some truth in the story, as *An Heroic Poem* of 1681 says that Bab May, Keeper of the Privy Purse, 'still keeps cast shitten Moll at the King's charge';[30] he also kept Lely's portrait of her with a guitar. Moll did not get 'turned off' for some time, got an annual pension of £1,000 and in 1672 bore Charles a daughter (Lady Mary Tudor, who went on to marry the Earl of Derwentwater). She herself was no pushover physically: there was a story of when, on a visit with Charles to Newmarket, a Colonel Abercromby spoke to her disrespectfully, she challenged him to a duel, which the colonel accepted. Dressed in men's clothes, she wounded him in the left shoulder. The colonel composed the quarrel and gave her 1,000 guineas in compensation.[31] She may have left the stage in 1668, but Nell continued for a few more years.

Nelly's fame even burst through dramatic convention in Dryden's *Tyrannic Love* in June 1669, which dealt with the martyrdom of St Catherine – a tactful gesture towards the Queen. In this melodramatic tragedy, to which she was not suited, she played Valeria, who stabs herself in the final scene. At the end, as she was about to be carried off, dead, she arose:

> *To the bearer:*
> Hold, are you mad? You damned confounded dog,
> I am to rise, and speak the epilogue.
> *To the audience:* I come, kind gentlemen, strange news to tell ye,
> I am the ghost of poor departed Nelly.
> Sweet ladies, be not frighted, I'll be civil,
> I'm what I was, a little harmless devil ...
> To tell you true, I walk because I die
> Out of my calling in a tragedy.
> O poet, damned dull poet, who could prove
> So senseless to make Nelly die for love! ...
> But farewell, gentlemen, make haste to me,
> I'm sure ere long to have your company.
> As for my epitaph when I am gone,
> I'll trust no poet, but will write my own:
> Here Nelly lies, who though she lived a slattern,
> Yet died a princess, acting in St Cathar'n.[32]

By now, she was a frequent visitor in the King's private bedroom.

Sir Francis Fane, occasional dramatist and friend of Rochester, told a story of how, in the summer of 1669, the King pretended to be a little unwell, in order to spend some more time in bed with her. One morning, the Queen decided to come round to see how he was, only just giving time for Nelly to slip out of bed 'in her nightgown and with one slipper on', and hide behind the wall hangings. The King genially invited the Queen to sit and chat for a while, but when she saw one slipper lying by the bed, she said, 'Me will not stay, for fear the pretty fool that owns that little slipper might take cold.' Her own hurt feelings are not recorded. The lost slipper fits well with the Cinderella legend, while a loose slipper was often taken to imply that the wearer was loose sexually.[33]

Another, more public, incident (made famous by a painting by Edward Matthew Ward in 1854), was recorded by John Evelyn, how he was walking with the King through the park past the houses in Pall Mall,

> when I both saw and heard a very familiar discourse between [the King] and Mrs Nelly as they called an impudent comedian, she being out of her garden on a terrace at the top of the wall, and [the King] standing on the green walk under it: I was heartily sorry for this scene: thence the King walked to the Duchess of Cleveland, another Lady of Pleasure and curse of our nation.[34]

Ward makes it look a very pleasant interlude. As Evelyn noted, Charles was still involved with Barbara, and about this time Lely did a frank nude portrait of Nelly, but a new player had arrived on the scene: Louise de Kéroualle.

During the secret negotiations of the Treaty of Dover, Charles's sister offered him a jewel as a thank-you present, when, according to legend, he said that pretty, chubby-cheeked Louise was the only jewel he wanted: could not Minette leave her behind? Replying that she was responsible to her parents, Henriette declined, and so they parted – for the last time. After her death that summer, Buckingham was sent over for the funeral and to negotiate a sham treaty (minus Charles's promise to become a Catholic, of which he was ignorant). While he was in Paris it was agreed that he should bring back Louise as a Maid of Honour to the Queen and present for the King (and agent on behalf of France). Buckingham had intended that Louise should be his ally but failed to escort her properly across the Channel, so making an enemy of her, though Arlington sent a yacht for her. (Last instance of telling this story.)

Louise-Renée de Penancoët de Kéroualle was born in September 1649 in Brittany to the Comte de Kéroualle, of an aristocratic but relatively impoverished family. In 1668 the Duke of Beaufort took her over, some said as his page-'boy', and got her made Maid of Honour to Henriette; there were suggestions that in return she was briefly his mistress – so thought Mme de Sévigné – and also, in 1669, of the Comte de Sault.[35] Years later, *A Satire* complained that, to get on at court, one had to

> Exalt my Lady Portsmouth's wit
> And vow she's only for a monarch fit –
> Although the fawning coxcombs know
> She's lain with Beaufort and the Count de Sault.[36]

Her family was anglophile, and her position with Charles's sister gave her associations with England. She soon agreed to the proposition put to her and was quickly set up in Whitehall. Dryden – of course – wrote some grovelling verses, but in general she was not welcomed, being French and Catholic.

The native mistresses, widely disapproved of on grounds of morality and public expense, were themselves the subjects of abuse and scandal. Notably, when in December 1670 the question of the imposition of taxes on the theatre was in debate in Parliament, the court party opposed the measure, as 'the players were the King's servants and a part of his pleasure'. For the 'opposition', one rash MP, Sir John Coventry, inquired, 'whether the King's pleasure lay among the men or the women that acted. Was it not known that the King had two harlots, Nell Gwyn and Moll Davis, in keeping?' This moralist insolence was too much for some at court; on the very night of Parliament being adjourned, a gang of Monmouth's King's Guards waylaid him near the Haymarket and slit his nose, to general outrage.

Early in 1671 appeared an angry *Ballad called the Haymarket Hectors*:

Our good King Charles the Second
Too flippant of treasure and moisture,
Stooped from the Queen infecund
To a wench of orange and oyster.
Consulting his cazzo, he found it expedient [penis]
To engender Don Johns on Nell the comedian ... [she gave birth in
    1670]
And he, our amorous Jove,
Whilst she lay dry-bobbed under, [unsatisfied]
To repair the defects of his love,
Must lend her his lightning and thunder;
And for one night prostitutes to her commands
Monmouth, his Life Guards, O'Brien and Sandys. [the Guards
    officers]
And now all the fears of the French
And pressing need of navy
Are dwindled into a salt wench
And *amo, amas, amavi.*
Nay, he'll venture his subsidy, so she may cloven see
In female revenge, the nostrils of Coventry. ...

But was it not ungrateful
In Monmouth, ap Sidney, ap Carlo, [suggested alternative fathers
    for Monmouth]
To contrive an act so hateful,

O Prince of Wales by Barlow?
Since the kind world has dispensed with his mother,
Might he not well have spared the nose of John Brother?

If the sister of Rose [Nell]
Be a whore so anointed
That the Parliament's nose
Must for her be disjointed,

Should you but name the prerogative whore,
How the bullets would whistle, the cannon would roar![37]

The writer suggests that the King was responsible; it seems unlikely that Nelly herself was at all responsible for the attack as it was not her style. The casual immorality and corruption of the 'merry monarch's' court were widely resented and not just by dismounted puritans.

With all this sort of thing going on, Mlle Kéroualle was not happy with the prospect of being just another mistress among others and held off for some time, despite Charles's efforts at wooing her and the discreet urgings of the French ambassadors. One admirer was the writer Charles Marguetel, Seigneur de Saint-Evremond, living as a sort of courtly, intellectual pimp. He wrote an encouraging piece:

Happy the woman who can discreetly manage her affairs without denying her desires. For even if there is scandal loving without reserve, it is a heavy hardship to go through life without love! Do not repulse temptations too severely – perhaps you are vain enough to be pleased only with yourself; but you will soon get tired of pleasing and loving yourself; and, whatever satisfaction you get from vanity, you will need another's love if your life is to be truly enjoyable. And so let yourself go into the sweets of temptation instead of listening to your pride. Your pride will make you return to France, and France will throw you, as has happened to so many others, into a convent.[38]

In September 1671, at a dinner, Louise briefly fainted, arousing speculations that she was pregnant, but at that time, this was not possible. As Ambassador Colbert told Louis, 'Her conduct while she was here and since she has been in England gave no grounds for belief that such good fortune would befall her so soon,'[39] but in October he reported, 'I believe I may assure you that if she makes sufficient progress in her friendship with the King to be able to serve His Majesty in any way, she will do her duty.'[40] She felt entitled to proceed at a slower pace, perhaps hanging on for the Queen's departure, one way or another.

Others would not wait. In October, de Croissy met with Lord and

Lady Arlington (the latter, it has been suggested, rather improbably, 'lived a lewd and shameless life. She belonged, with Harry Killigrew, her husband's secretary, and his wife, to a sort of club, the Ballers, whose members gathered to drink and then dance naked'.[41] It does seem that her association with the notorious Killigrew may have jaundiced the writer's view). A recent writer describes her as 'a skilful hostess, as serious and discreet as her husband'.[42] Nevertheless, it appears that together, 'with malice aforethought', they set up a large house party at Euston Hall, near Newmarket, the Arlingtons' country residence, for the King, de Croissy, a great many members of the court and, especially, Louise. John Evelyn was also there, who described how his fellow guests spent the mornings hunting and hawking and then playing cards and dice until very late, 'I must say without noise, swearing or confusion of any sort'. The mansion was magnificent, in the style of a French château (which would have pleased Louise), with fresco paintings by the Baroque artist Antonio Verrio in the King's apartment and hall and stairs, a chapel, a library and orange garden. Evelyn wrote that

> the whole house [was] filled from one end to the other with lords, ladies and gallants; there was such a furnished table as I had seldom seen, nor anything more splendid and free, so that [for] fifteen days there were entertained at least two hundred people, and half as many horses, besides servants and guards, at infinite expense.[43]

De Croissy reported that the King spent a lot of time with Louise, and 'small attentions which denote a great passion were lavished on her; and as she showed by her expressions of gratitude that she was not insensible to the kindness of a great king, we hope she will so behave that the attachment will be durable and exclude every other.'[44] Charles was never exclusive but determined, and with the help of the Arlingtons, de Croissy and Lady Sunderland, he got her. First she was put in a bed, and then he came to her. Evelyn recorded that

> It was universally reported that the fair lady was bedded one of these nights, and the stocking flung, after the manner of a married

bride; I acknowledge she was for the most part in her undress [in negligée and without stays] all day, and that there was fondness and toying with that young woman; nay, 'twas said, I was at the former ceremony, but 'tis utterly false; I neither saw nor heard of any such thing whilst I was there, tho' I had been in her chamber, and all over that apartment late enough; and was myself observing all passages made with curiosity enough; however 'twas with confidence believed that she was first made a *Miss*, as they call these unhappy creatures, with solemnity at this time.[45]

(G. D. Gilbert, in a note in his edition of Mme d'Aulnoy's *Memoirs*, suggests that the origin of 'miss' for a mistress/prostitute was from the Dutch, '*Meisje-van-pleizier*'.)

Louise did not like to think of herself as in any way socially or morally downgraded by her surrender, being reported to have said, 'Me no bad woman. If me taut me was one bad woman, me would cut my own trote.' Sometime later, she said that she was just as much the King's wife as the Queen, only she was not married by a bishop.[46] Her idea was that she should be recognised as the *maîtresse en titre*, a respected title in the French court. This in the context of the Newmarket party, where, as it went on, Evelyn later found 'jolly blades racing, dancing, feasting and revelling, more resembling a luxurious and abandoned rout than a Christian court'.[47] By 2 November, de Croissy wrote, 'I have given Mlle de Kéroualle much pleasure by telling her that his Majesty will be very pleased if she keeps in the good graces of the King'.[48] Meanwhile, Louis rewarded 'serious and discreet' Lady Arlington with a diamond necklace and £10,000.

The next year, 1672, was busy, notably with Charles's Declaration of Indulgence, to abolish discrimination against nonconformists and Catholics, followed by declaration of war against the Dutch. Louise had her first baby on 29 July (among the four that Charles had that year) – not yet formally acknowledged, but soon to become Charles Lennox. In December, the King granted her a pension of £10,000 from revenues from Irish lands. She was starting to have some influence in court affairs – curly hair like hers and French fashions were to be seen; among his women, she was the only one to show any interest in politics. Nelly had none, as a popular ballad declared:

> Hard by Pall Mall lives a wench called Nell,
> King Charles the Second he kept her.
> She hath a trick to handle his prick,
> But never lays hands on his sceptre.

> All matters of state from her soul she does hate,
> And leaves to the politic bitches.
> The whore's in the right, for 'tis her delight
> To be scratching just where it itches.[49]

Louise had been brought up at court and knew how to intervene discreetly; discussions between the Dukes of York and Lauderdale and Clifford took place in her residence, and she may have been one of those who advised Charles to appease Parliament by revoking the Declaration of Indulgence. On 25 July 1673, she was made a Lady of the Queen's Bedchamber (against Catherine's wishes) and, more important, Duchess of Portsmouth, Lady Petersfield and Countess of Fareham (while applying to change her nationality). Nelly was jealous and angry, wanting some equivalent acknowledgement and title; taking the King at his casual word, she arranged for patents to be drawn up to make her the Countess of Plymouth, but the King refused, saying it had been only a jest, much to her chagrin. Her low origins would always militate against her being raised to the peerage.

Madame de Sévigné took an interest in English court affairs and commented shrewdly on Louise's situation:

Mademoiselle de Kéroualle has been disappointed in nothing; she wished to be mistress of the King, and she is so. He takes up his abode with her almost every night in the face of the whole Court; she has had a son, who has been acknowledged and presented with two duchies. She amasses treasure, and makes herself feared and respected as much as she can. But she did not foresee that she should find a young actress in her way, whom the King dotes on; and she has it not in her power to withdraw him from her. He divides his care, his time and his health between these two. The actress is as haughty as the Duchess of Portsmouth; she insults her, makes faces at her, attacks her, frequently steals the King from her, and boasts of his preference for her. She is young, indiscreet, confident, meretricious and pleasant; she sings, dances and acts her part well. She has a son by the King, and wishes to have him acknowledged. She reasons thus, The Duchess claims to be a person of quality.

She claims that everyone in France is her relation; whenever any person of distinction dies, she puts on mourning. Well, if she is of such high quality, why does she play the whore? She ought to die of shame. As for me, it's my profession; I do not pretend to be anything else. The King keeps me, and I am constant to him at present. He has given me a son; I claim he ought to acknowledge him and I am sure he will, for he loves me as much as his Portsmouth ... I like these original characters.[50]

Nell counter-attacked whenever she could. One of their encounters is recorded when Nelly was looking particularly fine. Said Portsmouth, 'Nelly, you are grown rich, I believe, by your dress; why, woman, you are fine enough to be a queen.' Riposted Mistress Nelly, 'You are entirely right, madam, and I am whore enough to be a duchess.'[51] It was never a good idea to condescend to Nelly. She was consistently hostile to Louise – 'Squintabella', she called her, on account of a slight cast in one eye, and 'the weeping willow', because of Louise's tendency to weep when at all distressed or thwarted. When the Chevalier de Rohan, a French aristocrat, was beheaded for his part in a minor uprising, Louise went into mourning. The next day, Nelly appeared at court dressed in similar fashion. When asked why, she declared, with a great display of grief, 'The Cham of Tartary is dead, and he was as close to me as the Chevalier de Rohan was to the Duchess of Portsmouth.'[52]

Another, probably apocryphal story – though revelatory of the stories told of Nelly and Louise (and remembering that Nell was brought up in a rough school) – appeared in Smith's *The School of Venus* (1716), and relates that once falling out with the Duchess of Portsmouth, in a scuffle betwixt them, Nell having Squintabella on the floor (her Grace being so called from a cast she had in her eyes) and taking up her coats, she burned with a candle all the hair off those parts which modesty obliges to conceal. The King angrily reproved her, but she replied, 'May it please your Majesty, that as there is an Act of Parliament for burning all French commodities that are prohibited, she hoped he could not be angry at her care in putting the Act in force.'[53]

If there is any truth at all in the story, the King might have been amused; on one occasion, having been informed of one of Nell's pranks, he declared that he would not deny himself such diversions for any man or woman living.[54]

In the meantime, Parliament continued to press the King as regards Catholics, and, despite his earlier promises to Louis, in 1673 he was forced to approve the anti-Catholic Test Act. Lord Clifford had to be replaced as Lord Treasurer by Sir Thomas Osborne (later the Earl of Danby), who was initially keen to reform the royal budget. The royal mistresses were an obvious target: Barbara received £6,000 a year and £3,000 a year for each of her three sons, Louise and her son received £8,600 and Nell, a former orange-girl and actress, £4,000 plus £1,000 for her children. He soon stopped the warrants for captured Dutch goods to be transferred to Kéroualle, Gwyn and Cleveland. When the King told Nell he had no money for her, she replied, 'I will tell you how you shall never want. Send the French into France again, set me on the stage again, and lock up your own codpiece.'[55]

When Parliament met again on 20 October, there was the familiar struggle about money, with complaints about the choice of Catholic Mary of Modena as the Duke of York's second wife, together with fears of a standing army and complaints about the cost of the King's mistresses (Moll Davis gave birth on 19 October), and with threats that there would be no money unless these grievances were addressed. Now, about this time (as the story has it[56]), Louise set up a costly banquet for Charles; when it was nearly dawn, he was taken into a private room where Louise and 'two other great ladies' paraded naked before him, like the three goddesses before Paris, to be thoroughly examined. After some more drinking, they played 'Questions and Commands', in which Louise got him to admit that he would prefer to govern without Parliament, and that Louis XIV, an absolute monarch, was 'the happiest monarch in the world'. According to the story, she told him to prorogue Parliament, which, the next day, he did. Actually Parliament had been about to impeach Lord Lauderdale, Charles's right-hand man in Scotland, which was what led the King to prorogue Parliament. With no money coming from Parliament and no new subsidies from Louis, Charles had to withdraw from his French alliance and make peace with Holland on 9 February 1674.

By now Danby was better disposed towards Louise and allowed her money for an £8,000 pearl necklace and 3,000-guinea earrings; predictably, and not wholly unreasonably, gossip suggested that this was for favours received. The King himself also gave her something: a dose of the clap, presumably acquired from one of his more casual acquaintances, brought up the back stairs to his private chamber by William Chiffinch (Keeper of the King's Closet). On 14 May 1674, the French ambassador wrote to the French Foreign Minister:

> While the King [Louis] was winning provinces, the King of England was catching a malady which he has been at the trouble of communicating to the Duchess of Portsmouth. That prince is nearly cured, but to all appearance the lady will not so soon be rid of the virus. She has, however, in a degree been consoled for such a troublesome present by one more suitable to her charms – a pearl necklace worth four thousand jacobus, and a diamond worth six thousand, which have so rejoiced her that I should not wonder if she were not willing to risk another attack of the disease.[57]

Louise's avarice was by now well known.

Wounded in body and spirit (though not greatly), Louise went off to Tunbridge Wells for the healthful waters. Here, she found that the house she wished to rent was already occupied by the Marchioness of Worcester. Louise claimed precedence as Duchess, only for Lady Worcester to respond that prostitution conferred no privilege, refusing to budge. Louise complained to the King, who did no more than send some of the Household Guards to escort her to Windsor, where Nell was already in favour, to finish her cure there (no doubt in tears).

In that same month, her sister Henriette came over, eager to join in the pickings and was given a pension of £600. Soon she struck up a relationship with Philip, Earl of Pembroke, a violent, brutal man and the nastiest nobleman she could have found, and married him that December. In September 1675, when Louise complained that he had not made appropriate provision for his wife's lying-in and threatened to complain to the King, he in turn threatened to set her on her head with her skirts turned back so that everyone might see the cause of England's grief. This idea may not have been entirely his own invention: John Garfield wrote in the 1660s of the whore Priss Fotheringham who 'stood upon her head with naked breech and belly whilst four cully-rumpers chucked in sixteen half-crowns into her commodity'.[58] It is no wonder that there was a 'growing sense that the twin extremes of society, the court and the brothel, mirrored each other disturbingly',[59] as sex was traded for money at every level.

9

THE NEW PRETENDER: MAZARIN

In November 1675, after a storm in the Channel, a small ship anchored in the choppy waters of Sole Bay. From it emerged another, smaller storm – what appeared to be a dashing young man, but was actually an even more dashing young woman, scandalously dressed in men's clothes. This was the twenty-nine-year-old Hortense Mancini, Countess Mazarin, ready to cut a swathe through the English court and especially into the heart of the King. Accompanied by only a handful of servants and a black pageboy, rescued from a Mediterranean corsair, she made her way on horseback to Lady Elizabeth Harvey, in Covent Garden, and then to the residence of her cousin, Mary of Modena, the Duchess of York. Ostensibly she had come on a family visit, but this was a mere fetch to obscure the plans of the English ambassador to France, Ralph Montagu, who hoped she would oust the Duchess of Portsmouth from the King's bed and favour and further his own career in displacing the Earl of Danby.

There seemed a very good chance that she could bring this off – lively, highly experienced in all the necessary arts, magnificent, flamboyant, more glamorous than baby-faced Kéroualle, with black, curled hair, Roman nose and remarkable eyes. One dazzled admirer wrote that 'the colour of her eyes has no name, it is neither blue, nor grey, nor altogether black, but a mixture of all three, which participates of all the excellence that is found in them. They have the sweetness of the blue, the briskness of the grey, and, above all, the fire of the black'.[1]

In addition, she and Charles had had some dealings before, in 1659, when Henrietta Maria had been trying to find a rich wife for her cash-strapped son. Born in Rome in 1646, the daughter of Lorenzo Mancini and niece of the great French statesman, the Cardinal Mazarin, Hortense had had great expectations; at that time the cardinal did not rate Henrietta Maria's bid and Charles's hopes highly, and nothing came of it. By May 1660, when Charles became King, it was too late (despite the cardinal's gift of 20,000 *livres*): the King had to marry royalty. It would have been a remarkable marriage: her tempestuous nature would have stirred up the court and English politics and changed history. As it was, her career before Charles was to make her notorious; it is certainly entertaining and worth reviewing (like her predecessors').

In her youth, Hortense had had to hang around in Paris; marriage to the Duke of Savoy or a Portuguese prince was considered and the Comte de Coligny was in the offing. Then, in 1661, Armand Charles de la Porte, Marquis de la Meillerage, proposed (remarkably, and perhaps worryingly, he claimed to have fallen in love with her back in 1655, when she would have been about nine), and the cardinal approved, requiring only that the marquis took the title Duc Mazarin, and bequeathing on his death, that March, enormous wealth: 28 million *livres*, together with most of the Palais Mazarin and stacks of works of art (Titian, Raphael, Correggio ...).

Life at the Palais Mazarin should have been good, with a handsome husband and too much money; once, she threw 300 *pistoles* (gold coins each worth about £1) out of a palace window for the pleasure of watching the servants in the courtyard below scramble for them.[2] However, the Duc soon became obsessively jealous of his beautiful wife (especially in relation to Louis XIV, who had had Hortense's older sister as a mistress), even introducing a woman spy into her household. He took to having night-time visions, when the Archangel Gabriel came to advise him; fearing the unreliability of his staff, he made them draw lots to determine their places (God, he declared, knew best who most deserved to be a footman or cook or secretary). Sexual-religious neuroses developed, as women and girls were forbidden to milk cows in case that prompted sexual thoughts (presumably he was not so concerned about the men); he painted over nudes by Titian and Corregio, naked figures in costly tapestries were hacked and sliced and he was going to hammer off offending bits from nude statues in the park, but his Sunday day of rest gave the King time to put in a guard to prevent him. It became wrong for Hortense to drive out in her carriage in public or go to a play, to play at blind man's buff (an addiction among seventeenth-century court young ladies) or to go to bed late.[3]

Hortense ran away to her brother at Soissons and then to her sister Marianne, Duchesse de Bouillon. The King tried to reconcile Hortense and Armand, but in vain. Soon she found herself put into a nunnery of the Abbey of Chelles; here she was joined by the boisterous scapegrace fifteen-year-old Sidonie, Marquise de Courcelles, who helped her in tormenting the poor nuns. In her memoirs she wrote how they 'used to put ink in the holy water to smut the good old nuns ... used to run through their dormitory at the hour of their first sleep, with a great many dogs, yelping', [4] and put two large vats of water over the nuns' dormitory that overflowed onto the nuns' beds. Despite all this, the abbess refused to let her husband have her.

Eventually, she and Courcelles got away through a gap in a grating; Courcelles went off with her admirer, but Hortense had to go back to the Palais Mazarin. Armand's obsessive interference and jealousy continued, not without some cause, it would seem, as two noblemen fought a duel over her, and Louis gave up on his attempts at reconciliation. Armand had attempted to nail her down with frequent pregnancies: she had three daughters and a son during her seven years with him, but there was no restraining her.

In June 1668, with the help of her brother and the Chevalier de Rohan, she ran off again, to Milan, sending for her jewels, which Armand had taken, to be sent on to her. International court gossip was full of her, and Charles wrote to his sister, Minette, the Duchesse d'Orléans:

> The sudden retraite of Madame Mazarin is as extraordinaire an action as I have heard. She has exceeded my Lady Shrewsbury in point of discretion by robbing her husband. I see wives do not love devout husbands, which reason this woman had, besides many more as I hear, to be rid of her husband upon any terms, and so I wish her a good journey.[5]

Hortense and her maid, Nanon, were in men's clothes, accompanied by her brother's man and a gentleman named Courbeville. The Duke of Lorraine helped her on to Switzerland; despite their male disguise, the women's long hair gave them away, as in the inns 'the people watched us through the keyhole, when we had shut ourselves in, and saw our long tresses'.[6] Hortense engaged in vigorous games and horseplay with Nanon, during which she hurt her knee very painfully and had to continue her journey in a litter, while Courbeville attended to her other needs. They reached Milan, where they were put up by her brother-in-law, Prince Colonna, Constable of Naples, and joined by her brother, the Duc de Nevers, who quarrelled with them about her relationship with Courbeville; in Venice, Nevers got Courbeville imprisoned, but she had him released.

Staying in the home of an aunt, she heard just in time that Armand was trying to get her shut in a nunnery, so she moved on to another convent, where another aunt was the abbess. She wrote to Armand that she might be willing to return, but when he insisted she stay in a nunnery for two years, she again got away with her maid, with the help of her sister Marie Colonna, who, perhaps inspired by Hortense, had left her husband to accompany her. At some time about now, she became pregnant. 'Courbeville was probably responsible for her condition, though doubtless many a gallant cavalier could have claimed the honour of the infant's paternity, for during this stay in Italy she conducted a host of intrigues,' wrote her biographer.[7] Nothing is known of any results of this pregnancy.

Now short of money and moving on slowly, Hortense had to sell or pawn many of her jewels. King Louis gave her a choice of living in France with her husband or returning to Italy with a pension of 24,000 *livres*; she did not choose France. Help was at hand, as the Chevalier de Lorraine (brother of the Duc d'Orléans) and the Comte de Marsan took up with Marie and Hortense respectively, much to the anger of Constable Colonna. In May 1672, they left Rome, dressed in men's clothes (as so often) and with concealed pistols, for Civita Vecchia and then for Provence and Marseilles (Savoy was then separate from France).

The Duke of Savoy (her former suitor) now welcomed Hortense, and she resided in Chambéry for three years (without Maria). Here she had her own little court, mixing church-going with masked balls, games of blind man's buff and shooting practice with pistols given her by the Duke. This was where she was given the young Moorish boy Mustapha, who became her favourite pet, taking him everywhere and swimming with him in the lake at Aix. Here also she dictated her memoirs to her lover, one César Vicard, who called himself the Abbé de St-Réal. All was going well until the Duke died in June 1675, when his widow indicated that her early departure would be very welcome. And then came the invitation from Ralph Montagu, who had encountered her earlier, to visit her dear, if distant, cousin and there try her luck.

That autumn, Hortense initially stayed in the household of the Duchess of York until the Duke put her in a house in St James's Park and immediately caused a stir in London society. Her story had gone before her, and everyone remarked on her beauty, 'the men with admiration, the women with jealousy and alarm'.[8] Predictably, Gramont and Buckingham (who even took her to Bartholomew Fair) were quickest off the mark. Everyone knew what to expect. A burlesque of 1675 presented a *Coffee-house conversation*, in which the first 'coffist' observed that

'Since our good king, with all his good parts, has a weak side towards women ... I think it much more honourable for Great Britain to have its monarch subdued by a famous Roman dame, than by an obscure damsel of Little Britain [Louise] or by a frisking

comedian.' His French acquaintance replied (in French): 'The
Duchess Mazarin is truly so charming, that if your King kisses her
only once, I hold her of Portsmouth *foutue*.'⁹

(Coffee houses were becoming extremely popular among gentlemen
– *not* ladies – for conversations, often about political matters. By
1663 there were at least eighty-two in London and probably several
hundred by this time. As a customer, one paid a penny entrance
fee and a penny-halfpenny per dish. Many had back rooms where
young women awaited one's pleasure – often indicated by a
sign of a woman's arm holding a coffee pot. In 1675 there was
a government proclamation by the Privy Council against coffee
houses, but to no avail.)

Her first friend was the writer and conversationalist, the Seigneur
de St-Evremond, exiled for criticism of Cardinal Mazarin but now
a fervent admirer of the cardinal's niece. He was responsible for
a welcoming verse which could have won her few friends among
the ladies:

> Fair beauties of Whitehall give way,
> Hortensia does her charms display;
> She comes, she comes! Resign the day –
> She must reign, and you obey.¹⁰

For all this, Charles was slow to respond or yield to her well
advertised attractions, though he met her every day in the Duchess
of York's bedchamber, during that lady's confinement. Glamorous
and challenging though she was, she was not yet dressed to
maximum advantage, but still partially dependent on her cousin.
The French ambassador Ruvigny wrote to Louis to urge him to
persuade her husband to increase her pension: if she could get
money from Charles, she would not be grateful to, or work for,
France. However, Armand would not pay for his wife to stay and
live it up in England; he was prepared to have her back in France if
she lived quietly in the Abbaye de Montmartre, while she would go
only if she had her own household, had her jewels and furniture,
an allowance of 60,000 *francs* and would not have to receive him.

A new ambassador, Honoré de Courtin, urged Louis to either bring her back to France, or support her in England. Her most recent lover, César Vicard, was now in England and opposed her return to France, and so she stayed.

The Hortense-Charles affair developed slowly but surely. The good summer of 1676 allowed for plenty of entertainments; Charles was frequently away from his chamber at night, until the early hours. About this time, Edmund Waller sought to please (and profit) with *The Triple Combat*, a comment on the glamour competition at court:

> When thro' the world fair Mazarine had run,
> Bright as her fellow-traveller, the sun,
> Hither at length the Roman eagle flies,
> As the last triumph of her conqu'ring eyes.
> As heir to Julius, she may pretend
> A second time to make this island bend.
> But Portsmouth, springing from the ancient race
> Of Britons, which the Saxons here did chase,
> As they great Caesar did oppose, makes head,
> And does against this new invader lead ...
> Venus had been an equal friend to both,
> And Vict'ry to declare herself seems loth:
> Over the camp with doubtful wings she flies,
> Till Chloris shining in the field she spies. [Nelly]
> The lovely Chloris well attended came,
> A thousand Graces waited on the dame;
> Her matchless form made all the English glad,
> And foreign beauties less assurance had. ...
> Such killing looks! So thick the arrows fly!
> That 'tis unsafe to be a stander-by ...
> [There is no one winner, of course, but a triple score-draw:]
> Where Love gives law, Beauty the sceptre sways;
> And uncompell'd, the happy world obeys.[11]

Portsmouth could not conceal her anxiety and jealousy of her latest rival, weeping copiously, as was her wont; Nelly, not being in the contest for *maîtresse en titre*, was not greatly concerned. Meanwhile, stories abounded of Hortense's effect on others. St Evremond was in love with her, as, supposedly, was the Portuguese ambassador, while Montagu was interrupting his affair with the celebrated court beauty Mrs Myddelton (partly to keep an eye on his protégée). Ambassador Courtin saw her at parties given for her: 'If you had seen her last night dancing the *furlana* with a guitar, you would not have been able to stop yourself from supporting her cause ... I have been present every day, and seen the most surprising things in her salon.'[12]

Hortense herself, who now with the assistance of Vicard had a reputation for wit and intelligence as well as devastating beauty, had her own salon in her house in St James's Park, attended by all those with pretensions to wit and a taste for the delicacies provided by her French chef. When she went with the court to Newmarket, she could be seen at dawn riding fast over the gallops, and in the evening, gambling at cards, especially at basset. George Etherege wrote *A Song on Basset*:

> Let equipage and dress despair;
> Since Basset is come in,
> There's nothing can engage the fair
> But money and Morin.

> Is any Countess in distress?
> She flies not to the beau;
> 'Tis coney only can redress
> Her grief with a rouleau.

> By this bewitching game betrayed,
> Poor love is bought and sold,
> And that which should be free trade,
> Is all engrossed by gold.[13]

Little skill was required, as each player gambled against the dealer; Morin was an unscrupulous French croupier, especially at Mazarin's house. A *rouleau* was a roll of gold coins, here provided by some doting fool. At home, she played almost continuously (winning with Morin's unobtrusive assistance), as St Evremond's verse reported:

> *Hortense joue à la bassette,*
> *Aussi longtemps que veut Morin.*
> *Que le soleil vienne éclairer le monde*
> *Il vous voit la carte à la main;*
> *Que lasse de son cours il repose sous l'onde,*
> *Vous veillez jusqu'au lendemain.*[14]

As Montagu now realised, Hortense had no interest in politics, only in having a good time – with anyone she fancied. Her pleasures included a new close friend, Anne, the young Countess of Sussex, Charles's daughter by Barbara Villiers, now expecting her first child. Hortense visited Anne frequently and, despite her condition, persuaded her to play shuttlecock and take part in Italian dances; she also often spent the night with her.[15] Whenever Charles came to visit his daughter, Hortense, conveniently, was also there. Courtin reported to Louis that 'though the affair has so far been conducted with some secrecy, it is likely that this growing passion will take the first place in the prince's heart'.[16]

As it was, the passionate nature of the relationship between Hortense and Anne was becoming so blatant that the Earl of Sussex, 'a most upright and proper, but stupid and bad-tempered young man',[17] threatened to separate from her unless she came away to live in the country, which she refused to do. Apart from the presumed lesbian nature of the relationship, other sexual improprieties were popularly rumoured, as in the so-called *Rochester's Farewell* (possibly by Charles Sackville), which suggested that they were both having sex with the servant, Mustapha:

> Thou to our admiring age dost show [marvelling]
> More sin than inn'cent Rome did ever know,
> And having all her lewdnesses out ran,
> Tak'st up with devil, having tir'd out man;
> For what is else that loathsome filthy black
> Which thou and Sussex in your arms did take?[18]

That autumn, Hortense introduced Anne to fencing lessons, and one day they went into St James's Park 'with drawn swords under their nightgowns [evening coats] which they drew out and made several fine passes, much to the admiration of several men that was lookers-on in the Park', as Lady Chaworth reported.[19] The King now strongly encouraged Sussex to take his wife away to the country – Hurstmonceaux Castle – where she raged and lamented, but 'still kept [Hortense's] portrait always with her and would often take it out and cover it with kisses'. (Lady Chaworth again.)

Ambassador Courtin worked at developing better relationships between the two foreign mistresses, both to protect Louise, his main agent, and to prevent the growth of factions and greater anti-French sentiment – both were popularly loathed. To quote Rochester, who had the people pray,

> Now heaven preserve our faith's defender
> From Paris plot and Roman cunt,
> From Mazarin, that new pretender,
> And from that *politique* Gramont.[20]

At a dinner with Sophia Bulkeley, younger sister of La Belle Stuart, Courtin managed to get them both shut up in a closet or small room for some time, until they at last emerged hand in hand in apparent good humour; how long the truce lasted is not known.

Hortense went from strength to strength, ever more extravagant and paraded as the King's mistress: at the opening of Parliament in 1677 she attended in a very prominent position raised above all other ladies behind the throne. Her former friend or fellow prisoner at the Abbey of Chelles, Sidonie, the Marquise de Courcelles, showed up, also with hopes of a crack at Charles, but was briskly packed off to France and marriage (and an early death), before she could cause any trouble.[21] Charles granted Hortense a pension of £4,000, which led Armand to stop the pension he had been paying her. She was at the peak of her celebrity – or notoriety, as the King's seducer and presumed new ruler – frequently imaged as Cleopatra, Mark Antony's seducer and emasculator. Shakespeare's *Antony and Cleopatra* was revived; it is an improbable coincidence that Charles Sedley's *Antony and Cleopatra* was performed in the Duke's Theatre in February 1677 and Dryden's *All for Love, or the World Well Lost* in the Theatre Royal at the end of the year.[22] Aphra Behn dedicated *The History of the Nun, or the fair Vow-Breaker* to her with her usual fulsome gush, assuring her 'how infinitely one of your own sex adores you'.

With Lady Sussex unavailable, Hortense found other amusements; one of them proved one too many for Charles, when she had a fling with the freshly landed, new, young Prince of Monaco, in July 1677. For once, Charles was angered at a mistress's infidelity; there was a quarrel, and he even revoked her pension, but soon (characteristically) restored it. This marked the end of the sexual part of their relationship, though they remained on good terms, while Louise regained her dominant position in the court and with Charles.

Hortense now settled for a life of pleasure with enough money, and her salon became a centre for the intelligent and fashionable. Her career in London was notorious as she gambled night and day and mingled with the crowds at Newmarket to lay bets on horses, had lovers of both sexes (including, unreliable gossip suggested, Mary of Modena and Lady Jane Gerard) and even boarded ships in the London docks to buy trinkets and parrots. Like mother, like daughter: in France, her daughter ran away with the Marquis de Richelieu from the convent where she was supposed to be in training. Shut up by her husband, she climbed the walls to get out.[23] Predictably, Hortense was accused by Titus Oates in the 'Popish Plot' of 1678, but nothing came of it, though Louise was scared, even thinking of running away to France. Charles Sackville's comic poem *Colin*, imagining possible contenders for Louise's position, included Mazarin:

> Then in came dowdy Mazarin,
> That foreign antiquated quean, [aged about thirty-two]
> Who soon was told the King no more
> Would deal with an intriguing whore;
> That she already had about her
> Too good an *equipage de foutre*.[24]

In 1683, still a beauty in her late thirties, she attracted the ardent passion of her young nephew, the Chevalier de Soissons, who absurdly challenged and, unfortunately, killed another admirer, the Swedish Baron Banér. Mme de Sévigné remarked, tartly, 'One would not have thought that the eyes of a grandmother could have done such execution.'[25] His death, and Soissons' punishment, caused her great distress; she talked of retiring to a convent but soon went back to card play and drink. On one occasion, St Evremond was startled to find her on her knees before her confessor, only to discover she was engaged in piercing his ears for some earrings she was giving him.[26]

When Charles died in 1685, King James continued to pay her a pension, though she was in some financial difficulties. In turn, King William granted her a pension, but her income never matched her extravagances. Only her powerful friends protected her; the banquets she gave were in fact provided by friends, with the devoted St Evremond apparently providing the butter. In 1692, she moved to Kensington, and then in 1694 out to Chelsea, adopting a stringent diet spoiled by an excessive fondness for drink (white wine, anis, absinthe and whisky).

In 1699, she was known to be dying; her son, the Duc de la Meillerage, and the Duchesse de Bouillon crossed the Channel to see her. On reaching Dover on 2 July, they were told they were too late, so turned round and went back. In his funeral elegy, St Evremond declared, 'With the likeness of Helen, Madame Mazarin had the air and appanage of a Queen of the Amazons: she appeared equally ready to charm and to fight,' and observed, 'More conquests can be made by [beauty's] eyes than by the arms of great men.'[27]

Nevertheless, the bailiffs went through her house and took all they could. Her husband at last got her back and took the coffined body away with him in a bizarre pilgrimage around France, from Alsace to Brittany. Peasants treated the coffin with veneration, laying rosaries on it and touching it for a blessing. Finally, it was laid to rest in the tomb of the great Cardinal Mazarin in the Collège des Quatre Nations, in Paris. Later, four of her granddaughters became mistresses of Louis XV. At the Revolution in 1790, a mob seized the coffin, broke it open and threw the bones on a fire.

10

LOVE AND VALUE: LOUISE AND NELL

Louise's greed and presumed power over the King were widely known and resented. There was a story of her being held up in her coach near Newmarket by a notorious highwayman called Old Mobb. 'Do you know who I am?' she demanded haughtily. 'Yes, Madam,' he replied. 'I know you to be the greatest whore in the Kingdom and that you are maintained at the public charge ... and that the King himself is your slave ... You may say now, Madam, that a single highwayman has exercised his authority where Charles the Second has often begged a favour and thought himself fortunate to obtain it at the expense of his treasure.'[1] Public criticism of the King's behaviour was also expressed in a lampoon entitled *Britannia and Rawleigh* (possibly by John Ayliffe), describing how Charles,

> fair soul, transformed by that French dame
> Had lost all sense of Honour, Justice, Fame.
> Like a tame spinster in's seraglio he sits. [like Hercules, effetely
>   spinning at the feet of Omphale]
> Besieged by's whores, buffoons and bastard chits;
> Lulled in security, rolling in lust,

Resigns his Crown to angel Carwell's trust;
Her creature Osborne the revenue steals ...
[The writer goes on to complain that]
A colony of French possess the Court;
Pimps, priests, buffoons i'the Privy Chamber sport.
Such slimy masters ne'er approached a throne
Since Pharoah's reign, nor so defiled a crown ...
Thus fairy-like the King they steal away,
And in his place a Louis' changeling lay.
[He goes on to urge the spirit of Raleigh to]
Teach 'em to scorn the Carwells, Pembrokes, Nells,
The Clevelands, Osbornes, Barties [Danby's wife],
Lauderdales ...[2]

For all that, in April, Louis sent her earrings worth £18,000, while her income was increased by £10,000 from the sale of licences to wine merchants.

About now, in 1674, Louise had herself painted by the French painter Henri Gascar in full *Playboy* centre-fold fashion, as a half-naked Venus, lacy chemise open to the waist, reclining on a cushioned couch.[3] Nelly responded by having Gascar paint her in a similar chemise and pose, but with her two young sons by Charles (later to be Charles, Duke of St Albans, and James, Lord Beauclerk) fluttering over as Cupids – and, even more significantly, the King watching in the background.[4]

In May 1675, Louise's parents came to London, where they visited their married daughter Henriette; they did not see their unmarried daughter's child. Nevertheless, and despite Nell's pictured children, it was Louise's son who was honoured first, when she persuaded the King to make her little Charles Duke of Richmond and Lennox (titles previously held by the recently dead husband of the former favourite, La Belle Stuart, presumably deliberately chosen as a snub to Frances). She also managed to outwit Barbara, Lady Cleveland, over the matter of their respective sons: Barbara wanted her son by Charles, Henry Fitzroy, Duke of Grafton, to have precedence over Richmond. The King tactfully (and, knowing Barbara's rages, prudently) declined to commit himself when approached by the

Lord Treasurer, who had to sign the necessary forms, and advised him to adopt the principle of, 'first come, first served'. Louise got her new ally, Danby, to meet her lawyer at midnight, just before he left for Bath; when Barbara's lawyer arrived in the early morning, Danby had already gone. It is pleasing to know that, to this day, the aristocratic descendants of these two mistresses have to observe this precedence on appropriate occasions. Nell had to be content with being made a Lady of the Privy Chamber to the Queen (not very grand), and her son got a pension of £4,000.[5]

Then, that summer, out of the blue, arrived a new and dangerous competitor in the battle of the bedrooms: Hortense, Countess Mazarin. Barbara went off to France and different lovers, but Hortense seemed a real threat. In March 1676, Louise had a miscarriage, which put her back for a while; her distress increased, expressed in her usual tearful fashion. In August, the ambassador reported to Louis on a meeting he had had with their unhappy agent:

> She opened her heart to me in the presence of two of her maids ... [and] explained to me what grief the frequent visits of the King of England to Madame de Sussex [whom she suspected of conspiring with her lover, Mazarin] cause her every day. The two girls remained propped against the wall with downcast eyes. Their mistress let loose a torrent of tears. Sobs and sighs interrupted her speech. Indeed, I have never beheld a sadder or more touching sight.[6]

More to the point, as far as the French were concerned, was the risk that the investment in Louise might be wasted if she were indeed ousted by Mazarin. Her jealous distress was very apparent and even amusing to others. On one occasion, when some accident had caused her a black eye, the courtier Bab May 'remarked with impunity to the King that she would probably like to black the other one too, to make herself look more like Madame Mazarin'.[7] Her cascading tears did not always wear away Charles's relatively stony heart. Once, being told by Ambassador Courtin that she was in tears over something, he replied, "Ods fish! I don't believe a word of this. She's better than you or I are. She wants something, that makes her play her pranks over this. She has served me so often this way, that I am sure of what I say as if I were part of her.'[8] After her miscarriage, she went to Bath at the end of July; the King welcomed her on her return but did not spend the night with her going back to Nell instead. Her jealousy was well known; Nelly pretended that she would have to arm herself against Louise's resentment for Charles's many visits to her in her absence, while Charles himself blithely continued his interest in Mazarin. Edmund Waller wrote his attempted conciliatory poem *The Triple Combat*, hoping for a harmonious triple rule by the three women, while Rochester was coarser and funnier, with his first verse beginning with Nelly boasting,

> When to the King I bid good morrow,
> With tongue in mouth and hand on tarse,
> Portsmouth may rend her cunt in sorrow,
> And Mazarin may kiss mine arse.[9]

Courtin arranged a brief reconciliation between Louise and Hortense by shutting them together in a small room, until they emerged hand in hand (or so the story goes). He continued paying them both, in hopes of ensuring French influence; he also related the following incident, when Louise and Nelly independently came to visit Mazarin:

When Madame de Portsmouth had left, the actress, who is extremely merry, asked me in front of the whole company to obtain her a gift from the King of France, telling me that she well deserved it and that she served the King of England much better than the Duchess of Portsmouth, allowing myself and the entire gathering to understand that he slept much more often with her.

Mazarin had heard stories of the young woman from Coal Yard's delight in fine undergarments and asked whether they could be seen. Nelly stood up, and the splendid, layered petticoats were displayed in all their glory. 'They made her lift up one petticoat after another and I have never seen any so clean or so magnificent.'[10]

Nelly, because of her low origins, was never rewarded like the aristocratic Louise. In 1670–7, a Treasury clerk paid Louise a total of £36,073 in royal gifts, and Nell a total of £7,938 – though in 1674 she received £2,265 for silver ornaments for her bed (though this is to say nothing of their annual pensions).[11] Nell's silver four-poster bedstead, perhaps modelled on the King's state bed, had silver eagles, crowns and cherubs, with figures representing Charles and Nell. Also figured, in mockery, were Barbara's former lover Jacob Hall dancing on a silver wire rope and Louise lying in a grave with some eastern prince, with, above all, the King's head. Before the extra supplements, the cost was £1,135.[12]

Louise had more lavish, extensive, constantly refurbished apartments in Whitehall, at the other end of the gallery from the King's, overlooking the sundial court. On the door of her apartment someone pinned a note: 'Within this place a bed's appointed / For a French bitch and the Lord's anointed.' Charles's position at the far end of the gallery from Louise's entrance, and reputed declining sexual powers, provoked facetious anatomical metaphors, as in one verse ostensibly spoken by her and added to Rochester's *Signior Dildo*:

> Good sir, I pray, what do you intend,
> To fumble so long at the gallery's end.
> If you fuck me no better, I'll have you to know,
> I'll lay you aside for Signior Dildo.

Also from about the same time, in 1673, Charles's doting on Louise, and his sexual decline, were indicated in Rochester's notorious *On King Charles* ('In the isle of Great Britain'):

> To Carwell, the most dear of all his dears,
> The sure relief of his declining years, [aged forty-three]
> Oft he bewails his fortune and her fate:
> To love so well, and to be loved so late.
> For when in her he settles well his tarse,
> Yet his dull, graceless ballocks hang an arse.[13]
> [The last three words – an idiomatic phrase – mean to
>   delay or to take too long.]

With all this, Louise's trophies surpassed Nelly's petticoats and bedstead. Evelyn was shocked at what he saw in her apartments in September 1675: 'Luxuriously furnished, and with ten times the richness and glory beyond the Queen's, such massy pieces of plate, whole tables, stands etc of incredible value.' Later, on 4 October 1683, he was there again, when

> that which engaged my curiosity, was the rich and splendid furniture of this woman's apartment, now twice or thrice pulled down and rebuilt to satisfy her prodigal and expensive pleasures ... Here I saw a French tapestry, for design, tenderness of work and incomparable imitation of the best paintings, beyond anything I had ever beheld; some pieces had Versailles, St Germain, and other places of the French king with hunting, figures and landscapes, exotic fowl and all to the life rarely done [designed at impressing Charles with Louis and with French culture]. Then for Japan cabinets, screens, pendulum clocks, branches [candelabra], braziers etc, they were all of massive silver and without number, besides of His Majesty's best paintings.

It all provoked Evelyn into naïve moralism: 'Lord, what contentment can there be in the riches and splendour of this world, purchased with vice and dishonour.'[14] Louise could have told him.

For all her wealth, Louise could never match Nelly for wit. One night, according to one story, the two of them were dining with the King, and two boiled chickens were on the table. Trying to rise to the occasion, Louise claimed she could make three out of the two. 'That cannot be,' said Nell. 'Why,' said Louise, 'there's one, and there's two, and one and two make three.' 'Yes,' said Nell, 'so they do,' and putting one on the King's plate and the other on hers, invited Louise to take the third for her pains.[15]

Around this time, with Barbara away in France, Mazarin involved with the visiting Prince of Monaco, and Louise visited only occasionally, Nell was in favour again, which she sought to exploit. Once, when the King was visiting her, she called to her son, 'Come here, you little bastard, and say hello to your father.' When the King protested at such language being used to his son, she replied, 'Your

Majesty has given me no other name to call him by.'[16] (Part of the issue was that Barbara's sons had been made dukes before they were even adolescents.) Charles took her point, but also his time. It was not until December 1676 that young Charles Beauclerk became Baron of Headington and Earl of Burford and not until April 1677 that his brother received his own title of Lord Beauclerk, while Nell benefited from a grant of money from both properties.

Now Nell, who had been disappointed with Danby's unwillingness to help her to a title, became more sympathetic to the so-called Country Party and found herself involved in politics. When in February 1677 the King opened Parliament, Lords Shaftesbury and Buckingham cited an ancient statute to argue that a prorogation of over a year meant the automatic dissolution of Parliament; they were promptly sent to the Tower. Nell and her friend Rochester argued for their mutual friend, Buckingham; he was partially released, first to stay with Rochester and then with Nelly in Pall Mall. Danby arranged for various warnings – threats – to be sent to her, but she stayed defiantly loyal to her friend and received visitors, including Sir Carr Scrope, an ugly little man who fancied himself a ladies' man and tried his luck with her, and William Fanshawe, the poverty-stricken Master of Requests. When his child was due for christening, Nell advised that he should 'reserve himself a little [money] to buy him new shoes, that she might not smell him stink two storeys high' when he came to call.[17]

After Louise's return from Bath she had a slightly more retired life. In September 1667, Ambassador Courtin reported, 'I ascertain that for some time now she has been left alone; but if she keeps her good health, she has a beautiful skin, and I do not believe that anyone can be so often in her company without desiring her.'[18] Nevertheless, that winter, Louise fell seriously ill for some six weeks, giving her great fears for her life and soul. Mlle de Scudéry wrote that 'Kéroualle has preached to the King, the crucifix in her hand, trying to make him give up women' – a lost cause, if ever.[19] Henry Savile wrote to Rochester that

> The King imputes her recovery to drops, but her confessor to the Virgin Mary, to whom he is said to have promised in her name

that in case of recovery she should have no more commerce with that known enemy to virginity and chastity, the monarch of Great Britain, but that she should return to a cloister in little Brittany, and there end her days. I have not yet heard that her Grace has confirmed this bargain, but there are fools that believe it.[20]

Shortly afterwards, when recovered, she went to the theatre with Charles and Mazarin.

A year later, Louise was indeed thinking of a retreat to France, when the storm of the so-called 'Popish Plot' broke over England, which would have been absurd had not several people died as a result. Anti-Catholic frenzy raged; many Catholics were threatened and had to lie low, and even the Queen was accused. Charles Sackville's poem *Colin* imagined the court women applying for Louise's vacant position as *maîtresse en titre*; in the event, Louise stayed, increasingly in favour with Charles and out of favour with the people. He gave her jewels worth £13,000, originally intended for the Queen of Spain, but most people preferred Nell. The *London Chronicle* of August 1678 reported that when a goldsmith was making an expensive service of plate to give Louise, a crowd of people, watching, said 'it was a thousand pities His Majesty had not bestowed this bounty on Madam Ellen'.[21]

In that year, the female dramatist Aphra Behn dedicated her new play, *The Feign'd Courtesans*, to Nelly, in a grovelling dedication that Samuel Johnson in his *Lives of the Poets* was to declare surpassed even Dryden in 'meanness and servility of hyperbolic adulation'. In it she told Nelly that

succeeding ages who shall with joy survey your history shall envy us who lived in this, and saw those charming wonders which they can only read of, and whom we ought in charity to pity, since all the pictures, pens or pencils can draw will give 'em but a faint idea of what we have the honour to see in such absolute perfection; they can only guess she was infinitely fair, witty and deserving, but to what vast degrees in all they can only judge who lived to gaze and listen ...

To listen, apparently, to words of extraordinary wisdom:

> When you speak, men crowd to listen with that awful reverence as
> to holy oracles or divine prophecies, and bear away the precious
> words to tell at home to all the attentive family.

Furthermore, she insisted,

> to the utmost limits of the universe your mighty conquests are
> known. And who can doubt the powers of that illustrious beauty,
> the charms of that tongue, and the greatness of that mind, who
> has subdued the most powerful and glorious monarch of the
> world.[22]

(To quote Shakespeare's Rosalind: 'Wonderful, wonderful ... out
of all whooping.') Nell had performed in Behn's *The Rover* in
1677 and *Sir Patient Fancy* in January 1678, but, even by the
standards of the time, this was excessive repayment for a popular
comic actress – but Nelly (once she had stopped laughing) was in
a position to do Behn some good through her aristocratic friends.

Sadly for Nelly, in August 1679, her mother, a heavy boozer
(literally: according to one lampoon, consuming up to twenty
quarts a day, and nearly six feet in circumference), fell drunkenly
into a drainage ditch and drowned, but Nell did the funeral in
style, as the author of *A Panegyric* recorded:

> No cost, no velvet did the daughter spare,
> Five gilded scutcheons did the hearse enrich
> To celebrate the martyr of the ditch.
> Burnt brandy did in flaming brimmers flow,
> Drunk at her funeral, while her well-pleased shade
> Rejoiced, ev'n in the sober fields below.[23]

It was, apparently, quite an occasion: many of the 'merry gang'
attended – Buckingham, Rochester, Buckhurst, Sedley – as well as
representatives from the theatre (Charles Hart, Orange Moll) and
noted bawds (her mother's colleagues), such as Mrs Cresswell.

There was a procession from Coal Yard Alley, through Drury Lane and Covent Garden to the church of St Martin in the Fields, with plenty of drink en route to sustain the mourners in their grief. It made a splendid wake.[24]

Now the political scene became more troubled, and both Nell and Louise found themselves involved, in varying degrees. There were demands that James be excluded from the succession, possibly in favour of the illegitimate but Protestant Duke of Monmouth. The King had to insist that Monmouth had no claim or right, and forbade Nell (who was in the Protestant, anti-James camp) to receive her old friend Monmouth in her home – which command she obeyed, while meeting Monmouth in the Countess of Orrery's house. *A Panegyric* described her as

> True to the Protestant interest and cause,
> True to th'established Government and Laws ...
> ... 'twas her matchless loyalty alone
> That bid Prince Perkin [Monmouth] pack up and be gone.[25]

Shaftesbury, meanwhile, went to Louise, suggesting that if the Duke of York were indeed excluded, then Charles could choose his own heir, such as her Protestant son, the Duke of Richmond. This seemed an unlikely eventuality: the probable real cause of these conversations was to get her to emphasise to Charles that the English would not accept Catholic James as king.

The court moved to Windsor, as usual, with the normal racing and hunting, while Charles took up fishing. Monmouth, constantly looking for allies in his campaign for recognition, then approached Louise but received a cool response. A letter to him from her, dated 20 November, says that she had not urged Charles to take away his military commission but did approve it, while emphasising her own influence:

> The King loves me so well as to tell me everything he intends to do ... Lord Essex, Lord Halifax and Lord Sunderland [are] all my very good friends ... Had you not all this while very coldly and very unkindly dealt with me I had made you the greatest man in

the Kingdom, next to the Duke of York, as you may see by what I have done by my Lord Sunderland whom the King never had a good opinion of till I recommended him. I have made Lord Halifax an Earl, upon his application to me. The King was pleased to make the Earl of Essex a Commissioner of the Treasury ... nobody shall come to Court or to any preferment, but those who will be my creatures. The King of England hath promised to support me, and I am allied to most of the sovereign princes abroad, as you may see by my being so often obliged to be in mourning for them.[26]

The boasting becomes a trifle bathetic at the end – and would have caused Nelly some mirth. Contemporary opinion agreed with her self-estimate, as in a verse:

> *Portsmouth's Looking-Glass*
> Is there a Minister of State,
> Or any Treasurer of late,
> That's fawning and imperious too?
> He owes his greatness all to you:
> And as you see just cause to do't,
> You keep him in, or turn him out.
> — though another writer was not impressed:
> ... at her folly who can choose but smile?
> While them who always slight her, great she makes,
> And so much pains to be despised she takes.
> — remarking, resignedly,
> But what must we expect, who daily see
> Unthinking Charles ruled by unthinking thee.[27]

The French ambassador Barillon reported that Monmouth 'every night sups with Mistress Nesle', and she herself tried pleading with Charles for Monmouth but was told off (in June, her second son, James, died, aged eight). She had always been on good terms with Monmouth, while speaking to him with her usual frankness. To his face she called him Perkin Warbeck, after a pretender to the throne hanged by Henry VII for his presumption. When he tried to put her down, she bit back, as *A Panegyric* recorded:

'Ill bred thou art,' says Prince. Nell does reply,
'Was Mrs Barlow better bred than I?'[28]

His mother, Mrs Barlow, was gentry, unlike Nell, but like Nell, she was Charles's whore, and, unlike Nell, Monmouth was illegitimate.

Charles was still struggling with Parliament over money, while negotiating with Louis XIV in France. Through Ambassador Barillon, Louis offered Charles £500,000 to prorogue Parliament until March; Louise acted as an intermediary, as Barillon reported:

> I saw Madame de Portsmouth, to whom the King has confided his affairs. She told me that if your Majesty would pay four millions a year for three years, the King would agree to carry out your Majesty's wishes; but that without this sum, it would be impossible for him to refuse to call Parliament. The King said to me last night that he was ashamed and that he felt a profound displeasure in having to traffic in this way with your Majesty.[29]

Charles was little inclined to feel shame: the overriding object was to get enough money to rule independently; promises were another matter. As it was, Parliament intensified pressure against the Duke of York and his Catholic and French sympathisers. At the end of the year, an indictment, *Articles of High Treason and other High Crimes against the Duchess of Portsmouth*, was deposited in the House of Commons. It declared that, as everyone knew, 'the said Duchess hath and doth still cohabit … with the King, having had a foul, nauseous and contagious distemper' (very unfair, as it was almost certainly Charles who had infected her). She was criticised for receiving money from Louis, for pushing her friends into high positions, accused of having a Catholic confectioner who could poison the King and having the 'highest honours and rewards conferred on her and hers, to the … discouraging of virtue, whose rewards those high titles and honours ought to be'.[30] Nothing came of this.

In June 1680, the Whig Lords also put forward an indictment of James as a Popish recusant, two-thirds of whose property should be forfeited, and Shaftesbury declared to a jury that the Duchess of Portsmouth should be indicted as a public nuisance (prostitute), but the King had the jury dispersed and the case blocked. Not surprisingly, Louise got frightened again, stopped her dithering and became more sympathetic to the exclusionists. In October, she and her ally Lord Sunderland urged Charles to send James away, but he refused. Despite this, he remained steadfast in his affection for her, as a letter of 1680, from Newmarket, when she was unwell, suggests:

> Pray do not answer this yourself, except you are quite out of pain, all I will add is, that I should do myself wrong if I told you that I love you better than all the world besides, for that were making a comparison where 'tis impossible to express the true passion and kindness I have for my dearest dearest Fubs.[31]

Fubs was his pet name for her, perhaps to do with her rounded cheeks; his private yacht was also named Fubbs.

In November, the Commons passed an Exclusion Bill against James, but Charles strove to prevent it passing the Lords; eventually, on 18 January 1681, he declared Parliament dissolved and called a new one, to meet at Oxford, a Royalist-sympathetic city and easily dominated by the royal guards – if necessary. The court trailed up after him; famously, when a small mob gathered near Carfax, in the centre of the city, and threatened a coach they thought was Louise's, Nell put out her head and called, 'Good people, be civil; I am the *Protestant* whore', which went down very well – and led the author of *The Ladies March* to call her, sardonically, 'A Saint to be admired the more / Because a Church of England whore'.[32]

The French negotiations were completed, with Charles promised £85,000 over three years, while discussions with Parliament were proving fruitless. On 28 October, his robes and crown were smuggled into an ante-chamber to Christ Church Hall. When the Commons entered, they were confronted by their monarch in full regalia, who there and then dissolved Parliament in one sentence. He then had some lunch and he and Nell visited nearby Burford, the town from which their son took his title, before going hawking and watching some horse racing, and that was that.

Without Parliament's money, he would have to be a little careful, but the French money helped him to pay a few debts and help some friends. Louise's son, the Duke of Richmond, was made a Knight of the Garter; though the ribbon was traditionally worn round the neck, at the ceremony Charles slipped the ribbon round the lad's shoulder, as it has been worn ever since. Nelly had to settle for some useful leases of land. Her favoured position at court, despite moralist public criticism, was suggested in November 1682, when some man shouted abuse at her in the Duke's Theatre, and 'the Earl of Pembroke's brother vindicating, there were many swords drawn, and a great hubbub in the house'.[33] She was now more of the court entertainer, amusing the 'merry gang' of Lord Dorset, Harry Savile, George Etherege, Peg Hughes and her particular friend, Mall Knight, a singer and procuress.

It was with Mall Knight that Nell had a falling-out that summer; Etherege (possibly) wrote *Mrs Nelly's Complaint*, which incidentally suggests that Nell had not always been faithful to Charles. The dispute was about who had seduced young William Dutton Colt (Prince Rupert's well-named Master of Horse) away from whom. Apparently, Mall had broken off with Charles Greville, Lord Lansdowne, in favour of Colt, but then Nell got him away. Nell complains of

> Knight, cruel Knight, that once lay in my breast,
> My constant crony and eternal guest,
> Th'applauder of my beauty and my jest,
> She, she, that cruel she to France is fled ...
> [The king was brought in to sort out matters and sent Knight
>   abroad.]

Mall, being absent, acts as a sort of ghost, haunting Nell, and complains in turn:

> Wherein have I deserved so ill of thee,
> That thou shouldst part my dearest Colt and me?
> Of brawny blockheads hadst thou not before,
> By my industrious care, a numerous store?

Cleveland herself was never stuffed with more ...
Colt, for all his charms, had a squint:
... my false squinter thou didst lead astray,
And her that too much trusted thee betray.
Inevitably, he looked askance:
For while his melting eyes did mine survey,
They craftily still seemed another way.
But Nell concludes triumphantly:
To France my baffled squeaking rival's gone,
And Colt and all his eyes are now my own.
Should she pretend to what's so much my due,
She might as well take lovely Duncombe too –
[Lieutenant Duncombe of the King's Foot Guards, Colt's
    predecessor with Nell.]
Duncombe, by great sway and power preferred,
For mounting me well first now mounts the Guard.
Help, Church and State, to do a Princess right,
Guard me from wrongs and exorcise this spright,
Ev'n now in terror on my bed I lie,
Send Doctor Burnet to me, or I die.[34]

The Revd Burnet was famous – or notorious – for attending spiritually troubled dying libertines, notably Nell's friend the Earl of Rochester. Nell had claimed, earlier, to have been faithful to Charles; she may have wavered in the later years, though here, Etherege, as a jest, may have simply exaggerated some minor flirtations.

In August, the King and Nell went to Winchester to see the horse racing there. The Dean of Winchester was happy to give a bedroom in the deanery to the King, but Prebendary Thomas Ken would not have 'a woman of ill repute' in his house, 'not for the Kingdom'. A bedroom was found for her elsewhere, and the King and Nell were not offended (had it happened to Louise, she would have been in floods of tears; it was just as well it was not Barbara). Two years later, when the Bishopric of Bath and Wells became vacant, the King cried, "Ods fish! Who should have Bath and Wells but the little black fellow who would not give poor Nelly a lodging?"[35]

Nell was not so poor, with her various pensions; in 1682 she lost £1,400 to Mazarin, gambling at basset (gambling was one of Mazarin's main sources of income), but could afford to pay £4,250 for a pearl necklace. It was not all 'self' with her, though: when, in November, many people in Wapping were made homeless by a great fire, the King gave £2,000 in aid, a 'person of quality' £500 and Nell, of no quality, gave £100 (one twentieth of the King's donation). That year, Charles laid the foundation stone for the Royal Hospital in Chelsea for wounded and disabled soldiers – the story is, that this was at the urging of Nelly (whose father may have been in the army).

The previous year, 1681, had marked a rare wobble in Louise's carefully controlled sexuality – perhaps as a result of Charles's declining sexual powers (if gossip, and Rochester's mockery, are to be believed) – when the twenty-eight-year-old Philippe de Vendôme, so-called Grand Prior of France and a notorious rake, came to England to visit his aunt, Hortense Mancini, soon arousing the interest of the court ladies and especially Louise. Charles did not enjoy, and did not long tolerate, his presence at court, and vigorously encouraged his return to France. Philippe and Louise were very probably lovers, as a popular lampoon of the time assumed, in *A Dialogue between the Dutchess of Portsmouth and Madame Gwin at Parting*,[36] when Gwin says,

> Let Fame, that never yet spoke well of woman,
> Give out I was a strolling whore, and common,
> Yet have I been to him since the first hour
> As constant as the needle to the flower; [compass needle and rose]
> Whilst you to your eternal praise and fame
> To foreign scents betrayed the royal game:
> Witness the Prior in your bosom lay,
> And in that posture did your lust betray,
> For which now with a pox you're sent away.

In fact, Louise had chosen to make a triumphant return visit to France in 1682, chiefly to show off to the French court. Charles gave her £100,000 for the trip. In Paris, she paraded with four carriages of six horses (the equivalent of a stretch limo), some in the royal livery, and had a magnificent mansion furnished 'in the best possible taste', displaying enormous extravagance and making great, ostentatiously careless losses at gambling. She was sumptuously entertained and received by Louis (and saw the ascendancy over him of his mistress Madame de Maintenon), and she and Ambassador Barillon asked him for the same right as Countess Cleveland, to sit on a *tabouret* (low stool) when visiting the Queen. She went down to Brittany and cleared up debts on the family estate and presented the nuns there with a picture by Lely of the Madonna and child, which they were very pleased with until they realised who was the model.

Gossip and lampoons later accused her of having an affair there with Vendôme. For farewell presents Louis gave her diamond earrings, her son a fancy sword valued at £12,000 and an equerry a golden chain; not to be out-done, she gave the sword-bearer a £4,000 diamond.

Back in England, her supremacy was very clear, as she presided over diplomatic receptions. When a Moroccan delegation arrived for discussions about Tangier (proving a troublesome part of Catherine's dowry), the Queen sat enthroned beside the King for the formal audience. A few days later, a banquet was given for the delegation – in Louise's splendid dining chamber in Whitehall. Evelyn was there, impressed by the delegation's good manners: 'They drank a little milk and water but not a drop of wine. Also they drank of a sorbet and chocolate, did not look about or stare on the ladies, or express the least of surprise ... the Moors neither admiring nor seeming to regard anything.' He noted that they were 'placed about a long table, a lady between two Moors ... and most of these were the King's natural children, viz., the Lady Lichfield, Sussex, Duchess of Portsmouth, Nelly, etc, concubines and cattle of that sort, as splendid as jewels and excess of bravery could make them'.[37] For a 'thank you' present, the ambassador gave Charles two lions and thirty ostriches (the lions would have gone to the Tower; the feathers might have come in handy for fans and fine headgear).

In the spring of 1683 Philippe de Vendôme arrived again, as part of a mission sent by Louis, and eager to resume undiplomatic relations. His flirtation and amorous pursuit – apparently very welcome – were soon noticed in court, where it was assumed that Louise was his mistress. Charles, now unwilling to share as in the past, especially his dear Fubs, sent Sunderland to forbid Vendôme to attend Louise's card-table – a rather pathetic little gesture. When he learned a few days later that Vendôme had disobeyed, he told Barillon to tell him to leave the country. Vendôme said that he would go only when expressly ordered to do so, by the King in person. Charles agreed to this and told him to go, but he did not. The King then sent Lieutenant Griffin of the Guards, to make him go within two days or face arrest and deportation on a packet-boat for Calais. Vendôme told Barillon that he wished to retire to the country. Charles said he must leave. Now Louise was getting anxious in case he made public any letters of theirs (a standard blackmailer's threat). Eventually he condescended to leave for Holland late in November. Louis warned him that it would be very much in his interest to keep quiet thereafter about his relationship with the Duchess of Portsmouth.[38]

Louise did well to be anxious and tearful, but Charles forgave her and became even more doting. Burnet recorded that 'his fondness broke out in very indecent instances, and he caressed her in the view of all people, which he had never done on any occasion or to any person formerly.'[39] In January 1684, the King told Barillon, 'The Duchess of Portsmouth and her son, the Duke of Richmond, are the persons above all others in the world whom I love the most. I would be deeply obliged to the King of France if he were to reconvert the estate of Aubigny into a duchy for her, with the reversion to her son and his future issue.'[40] Barillon was not enthusiastic about this proposal regarding a duchy and the tabouret rights it would give Louise, but Sunderland and the Duke of York supported the request. Louis approved the revival of the Duchy, and Louise used her influence to get the Duke of York reinstated as Lord High Admiral in March 1684.

In November, Louise was ill and thought herself dying; worried Charles at her bedside was made to promise never to abandon James, while she also used the occasion to urge Louis to issue naturalisation papers for her son, so that he could inherit the money she had quietly stashed away in France. She soon recovered. When her sister's vile husband, the Duke of Pembroke, died, aged thirty, Henriette took the opportunity to return to France. It took several ships to ferry all her booty back: chests with fine cloths, cabinets, looking-glasses, Chinese lacquer cabinets, a bed of Genoese velvet, pearl necklaces, silks, gloves, etc. Despite having a small child, she was in a position to snap up the Marquis de Thors, Governor of Blois; her daughter, Lady Charlotte Herbert, later married the son of the notorious Judge Jeffreys.

Henry Jermyn, the old Earl of St Albans, 'full of soup and gold', as Marvell described him in *Last Instructions to a Painter*, reputed former court stallion and lover and secret husband of Queen Henrietta Maria (and ultimately responsible for Jermyn Street), had died in January 1684. Charles now made Nelly's thirteen-year-old son, Charles, the new Duke of St Albans, with lodgings in Whitehall and a pension of £1,500, while she got a pension of £5,000 and other benefits, including bragging rights ('my son, the Duke ...'). It was also arranged that he should marry Diana de Vere, heiress of the Earl of Oxford (who had seduced and refused to marry an actress, Roxalana), which took place in 1694.

In late 1684, the King's health declined. On Monday 2 February 1685, he collapsed, and despite all the doctors, weakened steadily. On his deathbed, he resigned the Crown to James, took the Catholic last rites, expressed his love for Louise and care for Nelly and, as narrated in the following chapter, died, shortly before midday, on Friday 6 February 1685.

His different mistresses now had to look to themselves. Barbara had been at court on the previous Sunday, but there is no report of her activities in the interim. Louise made preparations for a quick retreat to France, but Nelly was more worried. As her pension lapsed with the King's death, she was soon in financial difficulties, and creditors came calling. She mortgaged her estate at Bestwood Park, borrowed from bankers and got an advance of £1,000 from the Keeper of the Privy Purse. At the end of April, she dictated (she could hardly write) a letter to King James, hinting at what could be done for her – a title – and touchingly describing her relationship with Charles over seventeen years. She said that Charles,

had he lived, he told me before he died, that the world should see by
what he did for me that he had both love and value for me and that
he did not do for me as my mad Lady Worcester, he was my friend
and allowed me to tell him all my griefs and did like a friend advise
me and told me who was my friend and who was not.[41]

She continued to mingle with the remains of the libertine set,
making her mark in her own way. Mary Howard, the Duchess of
Norfolk, invited her to Windsor for a session of cards. In the Duke's
absence, the Duchess started flirting with Sir John Germaine. He
also tried it on with Nelly, who said afterwards that 'the dog would
have lain with her, but she would not lay the dog where the deer
laid'. Germaine then had a vigorous night with the Duchess; in the
morning, Nelly asked if she was rested. The Duchess apologised
for having her hair very untidy. Nelly wondered why, after such
a night as the Duchess had passed (had they been very noisy?),
her hair was not out of powder and curl also, and expected to see
Germaine crawl out 'like a drowned rat'.[42]

In September 1685, James paid off most of her debts, gave her
some £1,800 and an annual allowance of £1,500, and Queen
Catherine – perhaps recognising her need and good nature –
generously granted her a pension of £2,000 a year, though she was
never free of debt. She lived in Pall Mall, bedridden towards the
end, in pain and partially paralysed down the left side (thought
to be one of the symptoms of venereal disease, an occupational
hazard, from which she had suffered for some years). She died in
November 1687 and was buried at St Martin in the Fields, her
funeral sermon preached by Dr Tenison. Her son inherited her
estate and bills. In her will she left money for a decent pulpit cloth
and cushions for the church, £50 to Tenison and a Mr Warner, for
poor Catholics, 'for showing charity to those who differ from me
in religion'; her son was to provide £100 to rescue the poor, to buy
winter clothes for those with none and to pay for the release from
prison of poor debtors.

Alexander Smith printed Etherege's poem on Nell Gwyn ('I sing
of a scoundrel lass / Raised from a dunghill to a King's embrace')
in his collection *The School of Venus* (1716), but concluded, 'Sir

George may write as diminutive [disparagingly] as he pleases of Nell Gwyn; however, I must do this justice to her memory, as to say, she was endowed with more charity than all the King's mistresses, which covers a multitude of faults.'[43] Indeed, she was honest, frank, funny and good-hearted: there was a lot to be said for her.

Louise's situation on Charles's death was very different: an unpopular French Catholic aristocrat, she was soon off, with a pension from James of 3,000 guineas a year, plus 2,000 guineas a year for her son and another £7,000 a year from various estates, sailing away in August 1685. As with her sister, it took several ships to carry away her loot. She lived in Paris in a grand mansion, gambling for large stakes and losing. When her English pension was discontinued, Louis gave her an allowance of £12,000 in June 1689 and her son a further £20,000 in September. She came to London in May 1688 to attend the wedding of her niece; in March 1689, she asked her old friend Henry Sidney to persuade William III to provide another pension, but without success. For a while she was mistress of Henri de Lorraine, Duc d'Elboeuf, and then lived at Aubigny, her son's estate. In 1698, she was permitted to visit England, when she managed to obtain a pension of £1,000. Unable to live moderately, by 1708 she was again in financial difficulties, having to pledge some property against loans. She came over again for George I's coronation in 1714, when there was a brief meeting between her, Elizabeth Villiers, Countess of Orkney and former mistress of William III, and Catherine Sedley, Countess of Dorchester and former mistress of James II, who remarked, delightfully, 'Fancy we three whores meeting like this!', which must have gone down wonderfully with Louise. Her son, Richmond, died in 1723, and she herself died in Paris, in November 1734, aged eighty-five.

11

AFTER ALL THIS VANITY

As time went on, there seemed an increasing general weariness and disenchantment with the loose behaviour at court. Remarkably, even Charles Sackville, Lord Dorset, once one of the wildest libertines and debauchees of the 1660s, turned to a bitter denunciation of the court's endemic corruption and the cuckold King's futility, in his *A Faithful Catalogue of the most Eminent Ninnies*, in 1683:

> Go on, my muse, and with bold voice proclaim
> The vicious lives, and long detested fame,
> Of scoundrel lords, and their lewd wives' amours,
> Pimp statesmen, canting priests, court bawds and whores:
> Exalted vice its own vile name does found,
> Thro' climes remote, and distant shores renowned. [1]
> Thy strumpets, Charles, have 'scaped no nation's ear,
> Cleveland the van, and Portsmouth leads the rear:
> A brace of cherubs, of as vile a breed,
> As ever were produced of human seed.
> To all but thee, the punks were ever kind,
> Free as loose air, and gen'rous as the wind.

Both steered thy pego, and the nation's helm,
And both betrayed thy pintle, and the realm ...

The writer goes on to denounce in savage terms a string of
conniving courtiers, unfaithful wives and loose mistresses, as
evidence of the moral collapse instituted by the lax King, while
warning of what might ensue for the future, dull-witted King's
reign, subject to manipulative ministers and immoral women:

Oh sacred James! May thy dread noddle be
As far from danger, as from wit 'tis free,
But if that good and gracious monarch's charms
Could ne'er confine one woman to his arms,
What strange mysterious spell, what strong defence
Can guard that front, which has not half his sense?[1]

It has been suggested that politically, Charles had become passive,
leaving many initiatives to James and Lord Sunderland, but more
recently it has been argued that he was working unobtrusively
through James's advisers to establish a stronger, more absolute
monarchy, to provide him with a safe and quiet existence.[2]
Otherwise, he seems to have had a relaxed way of life with Louise
and Nell, though by November, 1684, his health was deteriorating,
and he ate and drank less. He was treating a sore on his leg with
mercury, the standard treatment for venereal disease (with which
he had been, and probably still was, afflicted). On Sunday 1
February 1685, Evelyn was at court:

I am never to forget the unexpressable luxury and profaneness,
gaming and all dissolution, and as it were total forgetfulness of God
(it being Sunday evening) which this day sennight [a week before]
I was witness of; the King, sitting and toying with his concubines
Portsmouth, Cleveland and Mazarin, etc; a French boy singing
love songs in that glorious gallery whilst about twenty of the great
courtiers and other dissolute persons were at basset round a large
table, a bank of at least 2,000 in gold before them, upon which two
gentlemen that were with me made reflexions with astonishment, it

being a scene of utmost vanity, and surely as they thought it would never have an end. Six days after, was all in the dust.[3]

The King felt unwell; by evening he had stomach trouble. On Monday morning, after a restless night, the Groom of the Bedchamber found his face very pale, and while he was dressing he continually stopped speaking in the middle of a sentence. The doctor, who was treating his bad leg, and the barber were admitted; the King settled in his chair, when he fell forward in a violent fit. The Duke of York was sent for. Sixteen ounces of blood were drawn to purge the body of infection. Over the next five days, the King suffered excruciating pain, as up to thirteen doctors bled him, gave him potions to make him vomit and empty his bowels, and inserted powders up his nose to clear his sinuses; hot cupping-glasses were applied, his head was shaved and blistering agents applied to his scalp. The Queen rubbed his feet with pigeons, as had been done to her when she was expected to die. Quinine (known as Jesuits' powders) put him into a coma, but did no more. He was very brave, thanked the doctors for their efforts and, famously, apologised for taking so long to die.

On Thursday, the Duke was told that the King would not last long. Offered a priest, the King waved him away. It is not clear what then happened, as Catholic commentators put out different stories as to whether it was the Queen, the Duke or even Louise (who had to withdraw) who was responsible for the summoning up the back stairs (the former entry of so many young women) of the Catholic priest, Father Hudleston, whom he had known at the Battle of Worcester in 1651, who gave him the last rites as a Catholic. How strongly Charles really wished this, or whether, at the last, he went along with family pressure, is unknowable.[4]

He then gave his blessings to his illegitimate sons gathered there (except his first, the Duke of Monmouth). The Queen sent a message asking his forgiveness, to which he replied, 'Alas, poor woman! She ask my pardon ... I beg hers with all my heart.' He resigned the Crown and kingdom to James 'with great joy' – according to official report (previously he had had no hopes for James's success as king – 'he will be obliged to travel again', (he had prophesied). He asked James to look after his mistresses, saying that he had always loved Louise and loved her now at the last, and, according to legend, added, 'Let not poor Nelly starve.' He asked for the curtains to be opened that he might once more see the sun, but sank back, and died, on Friday 6 February 1685, in his sixty-fourth year. Diagnosis, from a distance of some three centuries, is chronic granular kidney disease, accompanied by uraemic convulsions and coma.

> The courtiers went off to inaugurate the reign of King James II, leaving the body covered by a single sheet and watched by a page. Curious visitors raised the covering from time to time to gaze upon the corpse: in death, as in life, Charles was on stage. The slices, blisters and pricks left all over the body by the doctors had already begun to fester before death came, and in the succeeding hours they rapidly began to stink. The odour of human corruption rose to mingle with the perfume of the heavy velvet hangings of the royal bed.[5]

His mistresses made their various arrangements. Catherine was deeply grieved and went into profound mourning, retiring to her apartment in Whitehall, with black drapes and candles, for two months. She then transferred to Somerset House and to a nunnery in Hammersmith. She had some difficulties with William III and returned to Portugal in 1692, where, for some time, she acted as regent, before dying in 1705.

The Revd Gilbert Burnet, perhaps angered by his dismissal from a court position and having heard of Charles's conversion to Catholicism, wrote in his *History* a very sour and hostile account of his late King (who, in turn, had not thought highly of him):

> He had so ill an opinion of mankind, that he thought the great art of living and of governing was to manage all things and all persons with a depth of craft and dissimulation … He had great vices, but scarce any virtues to correct them … He was, during the active part of his life, given up to sloth and lewdness to such a degree that he hated business … And though he desired to become absolute, and

to overturn both our religion and our laws, yet he would neither run the risk, nor give himself the trouble, which so great a desire required. He had an appearance of gentleness in his outward deportment: but he seemed to have no bowels or tenderness in his nature ... He was apt to forgive crimes, even blood itself, yet he never forgave any thing that was done against himself ... He had the art of making people grow fond of him, at first, by a softness in his whole way of conversation, as he was certainly the best bred man of his age. But when it appeared how little could be built on his promise, they were cured of the fondness he was apt to raise in them ... Few things ever went near his heart.[6]

(It is not hard to read between the lines here.) John Evelyn, certainly a moral-minded man, who knew Charles and the court rather better, had this to say, regretfully, of his 'love of a voluptuous and sensual life, which a vicious court had brought into credit'.

Of the man himself, he wrote more generously than Burnet:

A prince of many virtues and many great imperfections, debonair, easy of access, of a vigorous and robust constitution, and in all appearance capable of a longer life ... his countenance fierce, his voice great, proper of person, every motion became him; a lover of the sea and skilful in shipping, not affecting other studies, yet he had a laboratory and knew of many empirical medicines and the easier mechanical mathematics; loved planting, building, and brought in a politer way of living, which passed to luxury and intolerable expense. He had a particular talent in telling stories and facetious passages, of which he had innumerable, which made some buffoons and vicious wretches too presumptuous and familiar, not worthy the favours they abused. He took delight to have a number of little spaniels follow him, and lie in his bedchamber, where often times he suffered the bitches to puppy and give suck, which rendered it very offensive, and indeed made the whole Court nasty and stinking. An excellent prince, doubtless, had he been less addicted to women, which made him uneasy and always in want to supply their unmeasurable profusion, and to the detriment of many indigent persons who had signally served both him and his father.

Easily and frequently he changed favourites to his great prejudice ... his too easy nature resigned him to be managed by crafty men, and some abandoned and profane wretches, who corrupted his otherwise sufficient parts, disciplined as he had been by many afflictions during his banishment; which gave him much experience and knowledge of men and things; but these wicked creatures took him off from all application becoming so great a king ... He was ever kind to me, and very gracious upon all occasions, and therefore I cannot without ingratitude but deplore his loss, which for many respects (as well as duty) I do with all my soul. [7]

While Burnet can find little good to say of Charles, Evelyn puts the blame for his failings on the 'vicious court' – which he had created, and for which, of course, he was responsible.

Burnet noted that, surprisingly, the King's 'funeral was very mean. He did not lie in state: no mournings [rings or garments] were given [though Evelyn reports that directions were given for the wearing of mourning]; and the expense of it was not equal to what an ordinary nobleman's funeral will rise to'.[8] James's economy seems more like sibling resentment (there was little fondness between the brothers). Evelyn phrased it more positively, or optimistically, in words that looked to mark the end of an era:

The King was very obscurely buried in a vault under Henry VIII's chapel in Westminster, without any manner of pomp, and soon forgotten after all this vanity, and the face of the whole Court exceedingly changed into a more solemn and moral behaviour.[9]

Of course, that wasn't going to last.

NOTES

Introduction: New Rants and Raptures

1. Bodleian MS Don.b.8
2. Butler, *Characters*, 210–11
3. Butler, *Satires*, 40
4. MacLeod, 17
5. Turner, J. G., 166
6. *Ibid.*, x
7. Bryson, 235
8. Sedley, I, 45
9. Wilson, J. H., *Court Wits*, 14
10. Pope, 639–41
11. Nussbaum, *Satires*, n.p.
12. Rochester (Hayward), 26–33
13. Turner, J. G., 167
14. Dryden, XI, 221–318
15. Rochester (Ellis), 31–4
16. Ward, 138
17. Etherege, *Plays*, 168
18. Rochester (Hayward), 26–33
19. *Poems on Affairs of State*, 1704
20. Bodl. Firth MS. C.15, 85
21. *Ibid.*
22. Bodl. Douce 357; *Poems on Affairs of State*, 1704
23. Bodl. MS. Don. b.8
24. *Poems on Affairs of State*, 1697
25. *Remains of the Right Honourable John, Earl of Rochester*, (London, 1718); Bodl. 8 O 21(2) Linc.
26. Gould, 141–54; Nussbaum, n.p.
27. Pope, 217–42
28. Nussbaum, n.p.
29. Radcliffe, *Works*, n.p.
30. Rochester (Hayward), 66–7
31. *Ibid.*, 71–3
32. McFarlane, 42–3
33. Radcliffe, *op. cit.* n.p.
34. Magalotti, 125
35. Bodl. MS.Firth.c.15
36. Margoliouth (I), 141–65
37. Radcliffe, *op. cit.*, n.p.; Bodl. MS. Firth.c.15

1 Before Dover: The First Buttered Buns

1. Hutton, 10
2. Clarendon, *History*, IV. 21–2
3. *Ibid.*, IX.18–19
4. Hutton, 12
5. Scott, 354
6. Hutton, 21
7. Carew, xxxv
8. Pepys, *Diary*, 22.11.1662
9. Hutton, 24
10. Evelyn, III, 40 & n.
11. Fea, *Beauties*, 119
12. Hutton, 26
13. Aulnoy, 4–5

14. Clarendon, *op.cit.*, V.1
15. Burnet, I. 52
16. Masters, 20
17. Hutton, 40
18. D. Wilson, 84
19. Hutton, 75
20. Clarendon, *op.cit.*, IV.296
21. Scott, 211
22. *Ibid.*, 116
23. Clarendon, *op. cit.* IV.268
24. Scott, 155
25. *Ibid.*, 411
26. Boyer, 48
27. Chesterfield, n.p.
28. Aulnoy, 111
29. *Ibid.*, 111
30. Aubrey (Dick), 89
31. Chesterfield, n.p.
32. *Ibid.*, n.p.
33. *Ibid.*, n.p.
34. *Ibid.*, n.p.
35. *Ibid.*, n.p.
36. Boyer, 48
37. Chesterfield, n.p.
38. *Ibid.*, n.p.
39. *Ibid.*, n.p.
40. Aubrey, I.75
41. Andrews, 22
42. *Ibid.*, 23
43. Halifax, II, 490
44. Chesterfield, n.p.

2 The King, the Quean and the Queen

1. Dryden, *Astraea Redux*, 284–7, *Works*, I.23–32
2. Clarendon, *op. cit.*, VI.234
3. *Poems on Affairs of State*, 1697
4. Magalotti, 71–2
5. Chesterfield, *op.cit.*, n.p.
6. Thurley, *Whitehall Palace*
7. Burnet, I. 307
8. Magalotti, 29
9. MacLeod, 26
10. Andrews, 53
11. Hartmann, *The King My Brother*, 39
12. Magalotti, 31
13. Chesterfield, n.p.
14. Rochester (Ellis), 329, n.11
15. Magalotti, 70
16. *Ibid.*, 30
17. *Ibid.*, 70–1
18. Pepys, *Diary*, 15.5.1663
19. Hartmann, *Charles II and Madame*, 50–1
20. The whole ensuing episode collected from Clarendon, in Andrews, 63–9
21. Gramont, VI. 71
22. *Ibid.*, X. 211
23. Aulnoy, 6–7
24. Andrews, 87
25. Gramont, Ix. 151–2
26. Buckingham, 7
27. Simpson, 145–7. The song was registered in 1637, and the song and phrase often reprinted. In 1660, in *Rats Rhimed to Death*, it is called 'London's true character'. The phrase once concluded the rhyme, 'Mary, Mary, quite contrary'.
28. Pepys, *Diary*, 31.12.62
29. *Ibid.*, 1.1.63
30. *Ibid.*, 8.2.1663
31. Gramont, X. 190
32. Rochester (Hayward), 122–6
33. Jusserand, 89
34. Pepys, *Diary*, 13.10.1663
35. *Ibid.*, 26.10.1663
36. Gramont, VII. 98
37. Andrews, 107
38. MacLeod, 128–9
39. *Ibid.*, 50, 59, 47
40. Andrews, 114,
41. Sackville, *Minor Poets*, I. 128–30
42. Wood, II. 68
43. Andrews, 128
44. *Ibid.*, 130–1
45. Pepys, *Diary*, 8.12.1666

46. Bodl. MS. Eng.Poet.e.4; *Poems on Affairs of State*, 1697
47. Bodl. Don.b.8; *Poems on Affairs of State*, 1697
48. Pepys, *Diary*, 27.8.1667
49. Gramont, VI. 70
50. Margoliouth I., 141–65
51. Pope, 667–73
52. Pepys, *Diary*, 29.7.1667
53. Gramont. X. 177

3 James, the Married Man

1. Gramont, VIII. 111
2. *Ibid.*, VIII. 112
3. *Ibid.*, VIII. 113
4. Andrews, 41; Fea, *James II*, 30–1
5. Gramont, VIII. 114
6. Pepys, *Diary*, 7.10.1660
7. Bodl. MS. Don. B.8; *POAS* II. 156
8. Burnet, I.171
9. *Ibid.*, I.169
10. Gramont, VIII. 114
11. Jusserand, 107
12. Gramont, X. 194
13. *Ibid.*, X. 194
14. Margoliouth, I. 141–65
15. Bodl. MS.Don. b.8
16. Bodl. Gough, (1666); *Third Advice to a Painter* (London, 1667)
17. *Poems on Affairs of State*, 1697
18. Gramont, VIII. 114,
19. *Ibid.* VIII. 116
20. *Ibid.*
21. Turner, J. G., *Libertines*, 41
22. Gramont, VIII. 117
23. Aubrey, I.216–21
24. Gramont, VIII. 118
25. *Ibid.*, V. 108–09
26. *Ibid.*, VII. 97
27. *Ibid.*, VIII. 122–3
28. *Ibid.*, VIII. 124
29. *Ibid.*, VIII. 126
30. *Ibid.*, VIII. 129

31. *Ibid.*, IX. 130
32. *Ibid.*, IX. 135
33. *Ibid.*, IX. 138
34. Denham, 22
35. *Ibid.*, 106
36. Gramont, IX. 134
37. Margoliouth, I. 141–65
38. *Poems on Affairs of State*, 1697
39. Denham, 96
40. *Ibid.*, 106
41. Andrews, 126
42. Gramont, IX. 156; for her portrait, see Macleod, 182
43. Jusserand, 154–6
44. Gramont, IX. 159
45. MacLeod, 92–3
46. Gramont, VI. 91–2
47. *Poems on Affairs of State*, 1697
48. Gramont, X. 195
49. *Ibid.*, X. 196–7
50. *Ibid.*, X. 201
51. Steinmann, *Myddelton*, n.p.
52. Magalotti, 36
53. *Ibid.*, 37–8
54. Fea, *Beauties*, 62
55. *Ibid.*, 62
56. *Ibid.*, 59
57. *Ibid.*, 62
58. Margoliouth, I., 141–65
59. Fea, *Beauties*, 148
60. Rochester (Hayward), 128–31
61. Rochester (Ellis), 225
62. *Ibid.*, 89–91
63. Evelyn, II. 84
64. Sedley, 134–5; for her portrait, see Dolman, 58
65. *Ibid.*, 135
66. *Ibid.*, 137
67. Sackville, *Minor Poets*, I. 139
68. Sackville, *A Complete Edition*, 511–12
69. Rochester (Hayward), 55–8
70. Sedley, 174
71. Fraser, 406
72. *Ibid.*, 407
73. Sedley, 218–19

4 The Glorious Court of the Prince d'Amour

1. Buckingham, 256–7
2. Davenant *Dramatic Works*, I, 336–7,
3. For a full description, see Thurley, *Whitehall Palace*
4. Magalotti, 72
5. Waller, 40–5
6. Keay, 194–5
7. Sedley, I. 19
8. Gramont, VIII. 119
9. *Ibid.*, VI. 75
10. Bodl. MS.Firth.c.15, 106
11. Gramont, IX. 147
12. *Ibid.*, IX. 149–50
13. *Ibid.*, IX. 151
14. *Ibid.*, IX 152
15. MacLeod, 92–3
16. Jusserand, 94–5
17. Gramont, VII. 83
18. *Ibid.*, IX. 154
19. *Ibid.*, VII. 88
20. *Ibid.*, VII. 90–1
21. *Ibid.*, VII. 91
22. *Ibid.*, X. 186
23. *Ibid.*, X. 188
24. Bodl. MS. Don. b.8, 179
25. Gramont., X. 193
26. *Ibid.*, X. 194
27. *Ibid.*, IX. 147
28. *Ibid.*, IX. 156
29. *Ibid.*, IX. 154–5
30. *Ibid.*, IX. 164
31. *Ibid.*, IX. 166
32. *Ibid.*, IX. 170–1
33. *Ibid.*, IX. 174
34. *Ibid.*, IX. 174
35. MacLeod, 182
36. Gramont, IX. 178
37. *Ibid.*, IX. 179
38. *Ibid.*, VI. 77
39. *Ibid.*, X. 183
40. *Ibid.*, X. 184
41. *Ibid.*, X. 185
42. *Ibid.*, X. 185
43. *Ibid.*, X. 197
44. Wilson, J. H., *Rochester-Savile Letters*, 55
45. Butler, *Satires*, 218
46. Fraser, 280; Pickford, 127–9
47. Cooper, 48
48. Wilson, J. H., *op.cit.*, 28
49. Rochester (Hayward), 76, 128
50. Fraser, 282
51. MacLeod, 189
52. Fraser, 284. For a full account, see Pickford, *passim*
53. Evelyn, II.386
54. Swift II, 151–2
55. Aulnoy, 130
56. Wilson, J. H., *Court Satires*, 239
57. Rochester (Hayward), 308; *Remains of the Right Honourable John Earl of Rochester*, 53–5
58. Bodl. MS.Don.b.8
59. Behn, VI. 374

5 Buckingham: The Wanton Hours

1. Anon. *Rochester's Farewell*, *Poems on Affairs of State*, 1697; Dryden, *Absalom and Achitophel*, 545–54, *Works*, II.2–36
2. Wilson, J. H., *A Rake*, 9
3. Clarendon, *Life*, III.133
4. Buckingham, II. 4–5
5. *Ibid.*, II. xxxii
6. *Ibid.*, II.52
7. *Ibid.*, II. 215, 192
8. Gramont, VI. 78
9. Bodl. MS Don.b.8, 179
10. Gramont, IX. 131
11. *Ibid.*, XI. 212
12. Buckingham, II. 195
13. Wilson, J. H., *A Rake*, 38–9; and see Reresby, 58–9
14. Bodl. MS. Rawl. Poet. 84
15. Gramont, XI. 213

16. Pepys, *Diary*, 21.10.1666
17. Wilson, J. H., *A Rake*, 50–3
18. *Ibid.*, 54–5
19. *Ibid.*, 64–5
20. *Ibid.*, 66
21. *Ibid.*, 73
22. *Ibid.*, 75
23. Clarendon, *Life*, III.280
24. Buckingham, II.208
25. Hartmann, *Charles II and Madame*, 194
26. Butler, *Characters*, 32–3
27. Margoliouth, I. 141–65
28. Wilson, J. H., *A Rake*, 94–5
29. *Poems on Affairs of State*, 1704
30. Wilson, J. H., *op.cit.*, 104–6
31. *Ibid.*, 119
32. Buckingham II. 14
33. Pepys, *Diary*, 30.5.1668
34. *Ibid.*, 19.5.1669
35. Waller, I. lxvi
36. Wilson, J.H., *op. cit.*, 132
37. Buckingham II.183
38. Melton, *HLQ*
39. Pope, 570–86
40. *Poems on Affairs of State*, 1704
41. McFadden, *YES*
42. Hanrahan, 147
43. Wilson, J. H., *op.cit.*, 172
44. Bodl. MS. Don.b.8, 482–3
45. Dennis, I. 218–19
46. Turner, J. G., 210
47. Wilson, J. H., *op.cit.*, 189
48. *Ibid.*, 191
49. *Ibid.*, 196
50. *Ibid.*, 200
51. Buckingham, II. 37
52. *Ibid.*, xxxix
53. Wilson, J.H., *op.cit.*, 201–3
54. Hanrahan, 168
55. *Ibid.*, 172–3
56. *Ibid.*, 178–80
57. Bodl. MS Don. b.8
58. Hanrahan, *op.cit.*, 206–08
59. Buckingham, II. 25
60. Sheffield, *Works*, I. 23–5; *Poems on Affairs of State*, 1697
61. Wilson, J. H., *op.cit.*, 213
62. Pope, 583
63. Buckingham, II. 231

6 The King and the Lady of Pleasure

1. Pepys, *Diary*, 14.1.1668, 31.5.1667
2. Bodl. MS. Don. b.8, 185
3. Gramont, VI. 77–8
4. *Ibid.*, X. 177
5. Evelyn, 4.2.1668
6. Pepys, *Diary*, 25.3.1668
7. Andrews, 177–8
8. Bodl. MS. Don.b.8, 190–3
9. *Ibid.*
10. Chesterfield, 18
11. Andrews, 223–4
12. Wilson, J. H., 112–14; *POAS* III. 170
13. Andrews, 182
14. Pepys, *Diary*, 28.4.1669
15. Hartmann, *The King My Brother*, 256
16. Magalotti, 29
17. Waller, II. 93, 94
18. *Poems on Affairs of State*, 1704; Bodl. MS. Don. b.8, 206–07
19. Clarendon, *Life*, III.172
20. Andrews, 199
21. Dennis. 216–17
22. Burnet, I.476
23. Pope, 668
24. Manley, n.p.
25. Andrews, 211–20
26. Aubrey, *Wiltshire*
27. Margoliouth, I. 141–65
28. Andrews, 214
29. *Ibid.*, 219
30. Rochester (Hayward), 236
31. Andrews, 175
32. *Ibid.*, 231
33. Hamilton, 165
34. Andrews, 242
35. *POAS* III.478
36. Bodl. MS. Douce 357

37. Andrews, 270
38. Wilson, J.H., *Rochester-Savile Letters*, 25
39. Andrews, 272–3
40. Hamilton, 206
41. Dryden, *Works*, II.3–37
42. *Poems on Affairs of State*, 1704
43. Buckingham II. 34
44. Margoliouth, I. 173–5
45. Evelyn, IV.359
46. Oldmixon, II. 576, Andrews, 256–7
47. Andrews, 262–5; Hamilton, 202–5
48. Dolman, 124
49. Bodl. MS. Don. b.8

7 La Belle Stuart

1. Hartmann, *Stuart*, 11
2. Gramont, VI. 77
3. *Ibid.*, VI. 76
4. Bodl. MS. Don. b.8
5. Hartmann, *op.cit.*, 55
6. Pepys, *Diary*, 9.11.1667
7. Gramont, VII. 95
8. *Ibid.*, VII. 95
9. *Ibid.*, VII. 96
10. *Ibid.*, VII. 97
11. *Ibid.*, VIII. 122
12. *Ibid.*, XI. 219
13. *Ibid.*, XI. 220
14. MacLeod, 96–7
15. Gramont, V. 98
16. *Ibid.*, V. 101
17. Wilson, J.H., *A Rake*, 133
18. Gramont, VII. 223
19. Waller, II.65
20. Gramont, XI. 211
21. Pepys, *Diary*, 19.3.1667
22. Turner, D.M., 92–3
23. Butler, *Satires*, 56
24. Gramont, XI. 223–5
25. Magalotti, 80
26. Burnet, I.452
27. Pepys, *Diary*, 3.4.1667
28. Burnet, II.252
29. Margoliouth, I. 141–65
30. Hartmann, *Stuart*, 146–7
31. *Poems on Affairs of State*, 1697
32. Hartmann, *op.cit.*, 151
33. Pepys, *Diary*, 26.3.1668
34. Hartmann, *op.cit.*, 153
35. Magalotti, 74–5
36. Sheffield, I. 23–5
37. Hartmann, *op. cit.*, 186
38. *Ibid.*, 189
39. Butler, *Characters*, 69–70
40. Bodl. Firth. MS. C.15, 85

8 Portsmouth but not Plymouth: Nell and Louise

1. Wilson, J. H., *Nell Gwyn*, 96
2. *Poems on Affairs of State*, 1697; Rochester (Hayward) 96–8
3. *Satire*, John Lacy, *Works of … Roscommon*
4. Rochester (Hayward), 96–8.
5. Aubrey, I. 205–06
6. Pepys, *Diary*, 21.12.1668
7. Wycherley, 206
8. Summers, II. 106
9. Bodl. MS. Firth. c.15
10. *The Covent Garden Drollery*, 4
11. Wilson, J. H., *Nell Gwyn*, 20
12. Fraser, 425
13. Wycherley, 214; Gould, 161–85
14. Rochester (Ellis), 102, 253
15. Wilson, J. H., *Rochester-Savile Letters*, 52
16. Smith, 83
17. MacLeod, 100–01
18. Wilson, J. H., *Court Satires*, 57
19. Buckingham I. 119, 17–22
20. Davenant, *Dramatic Works*, I. 396–7
21. Dolman, 68
22. Beauclerk, 102
23. Bodl. MS.Firth c.15, 254–60
24. *Ibid.*,
25. Wilson, J. H., *Nell Gwyn*, 66
26. Hopkins, 86

27. Bodl. MS. Firth c.15
28. Smith, 62
29. Turner, J. G., 41
30. *Remains of the Right Honourable ... Rochester*: Bodl. 8 O 2192) Linc.
31. Dasent, 170
32. Dryden, *Works* X. 192–3
33. MacLeod, 46
34. Evelyn, III. 573
35. Fea, *Some Beauties*, 75
36. *Poems on Affairs of State*, 1697
37. *Poems on Affairs of State*, 1704
38. Delpech, 59–60
39. Andrews, 208
40. Delpech, 59
41. *Ibid.*, 60
42. Uglow, 429
43. Fea, *op.cit.*, 75
44. Delpech, 42
45. *Ibid.*, 42
46. Wilson, J. H., *Nell Gwyn*, 152
47. Bevan, 41
48. Delpech, 62
49. *Works of ... Roscommon*
50. Sévigné II. 170
51. Beauclerk, 226
52. Wilson, Derek, 293
53. Smith, 64
54. Wilson, Derek, 293
55. Beauclerk, 231
56. Wilson, J. H., 120
57. Bevan, 63
58. Turner, J. G., 145
59. *Ibid.*, xiii

9 The New Pretender: Mazarin

1. Hartmann, *Vagabond Duchess*, 152
2. Fea, *Some Beauties*, 5
3. *Ibid.*, 6
4. *Ibid.*, 8
5. *Ibid.*, 12
6. *Ibid.*, 19
7. Hartmann, *op. cit.*, 112

8. *Ibid.*, 160
9. Alexander, 144–5
10. Fea, *op.cit.*, 1
11. Waller II. 77–8
12. Delpech, 107
13. *Choice Ayres and Songs*, 72
14. Hartmann, *op.cit.*, 236.
15. Delpech, 109
16. Hartmann, *op.cit.*, 168
17. *Ibid.*, 201
18. *Poems on Affairs of State*, 1697
19. Hartmann, *op.cit.*, 204
20. Rochester (Ellis), 102
21. Delpech, 121
22. Alexander, 147
23. Delpech, 172–3
24. *Poems on Affairs of State*, 1697
25. Hartmann, 242
26. Delpech, 173
27. Hartmann, *op. cit.*, 250

10 Love and Value: Louise and Nell

1. Dasent, 195
2. Margoliouth, I.184–9; *Poems on Affairs of State*, 1697
3. Dolman, 71
4. Falkus, 134–5
5. Beauclerk, 241
6. Hartmann, *Vagabond Duchess*, 96
7. *Ibid.*, 188
8. Bevan, 72
9. Rochester (Ellis), 101
10. Delpech, 114
11. Hutton, 385
12. Hopkins, 147
13. Rochester (Hayward), 104–05
14. Evelyn, IV. 343
15. Wilson, J. H., *Nell Gwyn*, 162
16. Wilson, Derek, 249
17. Wilson, J. H., *op.cit.*, 169
18. Delpech, 77
19. *Ibid.*, 120
20. Wilson, J. H., *Rochester-Savile Letters*, 52

21. Wilson, J. H., *Nell Gwyn*, 183–4
22. Behn, II. 305–06
23. *Works of ... Roscommon*, 98–103
24. Beauclerk, 292–6
25. *Works of ... Roscommon*, 98–103
26. Bevan, 118
27. *Poems on Affairs of State*, 1697
28. *Works of ... Roscommon*, 98–103
29. Delpech, 135–6
30. *Ibid.*, 142–3
31. Bevan, 125
32. Beauclerk, 307; Bodl. MS. Firth c.15, 106
33. Turner, J., 1
34. Bodl. MS. Firth. c.15, 129–32; *Miscellaneous Works*, I. 29–33
35. Wilson, Derek, 253
36. Beauclerk, 324–5
37. Evelyn, IV.395
38. Delpech, 170
39. Bevan, 148
40. *Ibid.*, 150
41. Beauclerk, 355
42. Masters, 110
43. Smith, 77

11 After All This Vanity

1. Sackville, *Minor Poets* II., n.p.; Bodl. MS. Firth. c.15, 232–53
2. Hutton, 430–41
3. Evelyn, IV. 409–14
4. Keay, 202–03
5. Hutton, 443, 445
6. Burnet II. 467–70
7. Evelyn IV. 409–11
8. Burnet II. 463
9. Evelyn IV. 415

BIBLIOGRAPHY

Alexander, Julia Marciari and Catherine MacLeod, eds., *Politics, Transgression, and Representation at the Court of Charles II* (London: Paul Mellon Centre, 2007)

Andrews, Allan, *The Royal Whore. Barbara Villiers, Countess of Castlemaine* (London: Hutchinson, 1971)

Anon., ed., *The Remains of the Right Honorable John, Earl of Rochester* (London, 1681)

Anon., ed., *The Works of the Earls of Rochester, Roscommon and Dorset* (London, 1739)

Aubrey, John, *Brief Lives*, (2 vols) ed. Andrew Clark (Oxford: Clarendon, 1898)

Aubrey, John, *Brief Lives*, ed. Oliver Lawson Dick (Harmondsworth: Penguin, 1949)

Aubrey, John, *The Natural History of Wiltshire*, ed. John Britton (London: Wiltshire Topographical Society, 1847)

Aulnoy, Baronne d', *Memoirs of the Court of England in 1675*, trans. W. H. Arthur, ed. and rev. G. D. Gilbert (London: Bodley Head, 1913)

Beauclerk, Charles, *Nell Gwyn* (New York: Atlantic Monthly Press, 2005)

Behn, Aphra, *The Works of Aphra Behn* (6 vols), ed. Montague Summers (London: Heinemann, 1915)

Bevan, Bryan, *Charles II's French Mistress* (London: R. Hale, 1972)

Bodleian Library, MS Don.b.8; Eng.Poet.e.4; MS. Firth.c.15; MS. Douce 357; MS Eng. Poet. D.49

Boyer, Abel, *The History of the Life and Reign of Queen Anne* (London, 1722)

Bryson, Anna, *From Courtesy to Civility. Changing Codes of Conduct in Early Modern England* (Oxford: Clarendon, 1998)

Buckingham, George, *Plays, Poems and Miscellaneous Writings associated with George Villiers, Second Duke of Buckingham* (2 vols), eds. Robert D. Hume and Harold Love (Oxford: OUP, 2007)

Burnet, Gilbert, *History of My Own Time*, (2 vols), ed. Osmund Airy (Oxford: Clarendon, 1890)

Butler, Samuel, *Characters*, ed., A. R. Waller (Cambridge: CUP, 1908)

Butler, Samuel, *Satires and Miscellaneous Poetry and Prose*, ed., René Lamar (Cambridge: CUP, 1928)

Carew, Thomas, *The Poems of Thomas Carew*, ed., Rhodes Dunlap (Oxford: OUP, 1949)

Chesterfield, Philip, Second Earl, *Correspondence with Various Ladies* (London: Fanfrolico, n.d., 1930?)

Choice Ayres and Songs, (Fourth Book), London, 1683

Clarendon, Edward, *The History of the Rebellion and Civil Wars*, (6 vols), ed. Dunn Macray (Oxford: Clarendon, 1888)

Clarendon, Edward, *The Life of Edward, Earl of Clarendon*, (3 vols) (Oxford: Clarendon, 1827)

Cooper, William Durrant, ed., *The Savile Correspondence* (London: Camden Society, 1858)

Covent Garden Drollery, The, ed. A. B. (London, E. Curll, 1672)

Dasent, Arthur Irwin, *The Private Life of Charles II* (London: Cassell, 1927)

Davenant, Sir William, *The Dramatic Works* (5 vols) (London, Sotheran, 1872)

Delpech, J., trans. Ann Lindsay, *The Life and Times of the Duchess of Portsmouth* (London: Elek Books, 1953)

Denham, John, *The Poetical Works of Sir John Denham*, ed. T. H. Banks (Hamden, Conn.: Archon Books, 1969)

Dennis, John, *Original Letters of John Dennis* (2 vols) (London, 1721)

Dolman, Brett, *et al.*, *Beauty, Sex and Power* (London: Scala, 2012)

Dryden, John, *Works*, (20 vols), eds E. N. Hooker, H. T. Swedenberg Jr. and Vincent A. Dearing (Berkeley, Calif.: UCalifP, 1956–2000)

Etherege, George, *The Works of George Etherege* (London: Tonson, 1715)

Evelyn, John, *The Diary of John Evelyn* (6 vols), ed. E. S. de Beer (Oxford: OUP, 1955)

Falkus, Christopher, *The Life and Times of Charles II* (London: Book Club Associates, 1972)

Fea, Allan, *Some Beauties of the Seventeenth Century* (London: Methuen, 1906)

Fea, Allan, *James II and his Wives* (London: Methuen, 1908)

Foxon, David, *Libertine Literature in England, 1660–1745* (London: The Book Collector, 1964)

Fraser, Antonia, *The Weaker Vessel. Women's Lot in Seventeenth Century England* (London: Weidenfeld & Nicolson, 1984, 1993)

Gould, Robert, *Poems chiefly consisting of Satyrs* (London, 1689)

Gramont, Philippe, *Memoirs of the Count de Grammont*, Anthony Hamilton, trans. (*c.* 1705) Horace Walpole (London: Bodley Head, 1928)

Halifax, *The Works of George Savile, Marquess of Halifax* (3 vols), ed. Mark Brown (Oxford: Clarendon, 1989)

Bibliography

Hamilton, Elizabeth, *The Illustrious Lady. A Life of Barbara Villiers* (London: Hamish Hamilton, 1980)

Hammond, Paul, ed., *Restoration Literature. An Anthology* (Oxford: OUP, 2000)

Hanrahan, David C., *Charles II and the Duke of Buckingham* (Stroud: Sutton, 2006)

Hartmann, C. H., *La Belle Stuart* (London: Routledge, 1924)

Hartmann, C. H., *The Vagabond Duchess. The Life of Hortense Mancini, Duchesse Mazarin* (London: Heinemann, 1926)

Hartmann, C. H., *Charles II and Madame* (London: Heinemann, 1934)

Hartmann, C. H., *The King My Brother* (London: Heinemann, 1954)

Hopkins, Graham, *Nell Gwynne* (London: Robson, 2000)

Howe, Elizabeth, *The First English Actresses. Women and Drama, 1660–1709* (Cambridge: CUP, 1992)

Hutton, Ronald, *Charles II, King of England, Scotland and Ireland* (Oxford: Clarendon, 1989)

Jusserand, J. J., *A French Ambassador at the Court of Charles the Second* (London: Unwin, 1892)

Keay, Anna, *The Magnificent Monarch. Charles II and the Ceremonies of Power* (London: Continuum, 2008)

Love, Harold, ed., *The Penguin Book of Restoration Verse* (Harmondsworth: Penguin, 1968)

Love, Harold, ed., *Restoration Literature. Critical Approaches* (London: Methuen, 1972)

Love, Harold, ed., *English Clandestine Satire, 1660–1702* (Oxford: OUP, 2004)

McFadden, George, 'Political Satire in *The Rehearsal*', 120–8, *Yearbook of English Studies* 4, 1974

McFarlane, Cameron, *The Sodomite in Fiction and Satire, 1660–1750* (NY: Columbia University Press, 1997)

MacLeod, C., and J. M. Alexander, eds., *Painted Ladies. Women at the Court of Charles II* (London: National Portrait Gallery, 2002)

Magalotti, Lorenzo, *Lorenzo Magalotti at the Court of Charles II. His 'Relazione d'Inghilterra' of 1668*, ed. and trans. W. E. Knowles Middleton (Waterloo, Ontario: Wilfred Laurier UP, 1980)

Manley, de la Rivière, Mary, *Memoirs* (London: E. Curll, 1717)

Margoliouth, H. M., *The Poems and Letters of Andrew Marvell* (2 vols) (Oxford: Clarendon, 1927)

Masters, Brian, *The Mistresses of Charles II* (London: Constable, 1997)

Melton, F. T., 'A Rake Refinanced. The Fortune of George Villiers', 297–316, *Huntington Library Quarterly*, 1998 *Miscellaneous Works, Written by ... Buckingham*, (I) (London, 1704)

Milton, John, *The Poetical Works of John Milton*, ed. H. C. Beeching, (Oxford: OUP, 1941)

Nussbaum, Felicity, ed. & intro., *Satires on Women* (Los Angeles: University of California Press, 1976)

Oldmixon, J., *The History of England during the Reign of the House of Stuart* (2 vols), (London: Pemberton, 1730)

Pepys, Samuel, *Diary*, (10 vols) ed. H. B. Wheatley (London: George Bell, 1893–9)

Pickford, N. A., *Lady Bette and the Murder of Mr Thynn* (London: Weidenfeld & Nicolson, 2014)

Poems on Affairs of State (London, 1697)

Poems on Affairs of State (London, 1704)

POAS: Poems on Affairs of State (7 vols), ed. George de F. Lord *et al.* (NH, London: Yale University Press, 1963–75)

Pope, Alexander, *The Works of Alexander Pope*, ed. W. Warburton (London: Daly, 1751)

Radcliffe, Alexander, *The Works of Capt. Alex Radcliffe* (London: Wellington, 1676)

Reresby, John, *Memoirs of Sir John Reresby* (London, 1734)

Rochester, John Wilmot, Earl of, *The Collected Works*, ed. John Hayward, (London: Nonesuch, 1926)

Rochester, John Wilmot, Earl of, *The Complete Works*, ed. Frank Ellis (Harmondsworth: Penguin, 1994)

Sackville, Charles, Earl of Dorset, *Poems on Several Occasions by the Earls of Roscommon and Dorset* (London: E. Curll, 1714)

Sackville, Charles, Earl of Dorset, ed. anon., *The Works of the most celebrated Minor Poets* (2 vols) (London, 1749)

Sackville, Charles, Earl of Dorset, *A Complete Edition of the Poets of Great Britain* (Edinburgh, 1793)

Scott, Lord George, *Lucy Walter, Wife or Mistress?* (London: G. Harrap, 1947)

Sedley, Charles, *The Poetical and Dramatic Works of Sir Charles Sedley* (2 vols), ed. V. de Sola Pinto (London: Constable, 1928)

Sévigné, Mme de, *Letters of Madame de Sévigné* (2 vols), sel. and ed., Richard Aldington (London: Routledge, 1927)

Sheffield, John, Earl of Mulgrave, *Works* (2 vols), (London, 1723)

Smith, Alexander, *The School of Venus or Cupid Restor'd* (London: J. Morphew, 1718)

Steinman, George S., *Some Particulars Contributed towards a Memoir of Mrs Myddelton* (Oxford: OUP, 1864)

Summers, Montague, ed., *The Restoration Theatre* (London: J. Paul, Trench, 1934)

Swift, Jonathan, *The Poems*, ed. W. E. Browning (2 vols) (Bell, London, 1910)

Thurley, Simon, *Whitehall Palace* (New Haven, London: Yale University Press, 1999)

Turner, David M., *Fashioning Adultery. Gender, Sex and Civility in England, 1660–1740* (Cambridge: CUP, 2002)

Turner, James Grantham, *Libertines and Radicals in Early Modern London.*

Sexuality, Politics and Literary Culture, 1660–1685 (Cambridge: CUP, 2002)

Uglow, Jenny, *A Gambling Man. Charles II and the Restoration, 1660–1670*, (London: Faber, 2000)

Waller, Edmund, *Poems*, ed. G. Thorn Drury (2 vols), (London: A. H. Bullen, 1901)

Ward, Ned, *The London Spy* (4th edition, 1709), ed. A. L. Hayward (London: Cassell, 1927)

Webster, Jeremy, *Performing Libertinism in Charles II's Court*, (Basingstoke: Palgrave Macmillan, 2005)

Wilson, Derek, *All the King's Women. Love, Sex and Politics in the Life of Charles II* (London: Pimlico, 2003)

Wilson, John Harold, ed., *The Rochester-Savile Letters 1671–80* (Col., Ohio: Ohio State UP, 1941)

Wilson, John Harold, *The Court Wits of the Restoration. An Introduction* (Princeton: Princeton University Press, 1948)

Wilson, John Harold, *Nell Gwyn, Royal Mistress* ((London: F. Muller, 1952)

Wilson, John Harold, *A Rake and his Times. George Villiers, Second Duke of Buckingham* (London: F. Muller, 1956)

Wilson, John Harold, ed., *Court Satires of the Restoration* (Colorado: Colorado University Press, 1976)

Wood, Anthony, *The Life and Times of Anthony Wood* (4 vols), ed. Andrew Clarke (Oxford: Clarendon, 1891)

Works of the Right Honourable the Earls of Rochester and Roscommon, (London, 1709)

Wycherley, William, *The Complete Works*, ed. Montague Summers (London: Nonesuch, 1924)

INDEX

Index

ABOUT THE AUTHOR

R. E. Pritchard formerly lectured on seventeenth-century and modern literature at Keele University. Among his publications are the anthology *Shakespeare's England*, studies of seventeenth-century writer-travellers and, more recently, *Passion for Living: John Wilmot, Earl of Rochester*, a biography of the outrageous wit and poet at Charles II's court. He now lives in West Oxfordshire.